# COCAINE QUAGMIRE

*Implementing the U.S. Anti-Drug Policy in the North Andes-Colombia*

Sewall H. Menzel

**University Press of America, Inc.**
Lanham • New York • Oxford

Copyright © 1997 by
**University Press of America,® Inc.**
4720 Boston Way
Lanham, Maryland 20706

12 Hid's Copse Rd.
Cummor Hill, Oxford OX2 9JJ

**Library of Congress Cataloging-in-Publication Data**

Menzel, Sewall H. (Sewall Hamm).
Cocaine quagmire : implementing the U.S. anti-drug policy in the north
Andes - Colombia / Sewall H. Menzel.
p.   cm.
Includes bibliographical references and index.
1. Narcotics, Control of--United States. 2. Narcotics, Control of--
Colombia. 3. Narcotics, Control of--International cooperation. 4.
Drug traffic--Colombia. 5. Cocaine industry--Colombia. 6. United
States--Foreign relations--Colombia. 7. Colombia--Foreign relations--
United States. I. Title.
HV5825.M376  1997    363.4'5'0973--dc21   97-9257  CIP

ISBN 0-7618-0751-9 (cloth: alk. ppr.)

To Patricia, William and Stewart

# Contents

# Introduction

The US anti-drug policy in the north-Andean country of Colombia has evolved considerably since the early to mid-1980s when it first became a paramount issue on the National Security Council's agenda. Perceptions of a threat to American society were highlighted and sharpened by reports of thousands of drug related deaths, an ever increasing level of cocaine addicts and the inability of prisons and rehabilitation centers to handle the social load. The considerable drain on national health care resources as well as the increasing number of American drug user casualties confirmed for many that here was a social threat with international dimensions. Towards the end of the decade in September of 1989, President George Bush stated that illicit drugs were the "greatest threat facing our nation today." (ONDCP 1993:1)

Because countering international cocaine trafficking became a key part of the national security strategy and foreign policy of the United States, Colombia has received substantial US financing, equipment, training, and advisors as part of an increasing US involvement in its international domestic affairs. All this has been designed to help Colombians resolve their own respective narco-trafficking problems, as well as lessen the impact of trafficking and drugs on the population of the US. Policies, programs, strategies and a variety of operations costing billions of dollars have been the result. By the late-1990s, Colombia remained a primary focus of the US anti-drug policy for Latin America. It is for this reason that this north-Andean nation derives its importance and is the focus of this study.

After an uneven beginning in its own anti-drug programs in Bolivia, from 1987 to 1989 the Reagan administration requested and Congress approved over $350 million in assistance for the Andean Ridge (a generic term for Colombia, Ecuador, Peru, Bolivia, Chile and Argentina through which the Andes Mountain chain runs) countries. The goal of this effort was not only to counter the production and trafficking in cocaine but also to buttress those countries' own respective efforts. Several years after the initiation of the Reagan administration's program, US government studies on Colombia indicated that thousands of additional metric tons of cocaine had been produced and were being transshipped for sale into the continental USA. The response was a Bush administration, five-year $2.2 billion program called the Andean Initiative which was focused on Bolivia, Peru and Colombia. Despite this additional program and other supportive efforts to combat cocaine and heroin trafficking through eradication, interdiction and the targeting of the leaders of the major drug trafficking organizations (cartels), coca and gum opium poppy production continued to increase, contributing in their way to an additional ten-thousand drug related deaths over a period of a decade or so and bringing into question the US anti-drug policy in the Andes. The declarations of Cartagena and San Antonio as well as the operations named *Snowcap* and *Support Justice*, among others, are tribute to the determined efforts of the US and Colombian governments to disrupt or otherwise halt narco-trafficking at its source - a supply-sided approach to solving the problem.

The focus of this book, written as a companion volume to my *Fire In The Andes - U.S. Foreign Policy And Cocaine Politics In Bolivia And Peru*, is on the US anti-drug policy as conceived in Washington, D.C. and implemented in Colombia. How this policy effort came about, where it has gone and where it appears to be going for better or worse in terms of its implementation in the 1990s are central interests of this study. In addition, a brief examination of the US government's perception of the drug threat and the related policies which emanated from this are presented. Finally, appropriate observations, lessons learned and conclusions concerning the case are rendered.

The central thesis of this study is that even if the White House's anti-drug policy for Colombia is successful in the short term, its greater *success* will be relative and very limited over the long term and the Colombian drug trade will continue to flourish. There are simply too many complicating factors, including high international demand, immense profits, a weak state system, and negative cultural attitudes and values towards law and justice which constantly undermine the ability of a supply-sided anti-drug strategy and its implementing efforts to successfully confront the traffickers decisively in Colombia. In laying out the case on Colombia, I have tried to demonstrate the strong dynamic of the supply and demand relationship which, in conjunction with the obstacles mentioned above and taken together as a whole, significantly prejudice the success of the US and Colombian anti-drug efforts. The US government has given the supply-side control effort in the north-Andes its best *shot*. Albeit a best shot, it has neither resolved the narco-trafficking problem in Colombia nor created the necessary conditions for political and economic development and stability in that country which could give the policy some chance for success. The winning of some battles does not necessarily win a war, and, as a respected US government report stated: "There appears to be a loss for every gain in the drug war...." (DOS INM 1993: 1)

When statistics are considered, the *Andean Strategy*, which for the best part of five years has been the center piece of the US international supply control efforts that were originally meant to reduce the amount of illicit drugs entering the United States by 15 percent over two years and by 60 percent over ten years, does not reveal a great deal of promise for success. Official US estimates show a 175 percent increase in the cocaine supply alone from 1988 to 1991 or from 400 metric tons to about 1,100 metric tons respectively. By the mid-1990s Colombia had even displaced Bolivia as a producer of coca leaf crops. In addition, heroin production has taken on ominous proportions as gum opium poppy crops have now been introduced into the Western Hemisphere's international drug markets. These facts have not been lost on the administration of President Bill Clinton which has promulgated another anti-drug policy approach in an effort to salvage the situation with an alternate set of "new" strategies and yet another drug *czar*, now with cabinet level status.

A principal criteria in this study to determine whether the US anti-drug policy in Colombia has worked is the *amount of cocaine* produced and the variation in its prices on the street. A rise in prices indicates a scarcity of cocaine coming into the US and a lowering of prices indicates a ready availability of cocaine or even a saturation of the market. Here too the size of the user population is an indicator of drug policy success or failure, although this may reflect domestic US demand reduction policies in play.

When the effort to control domestic drug usage in the United States was extended to the exterior and became part of the US foreign policy menu, this introduced a new dimension of political intervention into the US relationship with Colombia. The outcomes of this process, their repercussions and continuing interaction as influenced by the internal social, economic, political and security conditions and their related actors within Colombia have had an impact on the US policy in play. In addition, non-state actors, interest groups and social movements all play a part, interacting with the state actors and the Colombian domestic condition. As such, trafficking operations in Colombia and their respective markets very much impact on both the individual and state actors. Anti-government insurgencies, as well as economic exigencies, have influenced the state's reactions to trafficking in general. Other aspects of the narcotrafficking phenomenon involving Venezuela, Brazil, Ecuador, are also addressed in this study as the traffickers have attempted, in part, to circumvent US policy through trans-national operations.

In preparing this book, I first researched and read as much as I could about the US anti-drug policy and its implementation, and then travelled throughout the north-Andes and into Panama and Washington, D.C. to conduct further research and interviews. In so doing I was impressed by the variety and number of government reports and studies, such as those put out by the General Accounting Office (GAO) and the US Congress. They are often unvarnished and critical in their approach which helped to surface a number of countervailing factors in play. In addition I found that interviews with participating actors, as well as other keen observers of their respective national scenes, such as members of academia and journalists, were quite useful. No one primary source was overwhelmingly more useful than others. All melded together and, in conjunction with secondary sources such as books, magazines, and newspapers, made the picture that much more complete on US anti-drug policy implementation in Colombia. Often most revealing were the myriad of diverse reactions to my interviews by members of the US Embassy (Country Team) staff in Colombia. Attitudes and opinions on the US anti-drug policy ran the gamut from dismay and apparent hopelessness to overwhelming bureaucratic confidence in ultimate success and that all was going well.

During the interview process, I found that some persons, working for the US and foreign governments in particular, were often guarded and circumspect in their comments for fear they would reveal too much information to me and be duly chastised or punished by their respective offices. Others were often extremely forthright and open and only desired that their perceptions and the *facts* be known. Here a *damn the torpedoes* attitude prevailed. So as not to place in undue jeopardy and to accede to the personal desires of those who wished to retain their anonymity, I have accordingly coded for identification as best I could those interviews of interest for this study. For example, an interview with a knowledgeable or highly placed DEA official in Colombia (CO) would be referenced as: (Interview DEA:CO). Another example is a key member of a Country Team's (CT) staff, which would be referenced as: (Interview CT:CO). In order to simplify and maintain continuity for the reader, I have also coded references to US Embassy (Country Team) cable traffic for Colombia. An example would be: US Embassy (USE) Colombia (CO) coded as *USE-CO Cable* etc.

It should be remembered that this is a case study and not a history. As such it seeks to illuminate the US anti-drug policy in play, indicating its relative merits, successes and failures by examining enough of the nuts and bolts or events and processes which *make* or *break* a policy as it comes to fruition via its implementation process. Readers knowledgeable in the field may find that I have not included *all* the information available or that *something* has been left out. I can accept this as my premise is to demonstrate what can happen and why to a foreign policy initiative in the reality of the international world, no matter how well intentioned or motivated the perpetrators of the policy were and still are today.

While many specific anti-drug "battles" involving the capture or dismantling of entire drug cartels and prominent traffickers have been won, the drug war in general continues to be lost. This is not because of the amount of effort expended, which is considerable, but because of an improper focus on the key center of gravity of the narcotrafficking supply and demand relationship. More than anything else it is a lack of complete understanding of what underlies the drug issue - intense and continuing international demand from both the United States and Europe - which has stymied the US anti-drug policy implementation effort. This may be very discomforting, yet, when all is said and done, the reader should come to the conclusion, as I have done, that the US anti-drug policy in Colombia is indeed embedded in a *quagmire* of countervailing factors over which it has little or no control.

# Acknowledgements

The inspiration for this work emanated out of a lecture series on narcotrafficking in the Americas by Professor Bruce M. Bagley of the Graduate School of International Studies, University of Miami (Coral Gables) and my own endeavors while working in Colombia, Bolivia and Peru during the 1980s.

I wish to thank Ambassador Ambler H. Moss, Jr., Director of the University of Miami's North-South Center, Professors Bruce M. Bagley, Enrique Baloyra and Alexander H. McIntire, Jr. of the University of Miami and Professor Eduardo A. Gamarra, Director of the Florida International University's Latin American and Caribbean Center, who read the original manuscript. They offered advice and numerous insights which enhanced my own research efforts and the writing of this work. A special thanks also goes to Aldo Regalado of the University of Miami's Richter Library Staff who greatly facilitated the production of this book.

Caribbean Sea

Cnita n islands of the Airhip e ago de San Andres y Prov dencia (13° 00'N 81°30 W) and the Isla de Malpeic 3° 58 N 81 35 W) belong ng to Colombia are not shown on this map

NETHERLANDS ANTILLES (Netherlands)
Willemstad

North Pacific Ocean

PANAMA
Panama

VENEZUELA
Maracaibo
Lago de Maracaibo
Caracas
Valencia
La Guaira

Santa Marta
Riohacha
LA GUAJIRA
Barranquilla
ATLANTICO
Cienaga
Cartagena
Valledupar
MAGDALENA
CESAR
Tolu
Sincelejo
SUCRE
Monteria
Turbo
CORDOBA
BOLIVAR
NORTE DE SANTANDER
Cucuta
Pamplona
ANTIOQUIA
Bucaramanga
SANTANDER
ARAUCA
Arauca
Rio Meta
Puerto Carreño
Quibdo
Medellin
Barbosa
CHOCO
CALDAS
Paz de Rio
BOYACA
CASANARE
RISARALDA
Pereira
Tunja
Yopal
VICHADA
CUNDINAMARCA
QUINDIO
Armenia
Ibague
Girardot
Bogota
Puerto Lopez
VALLE
TOLIMA
Villavicencio
Buenaventura
Cali
DISTRITO ESPECIAL
META
Puerto Inirida
Neiva
CAUCA
HUILA
Popayan
GUAINIA
Rio Guaviare
San Jose del Guaviare
Rio Guainia
Tumaco
NARIÑO
Florencia
GUAVIARE
Pasto
Mocoa
Rio Vaupes
Mitu
Ipiales
PUTUMAYO
CAQUETA
VAUPES
Quito
Rio Napo
ECUADOR
Rio Caqueta
BRAZIL
Rio Japura
AMAZONAS
PERU
Amazon
Rio Ica
Iquitos
Leticia
Rio Putumayo

**Colombia**
— International boundary
-·-·- Internal administrative boundary
★ National capital
● Internal administrative capital
—— Railroad
—— Road

0    50    100   150 Kilometers
0    50    100   150 Miles

PERU

Maranon
Rio
Rio Javari

Boundary representation is not necessarily authoritative

EAM BJ0442 6 85

*xiv*

# Chapter 1

## A Narcotrafficker's Paradise

One of the issues of concern to American voters on the eve of the 1980 presidential election was the evolving domestic problem of ever-increasing drug usage. Prior to 1980 it was estimated that as little as 20 metric tons (mt) of cocaine from the Andean source countries of Bolivia, Peru and Colombia were sufficient to supply the US demand. (Walker 1989: 197) As the newly elected president Ronald Reagan took office, both the number of cocaine users and their respective supply of the illegal drug was steadily increasing. The Department of Health and Human Services reported that some 40 percent of the national population between the ages of 18 and 25 were using drugs and about ten percent of the adult population age 26 years and older or some 20 million people were also using drugs. (NIDA 1990-1991: 21) Over time the US Congress became more and more aware of the critical involvement of Colombia in the international cocaine trade as a major processor and transshipper of the drug. A series of debates took place among its members over what should be done to deal with the problem.

President Reagan was concerned over the drug issue and it had become readily apparent that local law enforcement officials needed help in dealing with the problem. In 1981 Senator Sam Nunn from Georgia and a number of his colleagues declared the need for a fuller government involvement in the anti-drug effort. To this end they were able to modify the Posse Comitatus Act of 1878 against the involvement of US military in civilian law enforcement functions by attaching an amending bill to the 1982 Defense Authorization Act, which would now allow the US armed forces to share drug-related intelligence derived from military sources with civilian offices. The military was also allowed to both operate and lend equipment in support of the Department of Justices's Drug Enforcement Administration (DEA), as well as allow the latter to use military facilities when and where needed. Nonetheless, the US military was prohibited from direct involvement in searches or arrests of civilians. Likewise, any assistance which would adversely affect military prepardness was also prohibited (Title 10 United States Code, Sectins 371-375). Exemptions were also made in 1981 by Congress to the 1973 Foreign Assistance Act, allowing the military as well as the DEA and the Federal Bureau of Investigation (FBI) to conduct police training in support of the US anti-drug policy. It was on this basis that a concerned Reagan administration and Congress initially pursued the anti-drug issue in Colombia. (House 1990: 9-10; GAO 1992b: 2-3; and Bagley 1991: 3-4)

Colombia is a country of paradoxes. While considered to be one of Latin Americas's oldest democracies with a population of about 32 million (1990 estimate), it also has one of the bloodiest histories involving endemic societal violence. (USE 1990: 1) For a country not at war, it has the highest murder rate in the world (25,000 to 30,000 annually); murder being its number one cause of death for those between the ages of fifteen and forty-five. (Miami Herald: 23 Sep 93 and 16 Apr 94; House 1990b: 82-83; USE 1990: 1; and Camacho Guizado 1991: passim) This is to say that on an average, during a period of about two years, as many Colombians often die as a result of homicides as the US military lost in combat during its ten year war in Vietnam. This situation is not entirely new to Colombia as during the late 1940s and early 1950s around 200,000 Colombians were reported as having been killed in the political power struggles (called "*La Violencia*") between the Liberal and Conservative parties. (Bagley 1987: 23) Lacking a respect for law and order and without a unifying national idea, a motivating ideology or a consensus on how to mediate disagreements, over the years feuding and wars between factions became quite common and contributed to this tradition of violence. Colombians were often not only involved in lethal conflict between themselves but also between themselves and the state. The trauma produced by this situation which culminated in *La Violencia* eventually resulted in a negotiated, power-sharing agreement in the 1960s which generally accommodated elite interests (called "*apaciguamiento*") and defined the Colombian political system for decades into the 1990s. (Camacho and Tokatlian 1993)

The concentration of power in the hands of the conservative and liberal elite groups was based on a mutual interest in the preservation of the current status quo. While agrarian reform and other redistribution formulas for helping to diffuse the nation's wealth in support of the landless poor were approved in general, the application was lax and the expectations of the potential beneficiaries were still left wanting. While privileges dominated and equal opportunity suffered, the elites controlled the economy and the law making processes to their advantage. (Thoumi 1990: 128-129 and 133-135; and Tokatlian 1993) As such, while maintaining their positions through patronage and a personalistic style of governance, the two ruling party elites failed to integrate a number of opposing groups and forces into the political process. While some people with varying degrees of education could propel themselves up the social-economic ladder of opportunity via business or government-linked jobs, this situation was not always available to everyone and the political doors of opportunity for groups pressing for reforms to rectify the situation remained essentially closed. As a result, beginning in the 1960s, those who felt themselves frustrated and marginalized sought to redress Colombia's social-economic and political injustices by forming armed insurgency movements which began to challenge the government for the allegiance and control of the population. (House 1990b: 83; Gros 1992: 6-7; and Sheahan 1987: 27) This was the setting which formed the backdrop for the emergence of the business known as narcotrafficking.

Conducive to narcotrafficking in Colombia was the up to 70 percent of the rural sector which was reported to be living in a general state of poverty, along with about 35 percent of the urban area population which was also reported to be little better off. Because of this situation, it was estimated that up to 70 percent of the people involved in the narcotraffickers' employ came from the rural poor. (Arrieta 1990: 209; New York Review: 22 Dec 88; and Sheahan 1987: 273-274) To redress their economic situation, many people looked to the traffickers and narcotrafficking in general for employment opportunities. Thus, an economy, based in part on the refinement and export of cocaine, took place despite otherwise steady national economic growth recorded in the export sectors involving coffee, cut flowers, coal, petroleum, and bananas.

In general the Colombian economy was far larger, healthier and more diversified and less dependent on the drug economy than say Bolivia and Peru. The GNP was reported at $40 billion with about $6 billion being earned through foreign exchange. (Bagley 1990: 446) Nonetheless, while macro-economic indicators were relatively impressive, the *distribution* of income in Colombia was still one of the most skewed in Latin America. Land ownership tended to be highly concentrated in the hands of a relatively small political and commercial elite, while wages for about half the population often stagnated or even declined with people earning not much more than between $50 and $100 per month. For many it was even less. (Sheahan 1987: 273 and 276; Camacho and Kalmanovitz 1993) As a result, some 300,000 Colombians gravitated towards direct or indirect employment in the cocaine trade during the late 1970s and early 1980s. (Camacho 1993)

This employment ranged all the way from coca growers, paste makers, security guards, radio operators and monitors, lawyers, accountants, pilots, mechanics, chemists, chemical engineers and laboratory workers to the big time traffickers or narcobarons who managed the effort using a corporate style system of control (Figure 1).

A Narcotrafficking Organization As A Corporation

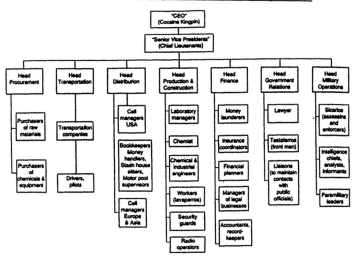

Source: USIA 1992 *Consequences of The Illegal Drug Trade.* p. 38.

Figure 1

Additional hundreds of thousands of Colombians worked in other legitimate businesses which, in part, serviced and otherwise supported the cocaine industry. (House 1990b: 81)

Colombia is reported to be the source of approximately 80 percent of the cocaine exported into the US and Europe, producing and refining in steadily increasing increments over the years at least 500 metric tons (mt) annually. It is second only to Peru in the production of coca leaves, eclipsing Bolivia in this capacity in the mid-1990's (Figure 2). The country's strategic location between the coca fields of its southern Andean neighbors and the Caribbean and Pacific shipping routes to the US and European markets has generally offered the narcotraffickers a comparative advantage in establishing control over the cocaine trade. (House 1990b: 80; and 1990c: 69 and INCSR 1996: 81) But why Colombia and not Venezuela or some other country?

### Andean Coca Cultivation 1989-1994

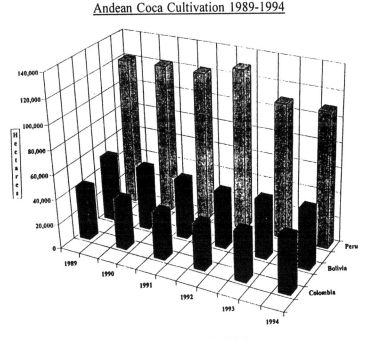

Source: INCSR 1995

Figure 2

While various factors have contributed to Colombia's unique position in fomenting the international trafficking of cocaine, it has been contended by Colombian scholar Francisco Thoumi that the key elements of ease of production and risk reduction form the basis for Colombia's success. To the degree that risk is reduced for the narcotraffickers' operations, certain factors became relevant in making Colombia an ideal narcotrafficker haven which has distinguished it from other potential trafficking regions. One of these factors involves the *general weakness of the state*, its institutions and values. Over the years, as the Colombian state became less accommodating and less responsive to the people it was supposed to serve, corruption in both the public and private sector abounded. In time a wide gap between written law (dejure) and socially acceptable behavior (defacto) took place. This *contemptuous attitude towards the law* on the part of much of the population generally found its expression in the phrase: *Yo obedezco pero no cumplo!* ("I comply but I do not obey!"). This is to say one obeyed the law to the degree that it was convenient, but otherwise ignored it. (Tokatlian 1993; and Thoumi 1990: 131) In short, one offered a deal to their friends and applied the law to their enemies.

In daily life this dichotomy was often played out in the *contraband activity* of numerous underground economies which flaunted the law in order to flourish. The informal economy's accelerated development during the 20th century reflected and reinforced a traditional lack of respect for state laws and regulations dating back into Spanish colonial times. People had become accustomed to living and operating in what North Americans would consider an illegal or quasi-legal manner. Along with this a long history of smuggling and contraband activities took place. Dishonesty was frequently accepted as "normal" in the struggle for survival. (Thoumi 1990: 131; and Tokatlian 1993) Whether it was with manufactured products entering and leaving the country, or livestock, coffee, emeralds or other items for which one sought to avoid export-import controls and tariffs, Colombians excelled at not only smuggling but also at the laundering of the proceeds from this often lucrative activity. In much of Colombia's society one's social status was based to a large degree on how wealthy one became. It was generally unimportant how the wealth was obtained and people did not ask questions. Society functioned on this basis and created a natural situation which was to be exploited by the narcotrafficker. (Thoumi 1992b: 51-52; and Kalmanovitz 1992: 9-11)

Another key factor bearing on why narcotrafficking particularly flourished in Colombia is that the government had lost control of or *never truly exercised real control over much of the nation's territory* of some 455,355 square miles which is approximately the size of Texas and California combined. (USE 1990: 1) This was due in part to the operations of various insurgencies which were contesting the government's legitimacy and right to rule and in part to the sheer magnitude and large expanse of the national territory itself. The problem of size was compounded by the nature of Colombia's geography which is characterized by its numerous and relatively isolated and remote regions formed by a series of rugged mountain chains, ridges, hills and rivers which naturally divide the country into zones and make communications and therefore control that much more difficult. This isolation not only encouraged the growth of relatively self-sufficient communities but also facilitated the use of bribes and coercive measures against the few government authorities present who generally stood alone and at high risk in confronting criminal elements in the outback of rural Colombia. That guerrilla groups generally dominated much of the countryside and that government officials were reluctant to challenge many of the illegal activities taking place within their respective zones, contributed to the provision of a natural safe haven which offered few or no risks to the narcotraffickers in their manufacturing and transshipping operations. Equipment and chemicals for processing cocaine were available through the various, albeit isolated, rural communities and numerous rivers traversing the region. (Thoumi 1992b: 52-54 and Gros 1992: 18-19)

A primary factor influencing the Colombian domination of the narcotrafficking markets in the Americas involved the use of *violence*. A legacy of the experience of La Violencia at mid-century has been the relatively low value placed on human life throughout much of Colombian society. To this end Colombians have been quicker than most to resort to violence in resolving personal problems or manifestations thereof which are often found in confrontational and competitive business situations. This served the Colombian traffickers well in their high-stakes, high-risk narco-business operations. Violence and the threat of violence were applied at will and without hesitation when dealing with Bolivian, Peruvian and US competitors, as well as within Colombia itself. The ruthless application of violence to resolve any and all problems which might otherwise be resolved through astute negotiations became a key characteristic of the Colombian narcotraffickers' modus operandi. (Thoumi 1992b: 50)

A final factor not generally recognized which also served the Colombians well in the establishment of their drug marketing systems was the presence of large numbers (about 450,000) of *Colombian migrants living within the US*. (Kalmanovitz 1992: 3) The natural emigration which took place over the years since the 1940s built up a large and diverse body of people, both legal and illegal, which facilitated the recruitment, organization, establishment and functioning of a US based network of traffickers for the distribution and sale of drugs, principally cocaine. In short, the familial ties of this relatively closely knit group made it both difficult for legal authorities to penetrate its operations and enabled it, in turn, to focus its proclivity to use violence on its competition, eliminating all who stood in its way. To this end the Colombian narcotraffickers were able to quickly establish themselves and eliminate any competitors, such as the Cubans in Miami, as they secured their domination of the US market. (Thoumi 1992b: 53 and Camacho Guizado 1991: passim)

The production of cocaine in Colombia has normally been carried out at the higher or more advanced levels of the process, converting coca paste or cocaine base into refined cocaine HCl. Nonetheless, as the world's second largest producer of coca leaf crops (INCSR 1996:81), the full production process from leaf to HCl also takes place, albeit on a much smaller scale than Peru. Unlike Bolivia and Peru, however, only a few indigenous Indian tribes actually chew coca with the result that there is little or no social legitimacy involved in its farming. Traditionally, while coca cultivation is considered illegal under Colombian law, it does not represent an important activity or threat to the state, sustaining about one percent of the total population. (Lee 1989: 56) Coca cultivation and farming take place for the most part in the remote plains and tropical regions of southeastern and southern Colombia which are comprised of the Departments of Meta, Guaviare and Vaupes to the east, Caqueta to the south and Putumayo along the Ecuadoran border. Nonetheless, some coca has also been produced in the Sierra Nevada Mountains near Santa Marta on the Caribbean coast, in the Department of Boyaca near Bogota, and in the Cauca Valley and the Amazon basin regions. (White 1989: 24)

Possibly the most important factor as to why coca has not been grown in great abundance in Colombia is the relatively low quality of its leaves which are affected by both the climate and the poor mineral composition of the soils. The two principal types of coca grown in Colombia are the *Ipadu* variety found in the lowland rain forest of the southern and eastern areas and the *Novogranatense* variety found in the hills or higher level hinterlands of west-central Colombia. (White 1989: 24; and Lee 1989: 21-22) The alkaloid content of the Colombian coca leaves is considerably less (.28 to .32 percent) or roughly a third to half of those grown in Bolivia and Peru (.50 to .75 percent). (Stickney 1993; USE-CO 1991: Cable 1484; Craig 1982: passim; and Lee 1989: 23) This means that it generally takes two to three times the number of Colombian grown leaves to produce a quantity of coca paste equal to that produced in Bolivia and Peru. (House 1990c: 70; and DOS INM 1992: 107)

The production cycle from leaves to cocaine is basically the same as in Bolivia and Peru. As such, the coca leaves are treated with kerosene and bicarbonate of soda, mashed together to produce the alkaloid which forms the coca paste. This paste is then treated with sulfuric acid and potassium permanganate to form the cocaine base. The base, in turn, is processed with ether and acetone to produce the final product of refined cocaine HCl. This last step in the refining process requires considerable technical expertise, capital investment in equipment and a skilled and trained work force that knows exactly how to bring about the chemical transformation process to convert base into HCl. To this end Colombia possessed the skilled labor, technology and assets, as well as the financing, to promote the mass production and marketing of cocaine in the international drug market. (Arrieta 1990: 49)

In contrast to coca and coca paste which are picked up directly from the farmers by a network of narcotrafficker buyers, the high cost of transportation from the farm to market for virtually all of the legitimate food crops grown by the poor *campesino* or rural farmers (such as rice, corn, yucca and bananas) makes agricultural farming an unprofitable venture for most. For this reason food crops are generally consumed on the farm itself as a basic food staple and coca remains the most remunerative cash crop available to the poor rural farmers in Colombia. (Tokatlian: 1993)

Most of the coca paste produced is picked up and transported to the refining laboratories which have been typically located at ranches in Antioquia and Cordoba or in the more remote jungle regions found along Colombia's border with Brazil and Peru. The relative isolation of the laboratories was important as the traffickers could then avoid to some degree having to deal with the often threatening and exploitive guerrilla organizations which sought to tax the cocaine production process to further their own respective anti-government causes. In addition to that produced within Colombia, cocaine base and HCl were generally picked up in Bolivia and Peru and flown into Colombia and its border regions for further refinement as required. (Senate 1989: 47; and Lee 1989: 31-32) To this end, by the mid-1980s 75 percent of the total amount of cocaine entering the US was refined in Colombia, while the remaining 25 percent was refined in Bolivia and Peru respectively. (DEA 1987: 36)

In the Guaviare Department, as well as other areas, the coca farmers initially enjoyed the boom of the early 1980s until around 1983 when the price of cocaine dropped on the international market and profits were cut in half. By this time the guerrilla organizations had moved into the regions and, while they were not involved to any large degree in production, they did levy a uniform 10 percent tax (*la vacuna* - "the vaccination") on both the farmers and the traffickers alike. (Chernick 1993) One of these groups was the *Fuerzas Armadas Revolucionarias de Colombia* (FARC - Armed Revolutionary Forces of Colombia). As its finances increased, the FARC became powerful enough to the degree that it actually assumed many of the functions of the state in the areas it dominated, imposing a draconian system of law, order and discipline which included the stamping out of drug addiction. In some cases if a campesino was found to consume *bazuco* (a mixture of coca paste and cocaine base), he received the choice of either desisting from the habit or being summarily shot. In addition the guerrillas defended the farmers against both the government and the traffickers, regulating the prices to be paid for coca and the forms of payment. In exchange for this service, the coca farmers also had to cultivate food crops for the guerrillas, as well as pay their otherwise extorted taxes to the latter. The guerrilla presence did bring considerable stability and a relative tranquility to the coca growing areas which previously had been known for their frequent cases of violence, often degenerating into chaos. (Bagley 1990: 457; Reyes Posada 1990: 131; and Rutledge: 1993)

While this arrangement endured for some time, it eventually broke down in later years as the traffickers more and more felt themselves threatened by guerrilla operations involving kidnapping and extortion. In short the guerrillas were increasing the overhead costs of the cocaine industry. If the traffickers did not pay their protection fees in the form of guerrilla "war taxes", they in turn found their expenses going up considerably as they were then forced to guard drug shipments, laboratories, clandestine airfields and courier routes, as well as themselves and their family members. Although seemingly high, the taxes were bearable and became part of the overall business expenses to be endured. The FARC sometimes even carried out its own coca cultivation, as well as taxing coca and paste production in the Vichada, Vaupes, Guaviare, Caqueta, Putumayo, Meta and Magdalena Departments, an area of approximately 160,000 square miles. (Chernick and Rutledge: 1993; and Lee 1992: 104)

The most profitable element in narcotrafficking was neither the growing of coca leaves nor the refining process which eventually produced the cocaine HCl, but the transportation and international market commercialization of the HCl which brought in huge profits for the traffickers (Domestically only about 2 percent of the Colombian population was involved in the actual consumption of cocaine products in the early 1980s). (Lee 1989: 195) The value added to the cocaine product at each level of its manufacturing and marketing processes was in direct proportion to the relative amount of risk attendant at that stage. For this reason coca farmers, running little or no risks, made the smallest profits, while refiners, smugglers and wholesalers took considerably higher risks and were rewarded in the process with vastly higher profits (Figure 3). (Thoumi 1992b: 46)

Price Growth of Cocaine

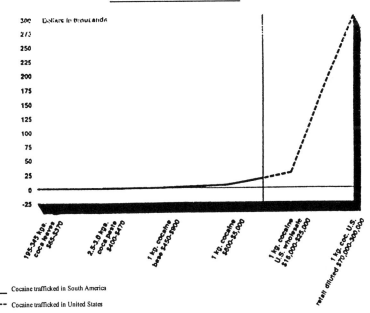

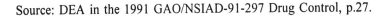

Source: DEA in the 1991 GAO/NSIAD-91-297 Drug Control, p.27.

Figure 3

To reduce their risks the traffickers were able to use bribes and intimidation to help market and transship their product, working around the Colombian governments' restrictions on coca and cocaine products. In this situation Panama, due to its geographical location immediately to the northwest of Colombia and its dominance by the corrupt General Manuel Noriega during the 1980s, served this purpose well. Noriega received some $4.6 million in bribes to enable the Medellin cartel alone to ship tons of cocaine through Panama to the US. Over time,

Colombian traffickers were even able to establish cocaine refineries in eastern Panama along its frontier with Colombia. (Lee 1989: 181; and Tokatlian 1993) The Colombians generally dominated the transportation and smuggling of cocaine into North America for its eventual wholesaling on the US drug markets. Beginning in the late 1970s, the now notoriously ruthless and violence prone Colombian traffickers seized control by force of virtually the entire wholesale US cocaine market from competing Cuban and mafia groups who, along with other non-Colombian traffickers, were relegated to the retail distribution networks on the lower end of the marketing system. When the costs of refining, transportation and wholesale commissions from distribution were totalled, the Colombian traffickers or refiners of the 1980s typically found themselves investing up to $2.4 million to successfully market a load of 300 kilos (660 lbs) of cocaine, earning at the end of the process a profit of about $4.65 million. (Lee 1989: 33) Yet the US market was not the only one of interest to the larger Medellin and Cali based narcotrafficking groups who also sought to exploit similar marketing opportunities in Europe. In any event total profits for the traffickers were estimated to be somewhere around $5 billion to $6 billion per year, with roughly $1.5 billion returning to Colombia, representing about 20 percent of Colombia's total export earnings. (House 1990b : 81; and Lee 1989: 34)

During the early to mid-1970s, or the years leading up to the advent of the Administration of Colombian President Julio Cesar Turbay in 1978, little was done in Colombia in terms of trying to understand or even stem the production and trafficking in drugs, whether it was cocaine or marijuana. The inability of the government to integrate its national territory, develop civil cohesion and resolve the social conflicts of the day all served to foster a climate condusive to the expansion of a myriad of narcotrafficking entrepreneurs and their respective commercial enterprises. (Arrieta 1990: 31) Nonetheless, the US Drug Enforcement Administration (DEA) and the US Department of State (DOS) as early sponsors of the US anti-drug policy in the Andean region became intensely interested in the trafficking taking place in Colombia during this period, attempting to bring attention to it as an illegal or criminal activity and questioning why it was that the Banco de la Republica in Bogota was allowing the return into Colombia of large amounts of drug monies. The bank's position was that discouraging the inflow of narco-dollars would merely drive the money into the black market or foreign banks. For this reason the government had declared tax amnesties to attract narco-dollars back into Colombia, exploiting this situation in favor of the local economy. The US anti-drug policy aimed to halt narcotrafficking in Colombia through programs which enhanced the law enforcement and criminal justice systems. Despite a US sponsored, four-year $6 million training program for some 600 law enforcement officials, high level corruption pervaded the Colombian national police agencies and trafficking continued unabated. Even anti-corruption purges under President Alfonzo Lopez Michelsen (1974-78) appeared to have no real impact as police-narcotrafficker linkages remained largely intact. (Sharpe 1988: 81) According to testimony by convicted trafficker Carlos Lehder, Lopez Michelsen was himself in league with the Medellin Cartel which supported him in his presidential campaigns, contributing up to $1 million. (El Nuevo Herald: 10 Apr 93)

The initial tolerance by both the Colombian society and government of drug usage, as well as production and trafficking, enabled the traffickers to launder their money by means of investments in urban and rural properties such as buildings for commercial enterprise, high-rises, restaurants, cattle ranches and farms, as well as construction and pharmaceutical companies. In addition, drug monies were used to support political campaigns, buy into radio stations, automobile dealerships, educational institutions, and even finance professional athletic teams and sports clubs. (Lee 1989: 3-4; and Castillo 1987: passim) One narcotrafficker, Pablo Escobar, and his family owned 96 registered pieces of property in the city of Medellin alone, including 16 residences. (Lee 1989: 5)

Roughly five loosely organized groups, each with up to about two hundred smaller trafficking elements and subgroups focused on the Medellin, Cali, Leticia, Pereira, and Baranquilla areas, were initially able to dominate the Colombian cocaine export market. To this end the groups not only collaborated among themselves but also cooperated, forming joint ventures in the refining of coca paste, cocaine base and HCl, insuring cocaine shipments, and working to thwart the government's anti-drug efforts. The remaining 30 percent of the drug trade not controlled by the principal cartel groups and syndicates was generally spread out among hundreds of other independent, small scale producers, refiners and smugglers, including in some cases elements of the insurgent-guerrilla organizations. (Lee 1989: 109; Chernick 1993) Among the more famous of the twenty or so Medellin-based drug barons and their families was an upper echelon of six persons who controlled the cartel's overseas operations and consisted of Pablo Escobar Gaviria, Jorge Ochoa Vasquez and his brothers Fabio and Juan

David, Hiro Mejira and Jose Gonzalo Rodriguez Gacha. (Senate 1989: 43 and 48-49) Leaders of the Cali-based cartel group were Gilberto Rodriguez Orejuela and Jose Cruz Londono. The profits of these two principal cartel groups alone have been estimated during the 1980s as being as much as $4 billion annually. This was despite wholesale cocaine prices in the US dropping from $55,000 per kilo in 1980 to about $15,000 in mid-1988 indicating a glut in the US cocaine market. (Senate 1989: 49 and 117; and Lee 1989: 8 - 9 and 109)

Most of the traffickers sought to prosper commercially and ply their trade without being disturbed. To accomplish this they generally tended to seek protection and avoid confrontational situations, using violence only when no other method would work. Corruption in the form of bribery was principally used to ensure that the trafficking operations remained not only protected but also effective. Efforts were continuously made to try and manipulate key Colombian institutions such as political parties, the press, police, military, judiciary and members of Congress as well as officials serving in the government at large. In Colombia there were always exceptions to this general rule and, if protection could not be accomplished by corruption in the form of bribes, then coercive intimidation or death threats were brought into play. The phrase *plata o plomo* (money or lead) signified that, if the approached party could not be persuaded to accommodate trafficker interests and receive the benefit of a large sum of money as a reward (bribe), then a lethal bullet would more than likely be forthcoming, making the intended victim an example to others who also might not be so inclined towards supporting narcotrafficker interests. (Lee 1989: 9 - 10)

The Colombian system of justice operated under what is known as an *inquisitorial* system of law whereby crimes were not investigated by the police or a district attorney, but by the judges themselves. Under this system a judge was expected to gather case related evidence, indict suspects, recommend verdicts and even suggest sentences. Once this work was completed, only then were their reports and recommendations forwarded to superior or circuit courts for review and actual sentencing. In the cases involving drug traffickers and political violence (terrorism), a group of up to several hundred judges who were specialists in these fields conducted not only the investigations but also the conviction and sentencing processes mentioned above. Only after the proceedings had been closed did a superior tribunal review (and generally endorse) the process. (House 1990c: 87) Thus, narcotrafficking cases were decided by a select group of judges without a jury process and this enabled the traffickers to influence the system directly through the leverage of bribes or intimidation focused on only one highly vulnerable person - the judge.

It was in this judicial system that the *plata o plomo* strategy became most flagrant in its application, whereby judges were offered the choice of death if they convicted a trafficker or a comfortable bribe if they allowed the accused to be released from jail or the charges set aside. Nonetheless, when dealing with other government officials in general, the desired accommodations of interest favoring the traffickers ran the gamut from merely providing information on proposed government anti-drug activities and looking the other way (seeing or hearing no evil), to actively attempting to create legislative obstacles to either thwart government anti-drug initiatives or hamstring government activities which might be prejudicial to the narcotraffickers themselves and their illicit trade. (Lee 1989: 10) The often relatively unclear and overlapping responsibilities among the understaffed Colombian law enforcement agencies, as well as their poorly trained and underpaid personnel, left this sector of the government highly vulnerable to systematic bribery and corruption by the traffickers. (Bagley 1988: 78)

In reality, the operations of a narcotrafficking cartel, clan or group tend to be highly fluid and no one person can be truly said to be a key center of gravity, keystone character or personality ("the brains") behind trafficking operations in Colombia more than anyone else. (Tokatlian and Stickney 1993) Operators and links in the production system and chain change constantly through an intricate system of contacts and subcontacts which are often arranged on a yearly, monthly, weekly and even daily basis. Much depends on where one fits into this production-transportation-marketing network. (Lee 1989: 99-100) Computer technology and modern communications systems with encryption devices and voice scramblers all have assisted the traffickers in protecting themselves and their operations from government interference, as well as coordinating the processing of precursor materials, construction and operation of laboratories, and the rental or purchase of boats, planes, helicopters and even submarines to ship cocaine products from the generally remote laboratory complexes to their respective international market destinations. Commercial carriers, human body carriers and especially private planes and boats have been the preferred means for smuggling cocaine out of Colombia into the US. Routing into the US is often done through Central America, Mexico, Jamaica, Cuba, Haiti and the Bahamas, as well as South America, Europe and Canada. (Senate 1989: 47 and 49; El Nuevo Herald: 7 Oct

93; and Lee 1989: 103) Networks of well placed informants throughout the government and its law enforcement agencies, as well as the monitoring of US and Colombian military, police and coast guard radio communication systems, have traditionally helped to provide the traffickers with early warning of threatening counter-drug operations. Narcotrafficker smugglers have proven themselves to be very adept at switching from planes to boats or vice versa as required to avoid US surveillance aircraft or ships running counter-narcotics interdiction operations. (Senate 1989: 47-48 and 52-53; and Lee 1989: 105-106)

Ironically, while mutually seeking to accomplish the same ends, cocaine trafficking and marijuana trafficking in Colombia appear to be controlled by distinctly different groups, with the cocaine traffickers holding the latter in low esteem. To some degree the difference in the type of product has produced a different trafficking pattern. While airplanes have traditionally been the primary mode of smuggling cocaine into the US, marijuana tends to be carried by boat to drop off points along the US and Mexican coasts where faster seagoing craft can make the final run into the shore. Nonetheless, traffickers such as Carlos Lehder ran a combined cocaine-marijuana smuggling operation from the Bahamas in the late 1970s, indicating that both products are sometimes handled by the same distributing and smuggling ring provided the price is right. (Lee 1989: 107)

While the various Colombian cartels and syndicates have specifically designated distribution markets and regions within the US (Medellin for example controlled Miami, Houston, New York and California), they routinely have assisted each other by mutually supplying cocaine products to each other to meet delivery and supply obligations and overcome potential market shortages. Likewise they have often taken turns in protecting the shipments through a form of rotating insurance systems, taking turns paying the transshipment costs. Frequently they pool their transportation assets and collaborate by piggy-backing on each others' means of transportation, while smuggling a joint cocaine shipment into the US. (Senate 1989: 50; and Lee 1989: 110) In 1981 traffickers were using a brokering process which enabled them to control both the volume of cocaine entering the US and its prices. By keeping the price high ($45,000 to $55,000 per kilo in Miami) on the wholesale market scale to maximize profits, they had in essence formed a cartel. This worked reasonably well into early 1984. After 1984 the cocaine industry had become too large, lucrative and diffuse for the cartels to control or even be bothered with controlling it. Although there were enough profits for everyone, competition based on the supply and demand process eventually did force the retail and street prices down accordingly. (Gugliotta 1992: 111-112) To further reduce risks, the Colombian traffickers have even shared information on both government and guerrilla operations which might have an inhibiting effect on their own operations.

Also included in the collaboration between traffickers are activities such as the assassination or elimination of government officials and individual citizens within the Colombian society who are deemed threatening to the former's livelihood. While on the one hand the Cali cartel groups have tended to prefer to use corruption or financial bribes to work their way around government sponsored anti-drug activities and policies, on the other hand the Medellin cartel, much in the violence-prone, contraband tradition of Colombia, often took on a confrontational position using violence as a principal operational methodology. In the mid-1980s it was reported that the Medellin cartel often coordinated and distributed these activities among its various clans. In some cases Pablo Escobar's group would be responsible for production and marketing and Jorge Ochoa's group responsible for enforcement and finance. Sometimes the roles would be reversed. (Senate 1989: 53 and 93; Lee 1989: 110-111) "Enforcement" meant the infamous carrot and stick combination of *plata o plomo* which was to have such tremendous impact and influence on how government officials carried out their responsibilities. To this end the traffickers felt they could exert enough pressure on government officials to influence or control their activities to such a degree that they were not a threat to the cartels' operations. Financial inducements or bribes in exchange for cooperation often ran from a few hundred dollars a month for a police constable to as much as $5,000 for a police captain. In this sense the government was perceived by the US as being a hostage of the traffickers. (Senate 1989: 59; Lee 1992: 101 and President's Commission 1986: 102) While the use of violence enabled the Medellin cartel to exert considerable coercive power over government officials, this also drew more attention to it as an organization, causing the Colombian government to formally target it more often than the relatively more passive Cali cartel. (House 1990b: 81)

Despite the fact that the Colombian traffickers have shared risks, pooled information, developed joint marketing enterprises and worked together to influence the government's anti-drug policies and efforts, falling outs have taken place within the cartels, such as those which occurred between the Ochoa and Escobar families. (El Espectador 29 Mar 86) Animosities between the cartel groups have often been raised to such high levels as to cause even the less confrontational Cali group to resort to the use of bombings and assassinations against the Medellin traffickers to resolve some of their more pressing unsettled disputes and turf battles over markets. (Semana: 29 Aug 88) Despite the apparent complexities of the trafficking operations, in the end little was accomplished by the Colombian government against the cartels during most of the 1970s and it was not until Julio Cesar Turbay Ayala took office that the Colombian government itself became interested in asserting some control over the narcotrafficking situation.

Almost from the start, the Colombian anti-drug policy at the end of the 1970s theoretically became very much aligned with that of the US, which was to eliminate all facets of the narcotrafficking then taking place. In essence the Turbay government declared war on the narcotraffickers. (Arrieta 1990: 293; and Bagley 1988: 79) At this time the Ministry of Justice and the Colombian National Police (CNP) coordinated Colombia's anti-drug effort through a policy making body called the *Consejo Nacional de Estupificantes* (CNE -National Council on Dangerous Drugs). Coca eradication and cocaine product interdiction was carried out by a 1,800 man *Directorio Anti-Narcoticos* (DAN - Anti-Narcotics Directorate) of the CNP. Besides an investigative and intelligence branch, the DAN had an operations branch and, over time, a supporting air wing of some twenty helicopters and other aircraft. The DAN was the "cutting edge" of the anti-drug, law enforcement portion of the CNP and was the office with which the US Embassy (Country Team) in Bogota coordinated and carried out much of the US anti-drug policy in Colombia.

The Ministry of Health was responsible for the drug prevention and media awareness programs of the government. The coca crop substitution program was run by the Ministry of Agriculture's Institute for Agrarian Reform (INCORA) and the National Institute of Natural Renewable Resources (INDERENA) which were responsible for all efforts to assist the coca farmers who desired to enter into other legitimate farming or other commercial occupations. Financing for the Colombian programs was roughly $25 million from an annual aid allocation of which the US was paying up to about half. (Interview DEA:CO 1993)

Since the later part of the 1970's or the beginning of the Turbay Ayala's liberal administration, Colombia had become the primary producer and exporter of marijuana destined for the US consumer market. Despite the fact that marijuana cultivation was illegal by national law, Colombian traffickers were involved in up to 65 percent of the growing, shipping and marketing processes. This involved some 10,000 metric tons (mt) of marijuana produced annually by up to 50,000 small plot farmers from an estimated 25,000 to 30,000 hectares (ha) located along Colombia's Caribbean coast (a hectare is equivalent to 2.5 acres). This brought the Colombian economy an estimated $300 million to $500 million per year in export revenues which were generally reinvested in the country. (House 1990c: 77; Bagley 1988: 74; and Arrieta 1990: 299)

The US government's anti-drug policy at the time had a primary focus on interdiction and eradication at the source (producing countries) in the hopes of disrupting the flow of drugs in quantity, thus avoiding to have to confront them once they had arrived and been dispersed for market consumption inside the US. Since marijuana was perceived as a significant problem in the US, it was only natural that on this basis alone Colombia should also become an anti-drug policy target of considerable note for the US government. Here too, Mexico and Jamaica had also been singled out as prominent in the trafficking of marijuana and were also being addressed by the US anti-drug policy. Nonetheless, it was Colombia which would receive a high priority focus in this regard during the early to mid-1980s. To this end the US placed great faith in the use of herbicides such as *paraquat* to be applied by either spraying or fumigation techniques to combat the growth of the marijuana crops. Having had considerable success in Mexico (also Jamaica) in reducing the marijuana crops there by as much as 90 percent, the US worked to persuade the Colombian government to follow suit and use herbicides in the same manner. (Arrieta 1990: 299) President Turbay, however, rejected this option and substituted instead the more conventional and traditional use of the Colombian armed forces and police to deal with marijuana through manual eradication. There were some reasonable grounds for this decision.

The CNE had been directed to look into the matter of the use of herbicides against marijuana and render a report. The result of the commission's investigation was the recommendation that no herbicides be utilized to eradicate marijuana crops until such time as proper experiments under Army control had been conducted in the Sierra Nevada Mountains near Santa Marta to determine if the chemicals could be used without endangering other types of crops. (Arrieta 1990: 301-302) The Army's ambivalent report was accepted by Turbay and served as the basis for his decision at that time not to proceed with the herbicide option until it was clear what would be its effect on the ecology of the targeted regions.

Nonetheless, Turbay was concerned about the various manifestations of the drug trafficking phenomenon in Colombia. Due to factors involving the corruption and contraband nature of the activities themselves, a new economic sector of considerable power and influence based on trafficking in both cocaine and marijuana was rapidly developing, over which the government had little or no control. In addition, the commerce in cocaine and marijuana was causing ever higher levels of crimes of violence which were also of concern to the government. (Arrieta 1990: 295) To deal with the marijuana problem which was generally focused on Colombia's Caribbean coast, the Colombian President issued his Decree 2144 in October of 1978 which directed that the Army assume the mission of suppressing the production of marijuana. To this end some 10,000 Army troops were deployed into the Guajira Peninsula region to execute *Operacion Fulminante* (Operation Fulminate). This operation lasted for the remainder of the year and throughout most of 1979, as the Army blockaded the Peninsula and achieved what appeared to be impressive results. Some 3,500 mt of marijuana were captured as well as 97 aircraft and 78 boats. Over 10,000 hectares (ha) of marijuana crops were destroyed and hundreds of persons were detained. (Arrieta 1990: 296-297)

While the results appeared impressive, not everything went well for the Army. Almost from the beginning of its eradication and interdiction operations it became subject to the corrupting influences of marijuana traffickers' bribes which tarnished the military's image. In addition it was accused of disrupting to some degree the general economy of the region which brought about the ire of a major portion of the civilian population. Likewise there were accusations of military heavy handedness or the excessive use of force resulting in human rights violations. (Tokatlian and Camacho 1993) In the end the growing of marijuana persevered in the face of the military's operations and the Army commander for the region, General Jose Maria Villarreal, contended that in order to be successful he would need five times the number of men then involved in the operation or some 40,000 additional soldiers. Even then he was not sure that he could guarantee a complete success against the flourishing marijuana business which always seemed to reappear in other parts of the country (Eastern Plains and Amazon regions) in a self-generating manner regardless of what efforts the Army attempted to take. It was for him a strange and highly irregular "war" to be fighting. That government anti-drug efforts would tend to merely displace drug production and shipping activities to other regions rather than eliminating them was very portentous for the US anti-drug policy to come. (Arrieta 1990: 297; and Bagley 1988: 80)

At the same time, the Army was complaining that anti-drug operations were interfering with its primary national security role and otherwise distracting it from confronting the various insurgencies then operating throughout Colombia. These were considered by the Army as threats to Colombia's internal security and were equated to being a national security issue or a *problema subversivo* (subversive problem) which was well within the legal purview of the Colombian armed forces to address. The guerrilla revolutionary movements of concern to the Army involved the rural based FARC with about 8,000 armed members, the much smaller urban based M-19 (*Movimiento 19 de Abril* - 19th of April Movement) and EPL (*Ejercito Popular de Liberacion* - Popular Liberation Army) organizations, and the both rural and urban based ELN (*Ejercito de Liberacion Nacional* - National Liberation Army) which numbered around 3,500 armed guerrillas. (Arrieta 1990: 298; and Chernick 1993) While the FARC hoped, through rural based campesino self-defense forces, to overthrow the government, the EPL was Maoist in orientation and operated in the mountains against the government. The ELN, operating in a north-central area or swath running from Arauca through Santander, Antioquia and Cordoba Departments to the Caribbean Sea, appealed to both students and campesinos, hoping to repeat the Cuban revolutionary phenomenon of Fidel Castro in that part of Colombia. (Zamosc 1990: 337-338; and Rutledge and Chernick: 1993)

These insurgencies were perceived by the Colombian Army to be threatening to the government of Colombia in the context of the successful Sandinista led revolution in Nicaragua of the late 1970s and the initiation of the civil war in El Salvador in the early 1980s by what were then to eventually become the Farabundo Marti National Liberation Front guerrillas. The Army could muster about 100,000 men which were faced by up to 20,000 guerrillas, not all of which were armed. While seemingly large in size, the Army did not have sufficient transportation and mobility in terms of helicopters and trucks to confront the highly mobile guerrillas who operated throughout Colombia. As such it had to be content with mounting selected operations against temporary concentrations of guerrillas which were only infrequently located in a timely manner by its intelligence services. (Thoumi 1990: 177)

During this time the US government was not idle and hoped to stimulate Colombian interest in supporting the US anti-drug policy

*Cocaine Quagmire*

efforts for combatting narcotrafficking in earnest at the source. To this end it had provided Colombia in 1978 with about $2.5 million for anti-narcotics activities. This was quickly followed in 1979 by grants in aid of about $3.8 million and again for 1980 at roughly $16 million or a considerably higher level of financing. (Arrieta 1990: 301)

While the US government and its US Embassy Country Team in Bogota desired to see enhanced Colombian military involvement in anti-drug operations, the Colombian Army took a dim view of this, claiming that anti-drug operations should be handled by an entity other than the military which desired to maintain its focus on the more traditional types of internal guerrilla-insurgency threats for which it had been conceived and trained. When the Army position became known, the US Congress barred the use of US funds for airborne radars, planes and communications equipment for the former because it feared they would be diverted for purposes other than fighting narcotrafficking. Based on what he saw transpire in Operation Fulminate, President Turbay tended to agree with his Army commanders and, while he declared that the traffickers were enemies of the state and that society in general should be mobilized against them, the police were ultimately singled out as the Colombian institution which should bare the brunt of the principal anti-drug mission. (Bagley 1988: 80; and Arrieta 1990: 298-299)

Despite the involvement of the Army in the marijuana eradication campaign along the Atlantic coast, the debate inside the country over the legalization of marijuana was causing considerable commotion. While Turbay advocated a *mano dura* (firm hand) against drug production and its usage, he was opposed by such highly visible personages in the form of the Mayor of Bogota (Bernardo Gaitan), a retired Army general (Jose Joaquin Matallana) and a number of other personalities involved in national politics. In addition, groups such as the Agricultural Society of Colombia and the National Association of Industries, as well as some north-coast departmental assemblies, also advocated legalization. While the debate raged on and the government maintained its staunch position against legalization, it was embarrassing to have such prominent and often vocal elements of Colombia's society visibly against the government's own anti-drug policy. Fortified by the strong anti-drug position of the US government's Country Team in Bogota, in the end Turbay successfully continued to reject any idea of legalization. (Arrieta 1990: 304-307)

In terms of supporting the US anti-drug policy, the Turbay government had entered into a bi-lateral extradition treaty with the US in 1979. This was done in part to reduce Colombia's negative international image of being weak in the face of narcotrafficking activities and to improve its relationship with the US. Traffickers wanted by the US government for violations of its laws were no longer immune inside Colombia and were now vulnerable to US prosecution. (Insight: 2 Apr 90; and Lee 1989: 211) To this end Colombia also signed during the period of 1979 - 1981 a series of bilateral agreements on the prevention and repression of illegal drugs and trafficking with Venezuela, Ecuador, Peru, Honduras, the Dominican Republic and Brazil. (Arrieta 1990: 308)

Yet, the extradition treaty with the US, while well intentioned on the part of Turbay, placed Colombia in a position of formally acknowledging that its laws and judicial system were insufficiently strong or effective and otherwise incapable of dealing with its own domestic trafficking situation. It also appeared to highlight a perception that only the laws of the US were efficient and correct for the judging of persons involved with narcotrafficking. Worse yet, it abrogated Colombia's sovereignty over its internal law enforcement institutions in respect to how the drug problem should be approached, adhering to US prescriptions of anti-drug policies instead of its own. For these reasons both the US and the Colombian governments played down the extradition issue.

The treaty, promulgated as Law 27 in Colombia and signed on 3 November 1980, did give Turbay his *mano dura* which he could always bring into play to beat down the traffickers or deal with other particularly obnoxious individuals. (Tokatlian and Silva Lujan 1993; and Arrieta 1990: 309-310) Nonetheless, the Colombian Supreme Court took exception to the fact that the treaty had not been actually signed by the President personally and overturned it! Here the matter stood until the advent of the next administration. (Lee 1989: 213) Throughout this time and into the mid-1980s, the Medellin cartel controlled the supply of up to 80 percent of the cocaine consumed in the US. (Arrieta 1990: 51) On the other hand, life was not always easy for the traffickers who themselves had to contend with other threats besides those of the government in the form of the insurgency movements inside Colombia.

While the guerrillas in Colombia could make a substantial claim to having a just cause on which to base their respective revolutionary movements, their efforts to raise monies to support their operations often placed them in a confrontational situation with the traffickers. Some FARC guerrillas attempted to displace the cartel middle men or coca paste buyers, only to find themselves ignored and their offers of paste for sale rejected. Confrontation became especially prevalent when kidnapping was indulged in by the guerrillas to exploit the potentially high payoffs offered by wealthy narcotrafficker kingpins and their family members. As the guerrillas' proclivity to use kidnapping as a primary means of raising large sums of money for their respective war chests increased and the traffickers became highly lucrative targets of opportunity, the latter began to organize to better protect themselves. (Chernick 1993; Arrieta 1990: 224; and Bagley 1988: 84) In 1981 various groups, such as the Cali and Medallin cartels, formed MAS (*Muerte A Secuestradores* - Death To Kidnappers) as a response to the threat of guerrilla kidnapping. This came about as the result of a meeting between a reported 223 leading traffickers who decided to form a paramilitary strike force numbering over 2,000 armed men, supported by a working capital of between $4.5 and $7.5 million. (Eddy 1988: 287; and Kolton 1990: 51) MAS represented the epitome of a violence prone society and would operate on almost a continuous basis throughout the decade of the 1980s, retaliating against the guerrillas, persecuting leftists, labor union organizers and anyone else who dared to harass or attempted to intimidate the traffickers. To this end some Colombian Army officers were also reported as being members of MAS and the paramilitary group enjoyed a tacitly warm working relationship with the Army. Ironically, later on during the 1990s MAS would also provide the infamous sicarios who would terrorize the nation at will. (Tokatlian and Camacho 1993)

The M-19 was one of the first guerrilla groups to cross swords with MAS. This occurred over the kidnapping of Marta Nieves Ochoa, the sister of Jorge Ochoa, in Medellin during January of 1982. (Gugliotta and Leen 1989: 91) At the direction of the Ochoa clan, MAS elements, having identified the M-19 guerrillas as the perpetrators of the deed, counter-attacked and did in weeks what the Colombian Army and police had been unable to do for years - virtually wiping out the M-19 as an operating force within the city of Medellin. The now terrorized M-19 survivors released Marta Nieves Ochoa without having received the $12 to $15 million demanded in ransom. Over time MAS extended its operations throughout the Departments of Cundinamarca, Valle and Antioquia, striking fear into the hearts of the guerrillas and winning the grudging admiration and respect of both the Army and police over its acknowledged efficiency in repressing kidnapping, extortion, and other similar harassments on the part of the guerrillas. (Gugliotta and Leen 1989: 92-93; Lee 1989: 163; and Chernick 1993)

Despite this, during the early 1980s Gonzalo Rodriguez Gacha, in exchange for paying a high rate of extorsive guerrilla war taxes, attempted to engage the FARC in formally protecting his airstrips and laboratories (Rodriguez Gacha also owned coca plantations as well as laboratories), which he planned to construct in remote, FARC controlled territory. The FARC refused and proceeded to raid Rodriguez's operations in the Guaviare Department, stealing weapons, some coca and a half million dollars in cash. A vendetta ensued over the years with each group killing off some of the other's supporters, including one of Colombia's highest ranking communists, Jaime Pardo Leal. (Castillo 1987: 234-235) To this end both the guerrilla and the narcotrafficking groups generally remained at loggerheads as the latter hired sicarios to protect their interests.

Turbay's anti-drug policy was based on the reality of the times in which some ten percent of the Colombian Congress was reported as having been elected in part through the use of narcotrafficker contributions. (Washington Post: 6 Jan 80) Trafficking groups had been encouraged by the less than unified position taken by individual Colombian politicians who often found both themselves and their immediate family members at high risk and vulnerable to extortion and intimidation in the form of reprisals, if their cooperation was not readily forthcoming on behalf the cartel groups. In addition the Colombian government's policy for actually dealing with the traffickers was not always clear, coherent or even sustained over the long run. (Arrieta 1990: 17) In this situation state policy oscillated between an often virtually complete tolerance on the one hand and strong repressive action on the other. Reflecting the confusion, government legislation failed to address the retrieval of trafficker funds from abroad for investment within the Colombian stock exchange or directly into domestic commercial enterprises involving real estate, construction and finances etc. (Arrieta 1990: 18) Annual exports of cocaine were estimated to be bringing Colombia between $1.5 billion and $4.1 billion in foreign exchange. While not particularly large in size relative to the remainder of the economy, the impact of this investment of narcotrafficker profits inside Colombia did have some positive effects on the economy. Narcodollars provided jobs for thousands of workers in construction and other related industries. (Arrieta 1990: 20; and Kalmanovitz 1993)

While benefiting the economy, trafficker investment operations also resulted in a corresponding rise in the index of violence. As the propensity for extortion and violence increased on the part of the Medellin traffickers over real estate acquisitions, both the poor campesinos and other indigenous land owners often found themselves uprooted, fostering in turn a propensity to take out their frustrations by joining the guerrilla groups which were attempting to expand their own influence over more and more of the national territory. (Arrieta 1990: 31; and Chernick 1993) As it was, the traffickers sought to obtain from the Colombian government and society at large both an acceptance of their operations as legitimate businesses and the elimination of any and all extradition treaties which might be directed at them. To this end intimidation and corruption were the methods used to seek judicial and congressional compliance with trafficker interests, as well as neutralizing portions of the state's anti-drug internal security apparatus. (Arrieta 1990: 30) As the Turbay administration came to an end in 1982, the US anti-drug policy in Colombia now found itself confronted by a series of cultural, socio-economic and political obstacles which would provide it with a formidable challenge for the years to come.

# Chapter 2

# The War On Drugs Comes To Colombia

In February of 1982 Ronald Reagan, cognizant of the ever escalating
drug usage and its effects on the health of significant portions of the
American population, declared war on drugs both at home and abroad.
The US government's focuses were to be on drug abuse and illegal drug
dealing within the continental USA, and the production, refining and
trafficking overseas in the source countries of which Colombia was
considered an acute case. To this end expenditures within the federal
government over the next seven years of the Reagan administration
were increased substantially to about $4.3 billion by 1988. To promote
his initiative Reagan made use of national television to dramatize his
perspective and to galvanize support for his mobilization of federal
resources to fight the war on drugs. The Congress supported the Reagan
initiative with anti-drug legislation to enhance law enforcement
programs in foreign source and transit countries such as Colombia. The
president's spouse, Mrs Nancy Reagan, launched her own public
relations campaign in an effort to educate and indoctrinate the American
public and its youth about the dangers of drug usage and abuse.
(Callahan 1993)

Over time, more information became known about the international
aspect of cocaine trafficking which emanated from Colombia. It was
supposed by Reagan and others within his administration that the supply
of cocaine and other drugs such as marijuana were exacerbating the
domestic drug problem within the US. If supply could be reduced
significantly or even cut off and stopped, then fewer people would be
involved in drug usage, or so the reasoning went. Eradication of coca
and marijuana could easily be measured and quantified in terms of how

many hectares of plants had been destroyed. Over time this became the principal yardstick by which the Congress and other government offices would measure the progress of the Andean anti-drug policy effort. All government agencies were expected to assist in their own way in addressing the drug issue. US embassies (Country Teams) throughout the Andes were urged to further develop coca eradication and other suitable drug control programs. (Interview NSC: 1993)

Government agencies went to work on the issue. The US National Security Agency (NSA) provided information on narcotrafficking operations which ultimately assisted the Colombian authorities in their March 1984 raids on the Tranquilandia cocaine refining complex. (Walker 1989: 211) It was also during this period of 1982 through 1985 that the US military began to support counter-drug smuggling detection and interdiction operations in the Caribbean. Almost immediately the traffickers reacted by establishing other transhipment routes through Central America and Mexico into the US. (Bagley 1991: 9-10) By that time the traffickers were known to be operating in groups whose operations were characterized as cartels. These groups in themselves were known to be centered in and around the cities of Cali and Medellin, Colombia, and were reported to control between 60 and 70 percent of the international cocaine market. (Lee 1989: 100)

The Reagan administration, to better address the drug issue, wanted to develop and coordinate anti-drug policy in a coherent manner as part of an integrated national strategy. The Congress assisted by creating the National Drug Policy Board (NDPB) which was chaired by the Attorney General, Edwin Meese III, and was comprised of the heads of some 15 US government departments and agencies. This was acceptable to President Reagan who opposed the concept of a drug czar or a single dominating agency whose all-encompassing powers would tend to eclipse all other agencies as it formulated general anti-drug policy and directed all drug related federal operations of the several dozen agencies involved to one degree or another in federal anti-drug efforts. (GAO 1988a: 15; and Van Wert 1988: 6) The NDPB, while establishing nine lead agencies to review issues and make recommendations for formulating the anti-drug policy, looked to the Department of State's Bureau of International Narcotics Matters (INM) to chair the International Standing Committee (ISC) which made policy and program recommendatins to the NDPB on all international narcotics control issues involving Colombia, as well as the other Andean countries. (Van Wert 1988: 6-7)

The Department of State (DOS) never really accepted the NDPB's involvement in overseas anti-drug issues and asserted its prerogative to represent the US government's international anti-drug position, using Section 400 of the Foreign Assistance Act legislation as its own justification as to why it should be in charge of all international narcotics matters. Irritating to the DOS was Meese's tendency to blend together foreign and domestic anti-drug policy issues. (Interview NSC 1993) The basic problem with the NDPB, however, was that it did not have the legal authority by statute to require other government agencies to redirect their plans and programs in support of anti-drug activities and perceived priorities or, even if they did, to coordinate the various diverse efforts toward a common goal. The NDPB strategy consisted of nothing more than a generally disjointed compilation of plans and ideas submitted by the separate US government departments and law enforcement agencies. In addition it was difficult to develop budgeting priorities because the NDPB also did not have the information required to determine which anti-drug initiatives merited priority attention. As a result anti-drug policies were frequently fragmented and uncoordinated. (House 1990: 1; and GAO 1988a 15)

With the advent of the conservative government of Colombian President Belisario Betancur Cuartas in August 1982, the US government began to exert pressure on the former to put the 1979 extradition treaty process into effect. To expedite this end the US Country Team in Bogota sent a note in early April of 1983 soliciting the extradition for trial in the US of one Emiro de Jesus Mejia Roman, a Colombian citizen then being held in Colombia on charges relating to narcotrafficking. Nonetheless, in a surprise turnabout, the Colombian Attorney General (*Procurador General*), Carlos Jimenez Gomez, declared unconstitutional the extradition treaty with the US. This caused considerable consternation among members of the Country Team in Bogota and the Reagan administration in Washington, D.C., since the Attorney General's office had previously been one of the principal instruments in support of an extradition treaty with the US in the first place. The affair dragged on until late October when the Colombian Supreme Court issued a pronouncement in favor of the extradition of Mejia Roman. Nonetheless, the following November President Betancur, by executive fiat, rejected the extradition of Mejia Roman and any other presumed narcotraffickers. (Arrieta 1990: 315-316)

The US, greatly incensed at this rebuff, directed its Ambassador to Colombia, Lewis A. Tambs, to castigate the Betancur government over its non-compliance in meeting the US extradition request, while the US Department of Justice protested formally to the Colombian Embassy in

Washington, D.C. The Colombian Minister of Justice, Rodrigo Lara Bonilla, feeling the US ire over the extradition issue, stated that while the Colombian government had the right to act independently in matters of this nature, it would review the treaty to better define the criteria for extradition. (Arrieta 1990: 316) Here too, the US Congress became more involved in the issue as House member Charles Rangel recommended retaliatory sanctions against Colombian cut flowers and other imports into the US. In November 1983 in its Public Law 98-164, known as the Hawkins-Gilman Amendment, the US Congress required that the Bureau of International Narcotics Matters (INM) of the DOS begin presenting an annual report on the compliance of Colombia and other nations with the US interests in the war on drugs. US anti-drug as well as military and economic assistance would be determined to a considerable extent on the findings presented in the INM reports. On this note the relations between Colombia and the US in late 1983 and early 1984 became tense, if not badly strained. (Arrieta 1990: 316-317)

During this time narcotrafficking inside Colombia saw a dramatic increase in its activity as it continued to meet international demand and provide at least 75 percent of the refined cocaine for the North American consumer market. The influence of the cartels also increased as both corruption and intimidation activities took place. Some traffickers such as Carlos Lehder, feeling relatively secure in their circumstances, founded their own political parties (Lehder founded the National Latin Movement - *Movimiento Latino Nacional* or MLN). By investing narco-dollars in public works projects in the Quindio and Risalda areas, Lehder was ultimately able to claim a following of around 100,000 friends and political supporters. (Arrieta 1990: 227) Another of the "social benefactors" or traffickers operating with a domestic agenda inside Colombia was Pablo Escobar Gaviria whose own civil works projects included the construction of up to 500 two-bedroom cement-block houses in a Medellin slum, as well as the provision of sanitation, sewer repair, clinics, educational facilities, lighting, and sports centers and buildings which had the primary purpose as well as ulterior motive of building a cordon sanitare of security around Escobar and promoting his own interests in gaining influence within the New Liberal Party movement. (Lee 1989: 11) Domestic construction, finance and farming all experienced booms as narco-dollars were reinvested in the Colombian economy. During this time, the Orejuela family of the Cali cartel controlled a financial empire comprising an automobile dealership, construction firms, drug stores, real estate and toy companies, an automobile racetrack, a bank (*Banco de los Trabajadores*) and some 28 radio stations. (Castillo 1987: 129-131)

By influencing the democratic system of politics, Escobar and others like him hoped to gain substantial protective influence within the Colombian Congress which could then be used to protect and support trafficking interests as needed. (Lee 1989: 5; and Arrieta 1990: 229) To assist in their endeavors to influence domestic politics on their behalf, both Lehder and Escobar even bought control of or founded magazines and newspapers, such as the *Quindio Libre* (Lehder) and the *Medellin Civico* (Escobar). These publications lobbied against extradition and promoted the traffickers' civic action activities as merely deeds of public-spirited citizens who had the people's welfare foremost in their minds. Escobar's efforts paid off as he was elected in 1982 as an alternate deputy for one of the seats in the Colombian House of Representatives. Lehder, on the other hand, was less than successful in his own bid for the Colombian Senate. (Bagley 1988: 77; and Lee 1989: 11)

During these years or beginning in 1983 with some U.S. urging, Betancur had become interested in bringing about a more extensive involvement on the part of the Colombian military in the anti-drug effort. To this end the military and police conducted joint operations against both the laboratory processing systems and the areas of actual coca production. Despite presidential emphasis along these lines, the Colombian armed forces, especially the Army, preferred a less obvious and more discrete anti-drug role. Well remembered was the trying period of Operation Fulminate. To offset the military's apprehension over conflicting priorities and proper national security roles, Betancur had been trying to negotiate an end to the insurgencies, opening a peace process based on dialogue with the various guerrilla groups. The Army, however, still viewed the guerrillas as the primary threat to Colombian society and, advocating *mano dura* or repression as a primary policy, was somewhat intransigent in terms of modifying its view to coincide with those of the President. This view contrasted with the president's policy of initiating social reforms, freeing hundreds of political prisoners and granting amnesty for the guerrillas as part of a peace process. While Betancur attempted to open the political process during 1983, over a thousand left-oriented political leaders and aspirants were murdered. With death threats and political murders escalating, the peace process floundered as both the military and police and the insurgents increasingly violated the government-guerrilla cease fire agreement. (House 1990b: 83) Played down during this time was the paramilitary threat offered by the narcotraffickers. Nonetheless, it was fear of corruption and the serious doubts on the part of the Army that it could play an effective role in successfully confronting and concluding the highly irregular drug war involving narcotrafficking commercial operations that produced most of its institutional apprehension and even some demoralization. (Arrieta 1990: 320-321)

More indicative of the actual situation in Colombia was the Army's willingness to sometimes protect the cocaine industry against the FARC guerrillas. At the end of 1983 an Army special forces unit from the 7th Brigade stationed at Villavicencio assisted the traffickers in relocating an entire cocaine production laboratory complex which had been threatened by extortion (up to $500,000) from the First FARC Front in Caqueta. After the laboratory, under Army protection, was moved in private planes to a remote site near the Brazilian border out of reach of the guerrillas, the special forces personnel involved each received payments for their services, ranging from about $500 to $2,500. (El Espectador: 1 Aug 85) Ironically, when the situation was exposed, those officers who were disciplined received punishments for taking bribes, not for helping the narcotraffickers. (El Espectador: 1 Aug 85) What had happened was, in part, a reflection of what had transpired earlier in 1983 when the 7th Brigade rescued 18 hostages and recovered two airplanes taken by the FARC guerrillas during a raid on a cocaine laboratory processing site located at a cattle ranch within the 7th Brigade's area of operational responsibility. (El Tiempo: 26 and 27 Jan 83) Apparently the collusion with and protection given the narcotraffickers in the face of guerrilla activities were seen as a way to enhance the Army's own counter-guerrilla missions in the future, implying that the traffickers might be helpful to the Army in combating guerrillas in other circumstances.

Yet violence, too, was noticeably on the increase and on 30 April 1984 narcotrafficker sicarios (gunmen) contracted by the Ochoa brothers, assassinated the Minister of Justice, Rodrigo Lara Bonilla. (Senate 1988a: 30) While the government had not shown a great deal of interest in implementing its extradition treaty with the US, Lara Bonilla himself had been working to denounce and block trafficking operations. To this end, using data provided by the DEA, he openly supported and worked to conduct an operation which on 10 March, or some weeks prior to his assassination, successfully targeted the southeastern Caqueta Department, destroying a cocaine refining complex in the Yari River and Guaviare Department involving 14 processing laboratories and 6 airstrips which were scattered throughout an area of about 3,000 square kilometers. Captured were some 14 mt of cocaine valued at a reported $1.2 billion on the international market - the largest amount of refined cocaine captured to date in a single operation. The laboratory complex, known as *Tranquilandia* (tranquil land) was estimated to have produced about ten percent of the 110 mt of cocaine thought at this time to be refined on an annual basis in Colombia. (Lee 1989: 171; Bagley 1988: 81; Miami Herald: 23 Mar 84; and Arrieta 1990: 317 and 223)

The *Tranquilandia* laboratory complex was reported as belonging to the Ochoa, Gonzalo Rodriguez Gacha and Pablo Escobar clans. Then too, there was another complicating factor which surfaced concerning the issue of guerrilla involvement in the protection of laboratories. When another airstrip and several other laboratories were found near La Loma in the general vicinity of the Yari site, equipment and documents belonging to the FARC were also found. (Lee 1989: 171-172) The FARC was then singled out by Ambassador Lewis Tambs as not only providing security for cocaine producing installations but also being involved in the actual production of coca and its marketing operations. In addition, the M-19 guerrillas were also linked to the issue when they claimed that they were in the process of retaliating against the government over the latter's highly successful operations in the Guaviare-Yari River region. (Arrieta 1990: 223-224; and Gugliotta and Leen 1989: 135-136)

The murder of the popular Lara Bonilla caused considerable consternation inside Colombia and President Betancur found himself confronting an image of a nation controlled by the drug barons and their cartels. The traffickers, in an effort to pressure the US government into desisting from its anti-drug activities, placed a $500,000 price on the US Ambassador's head and further offered $300,000 for the capture, dead or alive, of any DEA agent in Colombia. (Clutterbuck 1990: 93) Public opinion became highly animated over Lara Bonilla's death and demanded that action be taken to eliminate the narcotrafficker scourge now perceived as afflicting Colombian society. The heretofore "US problem" had now become Colombia's problem. (Gugliotta and Leen 1989: 170) For President Betancur extradition now appeared to be an acceptable solution. Under considerable internal pressure from the Colombian people, as well as external pressure from the US, Betancur began to implement the 1979 extradition treaty. Also at this time economic problems inside Colombia were becoming exacerbated and the government was badly in need of financial assistance to get it through this trying period. To this end it sought to mend its fences with the US and an unprecedented number of arrests, confiscations of property and destruction of cocaine laboratories took place. (Camacho and Tokatlian 1993)

During May, Carlos Lehder was apprehended and extradited to the US for trial. By the end of 1984 five other US requests for extradition had been favorably viewed and in January 1985 four Colombian traffickers were turned over to the US government to stand trial. In short, the use of extradition had set a precedent which the US would now use as a standard to evaluate in part its anti-drug policy concerning Colombia. (Arrieta 1990: 318) As it was, President Reagan congratulated Betancur on his decision to support the US anti-drug efforts and assist in the arrest and extradition of key traffickers to the US. (El Espectador: 13 Dec 84) The Washington, D.C. community also responded to the Colombian initiatives and increased anti-narcotics aid accordingly from about $3.5 million in 1983 to $10.6 million in 1986. The US also threw its weight into favorably influencing IMF financing for Colombia and invited Betancur to visit the White House - all actions symbolic of the now mended US-Colombian relationship. (Arrieta 1990: 319) At this point in time the US anti-drug policy had received a noticeable boost and the Country Team sought to exploit its now apparently favorable position to the fullest.

President Betancur had declared *guerra total* (total war) on narcotrafficking and Rodrigo Lara Bonilla's death served as a catalyst for action as no other event up to that time had been able to. (Arrieta 1990: 321) Invoking the extradition treaty was a transcendental event. Bringing the military into play against the narcotraffickers as a next step was another. These actions by the Colombian government would manifest themselves in several dimensions: operations, international support and judicial proceedings.

Action took place rapidly as the Colombian Executive issued its Decree 1038 on 1 May 1984, placing the entire country under an *estado de sitio* (state of siege). The Army was now granted the authority to conduct operations when and where it wanted. Legal writ was no longer required to confiscate or seize any and all private property including aircraft, electrical generators, precursor materials, houses and buildings or any other personal belongings thought to belong to the traffickers and their respective organizations. Destroying laboratories and coca-marijuana crop lands were also part and parcel of the government's offensive. Nonetheless, in accordance with the government's policy, all military operations were to be accomplished in close coordination with the national police. (Arrieta 1990: 321) The Army-police operations disrupted trafficking inside Colombia to the degree that the price of cocaine on the street in the US went form $15,000 per kilo (2.2 pounds) in Miami to highs ranging from $25,000 to $30,000, as the availability of cocaine lessened substantially. (Arrieta 1990: 242) The risks and costs of doing business inside Colombia had gone up significantly and the traffickers were now passing these off to the consumer by raising prices accordingly.

On 2 May, Decree 1042 was issued by the government to allow the military to apply its own penal codes against the civil population in general to help subdue and bring to trial the traffickers. Military justice and its related legal processes now supplanted the more lenient civilian courts and systems of law, placing much of Colombia under martial law and giving the military further unprecedented authority to act as it pleased. At the same time and at the encouragement of the Country Team, the government formed its own commission to investigate money laundering and study its political and economic impacts on the country. To this end investigations were conducted to determine how the traffickers were actually laundering their money and how the government might actually prevent this activity. (Lee 1989: 141; and Arrieta 1990: 242)

As part of the international linkages brought into play, the Colombian government and military extended and established close ties with the US Southern Command (SOUTHCOM) headquarters in Panama then under the command of General Paul Gorman. In this case the US military wanted to establish an anti-drug aerial surveillance search radar on either San Andres or Providencia Islands in the Caribbean. These Colombian controlled islands were located just off the coast of Nicaragua and astride some of the main narcotrafficking routes from Colombia into the US. Yet, there was a political incentive that was also in play in this situation. By acceding to US desires, Colombia would receive the always desired international recognition of its sovereignty over the two islands, an issue long contested by nearby Nicaragua. (Arrieta 1990: 321-322) An agreement was consummated and, in return for Colombian permission to allow the establishment of the radars for anti-drug operations which recognized its defacto as well as dejure control over the islands, the US Congress authorized an increase in the military aid program for Colombia, provided that it was used to engage the traffickers.

Another result of the Lara Bonilla murder which greatly favored the US anti-drug policy in Colombia was the decision by Betancur to accede to US requests to initiate the long sought use of herbicides to deal at least with the marijuana crops. Fumigation and spraying using the herbicide agent *paraquat* was the technique desired by the US with a principal focus on the Colombian Atlantic coast region. On 22 May 1984 the Council of Ministers reversed the previous policy and approved the use of herbicides to eradicate marijuana. The only exception to the US desired herbicide policy was the substitution of *glifosate* for paraquat. Glifosate was thought by the influential Agricultural Livestock Institute (ICA) to have less of a potential for collateral damage effecting the ecology of the target region than even the planting of marijuana itself could have. Roughly a week later or on 1 June orders were issued by the Colombian government to begin spraying and fumigation operations. Despite protests from the indigenous Indian groups such as the Arhuaco, Koguis and Malayos, spraying commenced as planned. (Lee 1989: 208-209; and Arrieta 1990: 323-324)

By the end of 1984 approximately 3,400 ha of marijuana crops had been eradicated principally through the use of glifosate. A year later or by the end of 1985 up to 8,000 ha were also eradicated. (Lee 1989: 209) The process continued and during 1986 up to 12,000 ha were further eradicated. Despite the obvious impact of the herbicide effort and the reduction of an estimated 22 percent of the Colombian marijuana production, by 1988 Colombia was still producing some 8,000 mt of marijuana, remaining the foremost producer of marijuana exported into the US. (Lee 1989: 210; and Arrieta 1990: 325) Under pressure from the government's eradication efforts, Marijuana farmers now moved away from the north coast into the Cauca Department where, ironically, the crop was even more favorably affected by the climate and soils there, increasing production levels up to 3.5 mt per hectare annually or well above the 1.1 mt per hectare achieved on the Caribbean coast. (Arrieta 1990: 326) Nonetheless, an eradication trend had been established which, by the end of 1989, was to show dramatic results.

At this time the Colombian government attempted to identify a herbicide which could be used successfully on coca crops without damaging adjacent legitimate agricultural crops. Beginning in December of 1985 a herbicide known as *Garlon* 4 was identified as a possible candidate and experimented with against some 1,000 ha of coca crops. By early 1986 it was decided to discontinue the use of the Garlon 4 chemical as it was found to have damaged or killed off most of the adjacent non-coca crops. In addition, the Dow Chemical Corporation, the manufacturer of Garlon-4, unable to obtain US and Colombian indemnification against potential law suits stemming from its use, opted to discontinue providing Colombia with the herbicide for fear of the potential adverse political and social repercussions which might occur, damaging the company's pharmaceutical reputation and business interests throughout Latin America. (GAO 1988c: 29; Arrieta 1990: 326; and Lee 1989: 210)

Beginning in mid-1984 the Colombian government was approached by over a hundred traffickers represented by Pablo Escobar, Jorge Ochoa, Gonzalo Rodriguez Gacha and others desiring to enter into a dialogue and negotiations. These traffickers, feeling the pressure of possible capture and the seizures by the Army and police of their personal possessions, met Colombian representatives in a series of secret meetings in Panama. Their serial aims were to try to have the stigma of being viewed in public as criminals formally removed, a guarantee of no extradition to the US agreed to by the Colombian government, and their reincorporation into Colombian society as normal citizens approved by the government. In exchange they offered to dismantle their respective organizations and retire from the narcotics trafficking trade. (Lee 1989: 110-111; El Tiempo 7 Jul 84; and Arrieta 1990: 329) President Betancur categorically rejected the traffickers' offer. In this he was supported by the majority of the Colombian mass media, the major political parties and the Congress. The heightened animosity of the media and the general population against the traffickers had been greatly exacerbated by the revelations concerning the secret meetings in Panama and the July 1984 murder of Judge Julio Manuel Castro Gil who was then leading the investigation of the assassination of the popular Lara Bonilla. (Lee 1989: 142; and Arrieta 1990: 330)

Yet the most spectacular action to take place involving narcotrafficker intimidation and terrorist type actions was the work of guerrillas operating on behalf of trafficking interests the following year. Here the M-19, reportedly paid about $1 million by the Medellin cartel, seized the building of the Ministry of Justice (Palacio de Justicia) on 6 November of 1985 with the apparent objective of destroying the documentation supporting a series of cases linking the principal cocaine traffickers to a number of pending extradition initiatives. During the operation which included a vicious government sponsored tank-led Army counter-attack that destroyed much of the Ministry of Justice building, over a hundred persons died, including 11 of 24 of Colombia's Supreme Court Justices and all of the members of the Council of State or Colombia's constitutional chamber. The Justices had recently declared a position in favor of the US-Colombian extradition treaty and for this reason may have been the real target of the Medellin cartel's inspired M-19 attack. (House 1990c: 88; Insight: 2 Apr 90; Claudio: 1991: 71; and Lee 1989: 172-173) The resulting outcry from the general population over the Palace of Justice attack encouraged the government to enter into what was the first joint US-Colombian judicial enhancement aid program which was administered by AID. Called Administration of Justice-One (AOJ-1), the program provided a total of $1.5 million over several years, focusing on administration, training and studies on how to improve the Colombian judicial system. (House 1990c: 88) In addition, the Colombian government expanded the horizons of its own operations.

As part of a series of cross-border operations called Condor I and II, the Colombian and Peruvian governments, exploiting US provided intelligence, coordinated interdiction operations and worked together to target laboratories and airstrips in the north-Peruvian Amazon region and along the Colombian border's Putumayo River. In this case Colombian helicopters carrying police para-commando units carried out a series of operations inside Peru which, although approved by the Peruvian Ministry of Interior, were viewed by the Peruvian military as a violation of Peruvian sovereignty and air space, diminishing their intended impact. (Lee 1989: 221) Feeling the government's ever increasing counter-narcotics pressures, for the remainder of the year and on into mid-1986 the traffickers continued to lobby the government on their own behalf to no avail. In late 1985 Pablo Escobar of the Medellin cartel even met secretly in Panama with Colombia's then Attorney General, Carlos Mario Hoyos Jimenez. There Escobar offered, in exchange for a revised extradition treaty with the US and a guarantee of no extradition for himself, to voluntarily turn himself over to Colombian authorities for a retroactive judicial prosecution without prejudice and to pay off the entire $15 billion Colombian national debt. (Claudio 1991: 71) While tempting to some members of the government, upon hearing about the offer, President Betancur rejected it and remained steadfast in his position which advocated strong action against all narcotraffickers. Time went on and in mid-1986 the Colombian democratic process came into play again as a new President was elected.

By the mid-1980s the US anti-drug policy found itself at a position of relative high tide compared to the decade of the 1970s. A somewhat lethargic Colombian government at the beginning of the decade had now been galvanized into action. This was due principally to the proclivity of some trafficker elements to engage in violence in an effort to intimidate or otherwise coerce government personalities into acquiescing in the traffickers' interests. Perceived as a potential threat to the state, narcotrafficker violence had became an issue which the highest levels of the Colombian government could not ignore. This produced a generally favorable effect in the form of public outcries and a government backlash against the trafficker inspired violence. This Colombian effort supported the US anti-drug policy.

Up to the mid-1980s the National Security Council (NSC) looked at the international narcotrafficking issue as merely peripheral and part of its Middle East focus concerning terrorism. This began to change as the intensifying domestic interest on the issue, along with a fear of international terrorism, competed for attention at the highest levels of the Reagan administration. A 1985 household survey which had considerable impact on government leaders indicated that cocaine client admissions since the advent of the Reagan administration had doubled! (DHHS 1987: cover page) Over ten percent of the population or some 23 million persons over twelve years of age were now reported to be using drugs in some form each year. These were startling figures for an administration which had supposedly declared war on drugs two years earlier. Every month the situation appeared to be getting worse rather than better. As a result the decision was made by President Reagan to highlight the problem for the American people by elevating and presenting the government's concern as a national security issue. (Interview ONDCP 1: 1993)

Besides attracting considerable public attention and support, it was expected that a national security emphasis would better focus the government's efforts and justify increased spending, as well as permit an ever greater role for the US military in the counter-drug effort. Both Reagan and the NSC thought that making the drug war a national security issue would both underscore the seriousness of the drug problem and send a signal to the international community that the US was very serious in its pursuit of the narcotrafficking scourge. The Andean countries, including Colombia, were now to receive an intensified special focus in order to deal with cocaine at its source. To this end, in the Fall of 1985, government agencies and Country Teams overseas were put on notice to this end, clearly signaling that dealing with drugs was now a national security imperative. (Intervies ONDCP 1: 1993; GAO 1988a: 14; and author observation)

It was, however, president Reagan's National Security Decision Directive (NSDD) 221 of 12 April 1986 that formally launched the process of intensive US government and military involvement in the

Andean narcotics situation. Drug trafficking was now officially declared a threat to US national security and not merely a domestic or social problem. National security threats were normally dealt with internationally and this favored the supply-side source targeting perspective which the administration advocated as the solution to the drug issue. While NSDD 221 sanctioned the expanded involvement of the US military in the drug war, certain protocols in the form of guide lines regulated US military employment. First, US forces had to be invited by the host country's government. Second, their actual operations had to be directed and coordinated by US civilian agencies and finally, their operations were to be limited to support functions only with no premeditated direct involvement in a potential lethal, confrontational situation with the traffickers which could lead to undue personal injury to the military personnel involved. (Bagley 1991: 5; and author recollection)

The US Country Team's early 1986 Bolivian Operation Blast Furnace proposal for a more militant approach in dealing with trafficking in that country was seized upon by the NSC as an easy way to get the Department of Defense more directly involved in the drug war at little cost. Ignoring the Country Team's position that an all-encompassing strategy and related anti-drug campaigns had to be thoroughly planned out and prepared for in order to achieve decisive results in Bolivia, the NSC made the decision to execute Blast Furnace more as an experiment than as a series of sequenced and integrated operations extending through both the dry and wet seasons over the period of a year or longer. (Interview ONDCP 1 and 2: 1993)

To this end the US Southern Command (SOUTHCOM) in Panama was notified by the JCS in early July 1986 and given only two weeks to prepare for and commence operations with a task force of 160 soldiers and six Blackhawk helicopters in support of the Country Team's anti-drug program in Bolivia. No attempt was made to coordinate Blast Furnace with other anti-drug programs then in place in Colombia and Peru or elsewhere. (Interview NSC 1993) The limited focus and duration of Blast Furnace insured that its impact was only temporary in nature and as such it had no long term impact in favor of the US anti-drug policy. Only the traffickers appeared to benefit from the operation as a learning experience as to what they could expect in the future from the Reagan administration's source oriented anti-drug efforts. Nonetheless, Blast Furnace set a precedent for the Andes region and the US policy for the drug war there was now becoming very much a militarized affair. The importance of this was not lost on Colombia.

(Bagley 1991: 11-12; and author observation)

Colombia's newly elected Conservative Party President Virgilio Barco Vargas inherited the US-Colombian anti-drug policy from his predecessor on 7 August 1986. At this time narcotrafficking in Colombia was allegedly accounting for national revenues of up to $2 billion annually compared to Colombia's $5.3 billion in official export revenues. (Lee 1989: 39 and 104; and Arrieta 1990: 331) As a result, the drug market was thought to be producing a multiplier effect, stimulating the national economy by as much as 15 percent of its $40 billion GNP. Demand for trafficker sponsored luxury housing and other projects benefitted the building and construction industries. Calls for cement, bricks, stone, glass and wood etc responded to the increased construction activities and, in turn, created an ever higher demand for labor and provided many needy persons with jobs. (Lee 1989: 6; Bagley 1990: 44; and Kalmanovitz 1992: 39)

An example of the positive economic effect the cocaine industry had on Colombia could be seen in the case of the city of Medellin which was in a state of relative decline as a major industrial center by the end of the 1970s. Its leading sector, textiles, had virtually collapsed due to competition from similar Asian based industries and the unfavorably high levels of international import tariffs. This state of depression and the related high unemployment rates (also felt in Cali, Bogota and Barranquilla) caused many Medellin residents to now become involved in the cocaine production industry and other forms of trafficking. This saved numerous businessmen, professionals and workers (both skilled and unskilled) from a state of bankruptcy or near total loss of income. (Arango Jaramillo 1988: 96) By 1987 some $313 million was reported as having flowed into the Medellin economy as the result of the flourishing cocaine industry. In short, the city's economy saw a resurgence and mini-boom in not only textiles but also in construction and other related industries. About 28,000 new jobs were created and the unemployment rate accordingly dropped by about 30 percent. (Gomez 1988: 109)

By lavishing their personal largesse on the local populations, particularly in poorer districts and slum areas, and financing a vast array of social services in their native towns and regions, narcotraffickers such as Lehder, Escobar and Rodriguez Gacha became Robin Hood-like legends in their time and complicated to a considerable degree the anti-drug programs of the US in Colombia. One Colombian Air Force base commander confided to the author during an official visit by the latter in 1988 that his regional command headquarters had been allocated

$10,000 towards civic action projects in the poor rural villages of the surrounding countryside. While normally impressive under most circumstances, given the military's limited budget, this funding for military civic action was more than outclassed by the local trafficking cartel which had spent up to $10 million to win the hearts and minds of the local population. To this end the Air Force's civic action program had been completely overwhelmed by the traffickers' own public welfare projects. (Author observation)

In other parts of Colombia it was known that the Pablo Escobar family traditionally provided some 5,000 toys every Christmas to the children of poor farmers in the Middle Magdalena Valley. (Arango Jaramillo and Child 1985: 128) Not to be out done, Carlos Lehder saw to it that 500-peso notes (about $4 in value) were regularly provided to each person who attended his "patriotic Saturdays" pep rallies where free lunches were also given out. (Lee 1989: 133) Escobar, in his public pronouncements, claimed that public indifference, apathy, negligence and irresponsibility on the part of the municipal administrators and ruling political oligarchy were the root cause of the Colombian rural population's poverty. (Lee 1989: 135) In this he found agreement from the various insurgencies who for decades had maintained much the same thing. The end result of the narcotrafficker welfare and civic-action campaigns was the creation of a group of staunch and loyal supporters made up of thousands of poor or otherwise marginalized people who could be drawn upon in the future to provide some form of protection or even serve the traffickers' production interests. (Tokatlian 1993)

In addition, other economic benefits accruing to Colombia in the short run from the narcotraffickers' activities was the financial support being given to the government's balance of payments and international reserves through the repatriation of *narcodollars* from the exterior. This enabled the government to avoid the devaluations and inflation which often afflicted other Latin American countries during the period of the 1980s. The various Colombian administrations throughout the 1980s were for those reasons adverse to diminishing this flow of repatriated capital, questioning its origin, or applying any form of sanctions which might reverse its flow into the Colombian economy. To this end tax amnesties were often declared for these and other types of otherwise unaccountable inflows of dollars from overseas. (Lee 1989: 38; and Arrieta 1990: 87)

As it was, government anti-drug repression often caused the traffickers to invest part of their monies overseas instead of inside the country. In the case of Panama, traffickers reportedly owned by 1987 real estate valued at $400 million, including over half of the 200 high-rise apartment buildings dotting the Panama City skyline. (Lee 1989: 37) To encourage the repatriation of money back into Colombia, the government had established a policy whereby it was not required by the banks to identify by name the transactor. While this was useful to the traffickers, there were other means by which they could launder their money, such as through the over-invoicing of exports in which the value of the export earnings was inflated to account for the additional narco-dollar earnings. (Lee 1989: 38)

Despite US and Colombian anti-drug policies, cocaine refining in the mid-1980s was escalating in scale going from a former production rate of about 198 mt to some 453.8 mt by 1988. The cumulative value of the production-refining effort to the traffickers in general was reported to be about $13 billion. (Arrieta 1990: 33) Since at that time Colombia's own coca crops in terms of total hectares never appeared to be more than about 11 percent of the total amount under cultivation in both Bolivia and Peru, it was in the transportation and marketing of the refined cocaine that the trafficker's real profits continued to be made. (Arrieta 1990: 59)

In the end, cocaine production tended to have an uneven impact on the economy, diverting some productive effort away from what might have been other commercial enterprises. Inflation did take place which inhibited the export of other potentially competing products, skewing the export market in favor of drugs. There was also the corresponding cost to the government for confronting and attempting to suppress narcotrafficking. In addition there was the social cost involving the corrupting impact that narcotrafficking had on popular values which tended to foment a more open, permissive attitude towards illegal activities in general. In practice, people generally attempted to avoid registering property and paying taxes. In the end a narco-dollar economy had developed which enabled considerable capital flight to take place as well. All this was to the detriment of the government's economy and societal values alike. (Arrieta 1990: 87-88)

During July of 1986 or the month prior to Barco assuming the Colombian Presidency, a series of narcotrafficker attributed assassinations took place in Colombia whereby a noted journalist (Roberto Camacho Prada), a police captain (Luis Alfredo Macana Rodriguez) and a government magistrate (Hernando Baquero Borda) were murdered. In addition, by Decemeber of 1986 the former director of the Anti-Narcotics Police, Jaime Ramirez Gomez (responsible for the seizures of some 27 mt of cocaine over a three year period), a congressman, a senator and the influential newspaper editor, Guillermo Cano, of the El Espectador were also assassinated. Of note was the fact that all the victims had been involved in working fervently against narcotrafficking in Colombia. (Senate 1988a:  30; and arrieta 1990: 336-337) The last case is interesting because, although a trafficker was specifically implicated in Cano's murder, he was eventually released because no Medellin judge was willing to try the case. *Plata o plomo* was having a serious undermining effect on the efficiency of the judicial system. (El Tiempo: 9 Feb 88)

Added to the government's embarrassment and tarnished image of having lost control of its internal domestic situation was the release of Pablo Escobar in November of 1986 after he had been arrested only a few days earlier at a police check point in the Antioquia Department. Escobar's escape was facilitated by a bribe to the local police of a reported half million dollars. (Lee 1989: 10) Escobar had reason to fear arrest as President Barco had acted to deal with earlier  Supreme Court opposition to the US-Colombian extradition treaty by drafting a new extradition law (Law 68) which he then implemented by fiat, signing it personally. (Lee 1989: 213)

President Barco also continued the US favored use of herbicides despite complaints from the Institute of National Resources (Instituto Nacional de Recursos) of the Ministry of Agriculture which claimed that there had been adverse ecological impacts in the Tayrona National Park from the use of glifosate. By 1987 in a determined government eradication effort, some 10,300 ha of marijuana had been sprayed. Yet, when an evaluation of the operation was completed, the total annual amount of hectares of marijuana in production had actually *increased* from about 8,000 ha in 1985 to a 16,000 ha high in 1987. (NAU 1987: 2-3; and Arrieta 1990: 332-333). The government's response was to try and redouble its efforts for the future.

While ecological factors and impacts from the use of herbicides were debated within the Colombian government and society in general, the local population in the Cauca Valley complained that there were no crop substitutes which were equally as remunerative as marijuana. On this basis and feeling unduly harassed, the local farmers began to organize and an effective opposition began to solidify against the government's anti-drug policy. There was also the presence of guerrilla groups which also began to threaten the progress of the marijuana eradication program. Nonetheless, marijuana cultivation ultimately stabilized at a level of about 14,000  to 16,000 ha as exportation into the US and European drug markets continued unabated and Colombia retained its position as the leading producer of marijuana in the Western Hemisphere. (NAU 1987: 2; and Arrieta 1990: 334-335)

Under the influence of a few traffickers in the areas of Cauca and Tolima, some farmers began to produce *amapola* (poppy) crops for sale and eventual refinement into heroin. In theory, one-tenth of a hectare of this type of crop could potentially bring a poppy farmer up to $5,000 in profits in the international heroin market which in itself had a profit potential of up to $100 billion. (Arrieta 1990: 333; and Dziedzic 1989: 535) Commercial-scale opium cultivations, reported in May of 1984 as seven cultivation sites of about one hectare in size (35,000 plants) each, were not considered to be capable of producing a substantial amount of heroin. By 1987 this situation had changed significantly. (NAU 1987: 7) At the same time Colombian traffickers were estimated by the Country Team in Bogota to be transshipping some 100 mt of cocaine through Colombia, with only about 5 percent of that amount having been actually intercepted by government authorities. (NAU 1987: 5)

Back in Washington the promoters and constructive critics of the Reagan policy, both Democrats and Republicans, wanted to see an all-out escalation of the drug war effort. This was to involve ever harsher US laws against drug consumption and trafficking, an increasingly larger employment of US resources in the form of weapons, equipment and even fire power to defeat the traffickers, and tougher international law enforcement and interdiction programs as part of an intensified diplomatic pressure on the Andean source and transit countries' governments, especially Colombia. (Bagley 1988: 193)

This was forthcoming in the October 1986 Anti-Drug Abuse Act authorized by Congress which allocated some $3.9 billion for FY 1987. Of these anti-drug monies, about three-quarters were ear-marked for expanded supply sided enforcement, involving interdiction and eradication and crop substitution programs. In addition other government offices pitched in to help out. The Agency for International Development (AID) transferred some of its funding to the Department of Justice to enable the later to enhance the investigative capability of law enforcement agencies in the Andes (International Criminal Investigative Training Assistance Program). The remaining amounts of anti-drug monies were dedicated to education, prevention, treatment and rehabilitation or the demand side. (Bagley 1988: 193-194; and GAO 1992b: 13)

Yet, just a few months after the passage of the 1986 anti-drug legislation, the severe fiscal deficit and the constraints of the US Congress' Graham-Rudman budget reduction requirements caused the

Reagan administration to cut approximately $1 billion from its anti-drug budget for 1987. To this end most cuts were made in the areas of education, treatment, rehabilitation and local law enforcement, which spared the international supply side focus and guaranteed its continued high priority and prominence in the US anti-drug policy. It was also reported at this time by the US media that the price of cocaine on the street had dropped from $35,000 to about $20,000 per kilogram (some reports stated $11,000 per kilogram), indicating that there was an abundance of cocaine available in the US consumer market. Also during this time, some 25 mt of cocaine HCl was captured in southern Florida alone, further indicating the escalating efforts of the traffickers to smuggle large quantities of the drug into the US from Colombia. (Miami Herald: 10 Feb 85; and Gugliotta and Leen 1989: 275; and House 1990: 6) Drug usage had intensified and up to six million people in the US were now reported as using cocaine at lease once a month with another quarter of a million known as compulsive users or addicts who consumed the drug every day. (DEA 1987: 26) Cocaine related deaths continued to escalate, reflecting a several-fold increase rising from 566 in 1984 to 1,793 in 1987 (DHHS 1987: 38; and 1991: 21)

Congressman Charles Rangel (D-NY) and Senators Alfonse D'Amato (R-NY) and Paula Hawkins (R-FL) repeatedly condemned or criticized the US government and President Reagan for not bringing a fuller range of US economic and political power to bear on foreign governments and Colombia in particular to force their more complete cooperation with the US anti-drug policy abroad. (Bagley 1988: 192) Congress in its Fiscal Year (FY) 1987 annual drug budget virtually doubled the Department of Defense's anti-drug funding from $200 million in FY 1986 to about $389 million for 1987. (GAO 1988a 20 and 29-30) At this time INM was writing and coordinating most of the NDPB's interagency anti-drug strategy and its implementation plans. For Latin America in general and specifically Colombia the policy goals were: first, to reduce the amount of cocaine shipped from Latin America to the US; second, eliminate major trafficking networks and cartels; and third, secure increased international cooperation. (DOS INM 1988: passim)

During the mid-1980s the smuggling dimension of the anti-drug policy problem for the US in terms of stopping cocaine and heroin was significant. Facilitating smuggling was the fact that every year some 290 million people were crossing the US border. Another 30 million air passengers were arriving on roughly 500,000 commercial airline flights from all parts of the world. In addition 7.5 million cargo containers entered the US through its seaports, 100 million pieces of mail arrived from overseas and 89 million land vehicles crossed into the US from both Mexico and Canada. Additional thousands of of pleasure boats and private aircraft came and went from the US mainland every year. The problem was so vast and complex that US Customs estimated that it was only able to seize some 27 of the 138 metric tons (mt) of cocaine estimated at that time to have been smuggled into the US during the period of a year. (Mabry 1988: 54) Nonetheless, buoying up the anti-drug effort's current course was the knowledge that enough evidence had become available to US authorities so that a formal indictment of a number of key Colombian Medellin cartel members took place on 18 November 1986. (Miami Herald: 19 Nov 86) Undermining any success of the policy was the acknowledgement that in FY 1987, after spending some $40 million on maritime interdiction operations, the Navy and Coast Guard reported seizing only 20 vessels, making some 110 arrests and capturing 550 pounds of cocaine. The Air Force spent $2.6 million, flying 591 hours which resulted in only six aircraft seizures and ten persons arrested. (GAO 1988a: 28-29) This was not an especially significant return for the amount of time and money invested.

In Colombia the use of herbicides continued apace and President Barco began to place more and more emphasis on the military and extradition as the principal instruments to repress the traffickers in his country. By June 1987 the US had submitted some 140 narcotrafficking related extradition requests of which 24 had been approved. Of the 16 persons actually extradited to the US, fourteen were Colombians and two were foreigners. (Lee 1989: 211) In part the US anti-drug policy had succeeded in working around the inefficient and corrupted Colombian system of criminal justice whereby only a small percentage of those tried for narcotics offenses were actually convicted. The use of *plata o plomo* or the combination of bribes and threats had successfully neutralized the Colombian judiciary. There was an observation expressed to the author that many judges were poorly trained or just incompetent when it came to drug-related cases. An overloaded judicial system often saw drug cases reduced to simple misdemeanors to expedite cases or get people out of jail to make way for others coming into the prison system. Conspiracy laws in Colombia did not have the same application or acceptance as in the US judicial system and this made it extremely difficult to prosecute anyone who was not actually caught in the act of trafficking or had narcotics in their possession.

Despite the apparent US success on the extradition issue, all did not go well for the US anti-drug policy. That June the Colombian Supreme

Court voted on the legality of Barco's Law 68. The evolving deadlock was eventually broken by a judge brought in from outside the Court which was then recorded as having voted against extradition. The Court's rationale was that Law 68's ratifying legislation was unconstitutional and that the government should submit new, implementing legislation to reapply for approval of a new law, a tedious bureaucratic process at best. The extradition process had for all intents and purposes come to a halt. Unfavorable public opinion towards extradition of Colombian nationals and reported death threats from the traffickers themselves were said to have been influential factors in the overturning of the US-Colombian extradition treaty. (GAO 1988c: 27; and Lee 1989: 213-214)

The heightened US interest in militantly confronting drug-trafficking through the use of military forces and the evident willingness of the traffickers and some guerrilla groups to use force to thwart the Colombian government's own anti-drug operations, now influenced President Barco to issue his Decree 3655 on 17 December 1987 to the effect of increasing the participatory role of the Colombian military and police in the drug war. The ferocity of the military's actions had such an impact on the general economy that labor earnings for the population at large were reported to have dropped off by up to 50 percent. (Arrieta 1990: 79) In addition, Decree 3671 of 19 December reaffirmed that the population was again subject to martial law. While this was well intentioned and issued in the context of the earlier state of siege which was still in effect from the previous Betancur administration, the Colombian Supreme Court declared that Decree 3671 was unconstitutional and that the Anti-Narcotics Police and the DAS should take the lead in the drug war, leaving the military free to concentrate on the various insurgencies, represented by the FARC and the ELN in particular. (Arrieta 1990: 337)

The Army was very satisfied with this new declaration and turn of events. The then Minister of Defense, General Rafael Samudio Molina, declared that the Army could produce better results if it focussed on the anti-guerrilla effort and did not fritter away its assets in police-related anti-drug activities. (Arrieta 1990: 338) Ironically, the Army found its anti-guerrilla efforts coinciding with mutual interests on the part of both the traffickers and rural agro-industrialists and plantation owners. Not to be deterred, the Colombian Executive issued a new Decree 1630 on 27 August 1987 which attempted to keep the military engaged in the anti-drug effort by confronting the trafficker sponsored sicarios and paramilitary groups which were now beginning to operate throughout the country. (Arrieta 1990: 338)

During 1987 US and Colombian interdiction operations had been noted by the US General Accounting Office (GAO) as probably being ineffective since the transportation costs to the traffickers was only about 10 percent of their actual earnings from the cocaine being sold on the street in the US. (GAO 1988a 17-18; and GAO 1991c: 26) In this regard the GAO was supported by the 1986 RAND Corporation study which implied that, even if one could triple the costs of production for coca farmers, cocaine prices in the US would rise by only about one percent. In short it would be extremely difficult to reduce cocaine consumption by as much as five percent through more stringent interdiction since the traffickers could always absorb the additional costs of business (Figure 3). (Senate 1990c: 34 and 95)

# Chapter 3

## Locking Arms - Washington, Colombia and The Andean Initiative

The advent of 1988 did not begin well for the Colombian government as on January 1st, Jorge Ochoa Vasquez, a key narcotrafficker kingpin, captured that previous November, was reported as having been released from the Carcel Modelo National Prison. In this case there appeared to be collusion on the part of a judge who had granted Ochoa his freedom based on a legal technicality. (Tokatlian: 1993) The US denounced the affair and, venting its obvious displeasure, announced on 5 January retaliatory measures intended to castigate the Colombian government for its ineptitude in allowing such an event to happen. Both Colombian exports into the US and its tourists were penalized by being harassed by both US Customs and Immigration personnel. Colombian exporters of perishable goods such as shrimp, avocados and bananas lost a reported $25 million due to US Customs' delays in processing the entry of the produce into the US, causing most of it to rot at the entry ports. (Lee 1989: 235; and Bagley 1988: 88)

These actions by the US caused considerable furor as Colombia complained to the Organization of American States (OAS) and a flurry of notes were exchanged between Presidents Barco and Reagan. Tensions between the US and Colombia became exacerbated. (New York Times: 13 Jan 88; and El Espectador: 26 Jan 88) In contrast to the damage caused the Colombian economy by the US policy, the traffickers were reported as repatriating to Colombia between $500 million and $1 billion or an equivalent equal to between 10 and 20 percent of Colombia's export economy. (Lee 1989: 3)

In 1988 the US government still believed that by reducing the supply of drugs flowing into the US one could reduce drug abuse by its citizens. The idea was to discourage people from experimenting with or becoming chronic drug users by making drugs difficult to obtain and increasingly expensive to use. Supply reduction in this sense was to stop the traffickers from smuggling their illegal goods and services to the American people by seizing their products and production infrastructure, their profits and investments and otherwise prosecuting them for engaging in a criminal enterprise. It was presumed that attacking the traffickers at the source would also defend countries friendly to the US whose own security and stability might also be affected by the power and influence of the traffickers themselves. (Van Wert 1988: 1)

Nonetheless, there was no coherent policy and related strategy and only a series of operations and programs, sometimes operating in tandem and sometimes not. Highlighting this fact was General Fred Woerner's annual SOUTHCOM conference on Latin American issues in early 1988. At the conference Ann Wroblesky, the Department of State's Assistant Secretary for International Narcotics Matters stated openly to those in attendance that there was no US anti-drug strategy for the Andean region. "We just operate!" was the INM leader's reply to a question as to whether an anti-drug strategy existed for the region. An Army general in the SOUTHCOM audience responded to Wroblesky's statement: "This is a prime example of a train going down the track without an engineer." (Author recollection 1988)

The US Congress' approach to dealing with the issue of narcotrafficking was to look to the source of supply as the basic cause of the addiction problem inside the US. To this end its sixteen distinct committees involved in anti-drug matters advocated bilateral arrangements and anti-drug policy goals which used coercive means in some form of sanctions to obtain the US anti-drug policy objectives, if persuasive methods proved incapable of producing satisfactory results. (Perl 1988: 20) Congressional interest in the drug policy issue at this time was intense and was reflected in its legislative process. Of the some 1,100 bills introduced into the House of Representatives during the first six months of 1988, about 20 percent dealt with some aspect of the drug policy issue. (Perl 1988: 45) The Congressional concern reflected to a significant degree the reported statistics which showed that drug usage was apparently still rising during the year as the number of cocaine-related emergency room mentions for the nation's principal metropolitan areas was reported at 60,141. Ominously, another 20,599 of heroin-related mentions were also reported at this time. (DHHS 1991: 22)

Among the 1988 presidential campaign issues, drugs had been at the forefront as there had been considerable frustration over the lack of visible progress in shutting down narcotrafficking in general. Consumption rates within the US were reported on the rise as was drug related violence and presidential candidate George Bush indicated that to resolve the situation he would assign a high profile to international anti-narcotics efforts within his future administration. At this time Congress very much wanted to centralize the management of the US anti-drug programs to bring about better control and continuity. Some members thought that a "drug czar" should be created to provide for a more unified approach to policy making and policy implementation. At this time considerable thought was being given at the NSC to place all counter-drug aerial means and operations under the DEA. Later on it was felt that a powerful anti-dug agency with budget certification authority mandated by law could achieve enough influence to insure that Congressionally allocated anti-drug monies could not be diverted for other purposes. This was important, as prior to 1988 there was neither a single document which outlined the priorities and policies of the federal government in its war on drugs nor a single high-level official accountable for the success or failure of the anti-drug effort. (Interview ONDCP 1: 1993)

With drug control being reflected in national polls during the first half of 1988 as the number one issue of concern to US citizens, the Congress responded with its Omnibus Anti-Drug Abuse Act of 21 October 1988 (Public Law 100-690) which built on earlier legislation promulgated in 1986. Monies were now not only allocated in quantity for interdiction but also for some demand related programs, indicating that Congress was not entirely satisfied with the supply sided approach. (Bagley 1991: 13) Of the $9.4 billion to be authorized for anti-drug purposes, about half was now earmarked for domestic control and enforcement programs. There was now a balanced spending effort indicating the more equal importance that Congress was now giving the demand side, compared to the Reagan administration's overwhelming emphasis (70 percent) on supply sided efforts. (Bagley 1992: 3)

Created at the mandate of Congress under the Omnibus Act was the Office for National Drug Control Policy (ONDCP). To demonstrate its importance, it was to be headed by an Executive Level 1, cabinet level official or Director, known as the *drug czar*. William Bennet was appointed as the ONDCP's Director. Nonetheless, while Bennet was technically serving at the cabinet level, President Bush did not want him present at cabinet meetings unless drugs were being discussed. While the ONDCP did take some authority away from the Department of Justice, it was felt that under the circumstances it could better define the anti-drug problem and begin to understand what was needed to attain a solution to the war on drugs. (Interview ONDCP 1: 1993) The ONDCP's primary function was to develop a comprehensive anti-drug strategy and to then coordinate the anti-drug policy implementation effort. (House 1990: 1)

The problems the ONDCP faced were considerable. While policy formulation could always be achieved in a relatively easy manner, the overseeing of its implementation was a significant problem which was never wholly resolved. That the ONDCP did not directly control the anti-drug budget process after it had been approved and therefore could not shift Congressionally earmarked anti-drug monies to better focus on priorities or influence the solutions to demanding and ever evolving problems meant that each government agency was essentially in control of its own affairs in terms of spending the monies allocated to it by the Congress. What the ONDCP could do to influence the general thrust of the US anti-drug policy among the various federal agencies was to use its stipulated authority to certify the budget requests of each agency in terms of the latter's role in the drug war. If an agency's budget was insufficient to meet its anti-drug obligations, it would be decertified and both the president and the Congress informed immediately. The idea was to ensure that the goals and objectives contained in the national anti-drug strategy were matched with sufficient resources to accomplish the agencies' respective goals. To this end the concept was considered generally successful. (Interview ONDCP 1: 1993)

Invariably it was found that implementation of the anti-drug policy would have to be carried out by each government agency. Here inevitable conflicts over priorities took place as each agency had its own agenda and interests. Nonetheless, the drug czar would be held responsible. While the Department of State as an institution and agency of the US government was to control the anti-drug activities of each Country Team, it also had other interests in each country, including promoting democracy, open and competitive economies and human rights issues among others. (Interviews DEA and ONDCP 1: 1993; and House 1990: 1)

Still, the coordination of the activities of several dozen federal agencies had to be carried out within a general plan. The Drug Interdiction Committee (made up of the FBI, DEA, Customs and Coast

Guard) was a case in point. No strategy existed and no one had bothered to sort out where some missions began and others ended. In short there was no team or fully integrated effort. To resolve some of the problems it was confronting over this issue, the ONDCP fomented the formation of a national drug intelligence authority which was to operate in the manner of the CIA but focus exclusively on drugs. As a result, El Paso, Texas became the site of the El Paso Intelligence Center (EPIC) which conducted drug intelligence collection and analyis operations in support of all federal agencies involved in the anti-drug effort. (Interviews ONDCP 2: 1993) In addition, Congress passed in October 1988 the 1989 National Defense Authorization Act which directed that the Department of Defense (DOD) would serve as the lead agency of the US government in the detection and monitoring of aerial and maritime transits of illegal drugs into the US. This also applied to the Andean region and Colombia. DOD's funding for this anti-drug activity accordingly rose to some $450 million. (Bagley 1991: 14; and Interview ONDCP 2: 1993)

Here also the Congress asserted its authority whereby the cooperation of drug-producing and transit countries with US anti-drug policy was linked to determining the eligibility of those countries for US foreign aid. Colombia was an obvious target in this case. The process, called *certification*, required the president to withhold at the beginning of each fiscal year (1 October) some 50 percent of the US foreign assistance to be dispensed to a given country until such time as a favorable anti-drug policy determination and certification was granted on or after the beginning of March of the following year. In short it meant that each fiscal year some five or more months might pass before allocated monies could be fully brought into play on behalf of US interests in the Andean countries. To obtain certification, either support of a vital national interest to the US on the part of the receiving country had to be demonstrated or that full cooperation was forthcoming in terms of preventing drug production, processing, trafficking, drug-related money laundering, bribery and public corruption. (Perl 1988: 24-25)

To stem the flow of precursor chemicals flowing into the Andes and Colombia in particular in 1988, Congress enacted the Chemical Diversion and Trafficking Act which imposed stringent monitoring requirements on all US based chemical companies that produced the so-called precursor and essential chemicals which could be used in the manufacture of coca paste and cocaine products. Violations of these requirements could result in criminal prosecution. In addition, the United Nation's 1988 convention to deal with the international trafficking problem world wide was sponsored by the US. The Financial Action and Chemical Action Task Forces were formed, involving up to some twenty-five of the more industrialized nations of the world. As a result, shipments of chemicals into the Colombia and the Andean region from US ports fell off dramatically. Nonetheless, there was a corresponding increase of chemicals flowing into Colombia from Brazil, Ecuador and Venezuela which offset the US effort. (GAO 1992a: passim) The DEA also began its efforts in conjunction with the Department of the Treasury's own Financial Action Task Force to freeze or otherwise seize narcotrafficker financial assets throughout the world. (Interview ONDCP 2 and DEA 1993)

As part of the Omnibus Anti-Drug Abuse Act's Title IV, the Secretary of State was responsible for coordinating all US assistance to be spent in international efforts to combat the production and trafficking of illegal drugs within each target country. Previously, certification had been based principally on the willingness of a country to reduce its production of illicit drugs. As mentioned previously this aspect was now reduced in importance to just one of a number of criteria or issues involving the taking of law enforcement steps to curb corruption, the entering into a bilateral counter-narcotics agreement with the US and the general nature of its support for US anti-narcotics policies and programs. Nonetheless, eradication goals for Colombia were still to be adhered to as a primary US government means for measuring progress inside Colombia. The US also hoped to exploit its initiative in the UN Commission on Narcotic Drugs' resolution of February 1986 which sponsored a Convention which included an article promoting the required extradition of drug traffickers to stand trial in those countries that desired to formally carry out a prosecution effort. (Perl 1988: 24-25; and Interview INM 1993)

The US armed services with their own two million trained personnel, extensive resources in equipment, and an ability to project and sustain its power worldwide was looked upon as the only national institution which could actually carry out an attack on the traffickers inside a source country. If otherwise idle in the Cold War, why not exercise its capabilities on behalf of the US counter-narcotics' efforts? If nothing else, the intelligence gathering capability of the Army, Navy and Air Force could be used to track and assist in the capture of the traffickers, or so the thinking at the ONDCP went. (Mabry 1988: 56; and Interview ONDCP 1: 1993)

While the use of the US military in an international role, as well as in a domestic role to seal the US borders, was seriously entertained by some policy planners, Secretary of Defense Frank Carlucci, as well as his predecessor, Caspar Weinberger, both argued against a combat role for the military in what they perceived was esentially a law enforcement problem. They contended that the mission of the armed forces of the the US was to protect the nation against attack from foreign armies and not narcotraffickers. (Carlucci 1988: passim; and Washington Post: 22 May 88) Admiral A.H. Trost, then Chief of Naval Operations, spoke out publicly, declaring that the smuggling of drugs into the US from Colombia could not be stopped through interdiction measures because "the economic incentives are so potent and the network of communications from farm to market via thousands of boats and small planes is so extensive." (New York times: 23 Jul 88) While the DOD was reluctant to enter into the anti-drug fray, it was finally persuaded and authorized by Congress to support the anti-drug effort as the lead agency responsible for detection and monitoring of aerial and maritime drug smuggling. To this end the JCS became more directly involved as the US Atlantic, Pacific and Southern  Commands were incorporated into the Andean anti-drug effort. (House 1989: 4 and 13-14)

With the ONDCP's encouragement, the INM increased its operational role by developing an air wing within the Department of State which used both contract and its own personnel to fly the aircraft. This was done over the objection of the DEA, which wanted to control all avionics activities in support of anti-drug operations as part of its Operation Snowcap activities. While this was a distraction from INM's fundamental mission of policy development and coordination, it was thought that assets being brought into play in Colombia and the Andes could be better controlled and focused in the anti-drug role through the INM representatives on each Country Team. (Interview NSC and ONDCP 2: 1993) In sum the ONDCP had better defined the roles of its players and could now promulgate anti-drug policies and strategies, but it still lacked the clout necessary to ensure that all the various governemnt offices and agencies responsible for anti-drug programs were operating the way they should. The election of George Bush in 1988 as the new president did eventually give the US anti-drug policy some needed clout and focus that it had not had before.

Congress specifically authorized Colombia $15 million in FY 1989 for defense equipment and $5 million to protect government officials and members of the press against narco-terrorist attacks. Likewise the strength of the US military assistance mission to Colombia was expanded well beyond the six personnel normally authorized by law. Possibly the most important aspect of the new law (Section 4305 of the

1988 Act) was the exemption of Colombia from the prohibitions of the Foreign Assistance Act (FAA) concerning training and financial support involving foreign police forces (Section 660 of the FAA of 1961). (Perl 1988: 38) In addition, the President was directed to evaluate and then certify to Congress (Sections 4407 and 4408 of the 1988 Act) that Colombia was eliminating bribery, corruption, narcotics production and distribution, and investigating and prosecuting any public officials involved in the drug trade or crimes of violence perpetrated against DEA agents. In addition Colombia had to show that it was cooperating with the US anti-drug policy to include changing its legal codes and laws as well as expediting extradition cases that the US had an interest in. (Perl 1988: 36-37) In this manner the US Congress thought it could better justify its approval of expenditures in the face of any criticism that might be directed at it over the issue of Colombian compliance with the US anti-drug policy.

An additional crisis ensued for Colombian President Barco when on 24 January a group of traffickers, calling themselves the *Extraditables* (vulnerable to extradition), declared war on any Colombian officials who attempted to extradite them to the US. The next day or the 25th of January a candidate for the mayoralty of Bogota was kidnapped and the Colombian Attorney General, Carlos Mauro Hoyos, was kidnapped and then eventually murdered by trafficker sponsored sicarios in Medellin on 25 January. Mauro Hoyos was in the process of investigating the unauthorized release of Ochoa. His murder effectively brought the investigation to a halt. (Senate 1989: 3) Invoking state of siege powers to combat this situation, and vowing he would not submit to trafficker blackmail or intimidation, Barco ordered the military and police into action. To this end the CNP was increased in size some five-thousand personnel or a new manning level of about 75,000. (Bagley 1988: 87)

Aware of the criticism it was receiving from campesino farmers, the high risks of corruption among its ranks, and the difficulty of attacking simultaneously the entire narcotrafficking commercial or business infrastructure and networks, the Colombian military, responding to Decree 1630 as well as its new orders, tended to focus on the more easily targeted urban based laboratories, large rural processing centers, and selected groups of sicarios and high level cartel leaders such as could be found in Medellin. While this was taking place over a period of a year or so, US aid to Colombia for anti-drug operations had experienced a slight drop, going from about $11.5 million in 1987 to around $9.8 million in 1988. This reflected US Congressional disenchantment over what had transpired in Colombia the previous year

and the seemingly ever increasing amount of cocaine entering the US.
(NAU 1987: 5; Arrieta 1990: 335-336)

The Colombian army now deployed a brigade into the area of
Medellin, attacking laboratories and production and refining facilities,
as well as properties belonging to known traffickers. In addition, in the
eastern plains region of Colombia (Llanos Orientales) another brigade
was deployed to engage in anti-drug activities. Similar to what had
happened roughly a year earlier in response to the Cano Laza murder,
the government's anti-drug operations again produced some results.
During the two months following the Hoyos murder, labor earnings
were once again reported by the Banco de la Republica as having
declined some 50 percent. (Arrieta 1990: 80) This reflected the anti-
drug effort for 1988 in which more than 22 mt of cocaine HCl had been
seized and up to 600 persons arrested for being involved in trafficking
operations. (House 1990c: 73)

The impact of the government's operations can be seen in the balloon
effect which often takes place when the traffickers begin to feel
uncomfortable and perceive their risks as rising. In this case Ecuador,
bordering Colombia to the south, began to serve increasingly as a
smuggling route for precursor chemicals into Colombia. This infiltration
effort exploited the Putumayo River and other Amazon river routes
from Ecuador. (Ortiz Crespo 1990: 34-35) The northwestern part of
Brazil and its Amazon region were also part of this balloon effect and
not only furnished a number of laboratory sites for the Colombian
traffickers but also considerable transportation routes into and out of
Colombia. These two countries provided most of the smuggling routes
which had supported the infamous *Tranqilandia* laboratory complex in
eastern Colombia. In addition, the riverine networks were plied by not
only ships and small boats but also *Mallard* and *Widget* seaplanes in the
service of the cartels. Since seaplanes do not leave a trace as to where
they are landing and taking off, it was that much more difficult to
detect a cocaine production laboratory which traditionally could be
identified by the telltale grass airstrip in its vicinity. (Senate 1989: 47-
48) Nonetheless, the government's operations had now become so
disruptive for some traffickers that they began to establish cocaine
refineries in Panama and even New Orleans. (Lee 1989: 181; and Senate
1989: 63)

While the disruption of trafficker activities by the Colombian
government was promising from a US anti-drug policy standpoint, there
was one countervailing factor which raised its head to all this -
corruption. Over the past five years numerous cases of high ranking

military officials' involvement in corruption of one sort or another had come to light. The police were also tainted in this respect and some 150 officers had been challenged and forced to retire. In Medellin alone it was thought that up to 80 percent of the police were involved in some form of corruption or illegal self-enrichment activities associated with drug trafficking. By the beginning of 1989, a number of Army colonels were being accused of selling arms to the Medellin cartel, while captured bank records pertaining to Gonzalo Rodriguez Gacha detailed multi-million dollar pay-offs to entire brigades of the Colombian Army in return for "protection." (House 1990b: 95; and Arrieta 1990: 254) Another colonel, this time from the police, was linked to the traffickers and additionally discovered with some 400 kilos of cocaine, worth millions of dollars, in his possession. In another case the police in the Valle Department were linked to various *sicarios* and were themselves carrying out assassination attempts on behalf of the traffickers. (Arrieta 1990: 255)

In addition, paramilitary activity involving military and police collaboration with the traffickers also surfaced. In March 1988 Pablo Escobar and Gonzalo Rodriguez Gacha, three Army officers, a police officer and a local mayor in the Uraba region of the Choco Department were indicted for planning and carrying out the massacre of 22 union leaders at a banana plantation. In another case, the Army took no action when a massacre of some 100 persons was discovered in the same area. These persons had been murdered and then buried by paramilitary groups sponsored and funded by the traffickers. Judges who were involved in the investigations relating to these cases, after receiving death threats, often found themselves forced to leave Colombia or face the very real possibility of themselves or their family members being assassinated. (House 1990b: 95)

That the traffickers controlled significant amounts of land, especially in the departments of Meta, Magdalena Medio, Cordoba and Sucre also came to the attention of the Colombian government. As part of their personal investment programs, the narcotraffickers bought up small and medium-sized properties, as well as those abandoned by their owners in the face of narco-guerrilla threats. Over time the traffickers' landholdings involved the control of large estates and other vast tracts of farm land. Formed to protect these holding were paramilitary self-defense groups made up of gun-wielding *sicarios*. The traffickers were so successful in these enterprises that the Colombian government's agrarian reform projects were now in jeopardy as new small plot, campesino land owners were now coerced into giving up prime farm land by selling out to the traffickers and fleeing to more isolated mountainous and less desirable farming regions. (Thoumi 1992: 66; and Arrieta 1990: 262)

Over a million hectares of the best farm lands in Colombia were now reported to be in the hands of the traffickers who viewed themselves as an emergent entrepreneurial class on a par with Colombia's traditional landowning elites. (House 1990c: 86; New York Times: 21 Dec 88; and Dziedzic 1989: 537) Given the propensity of the traffickers to use violence and the apparent lust by some for political power as well as large profits, the social, political and economic implications for the Colombian government were becoming even more serious. Up to half a million campesino families were again without arable land and the million hectares of high grade farmland obtained by the traffickers over the period of a decade contrasted starkly with the nine-hundred thousand hectares of land laboriously distributed by the government over a twenty-five year period or quarter-century to the rural poor. (Semana: 5 Dec 88; and Bagley 1989-90: 161)

That narcotrafficker violence had played a role in creating this situation there was no doubt as more than 130 paramilitary groups were reported as having ambushed or massacred as many as 1,300 persons involving farm workers, poor *campesino* farmers, civil administrators, guerrillas, and judges and government officials conducting investigations into the agrarian-reform and land control situations. (House 1990b: 84; and Arrieta 1990: 263) Nonetheless, some trafficker paramilitary forces were received with considerable favor as happened in the region of Magdalena Medio where the MAS, the military and the local large land holders, including numerous traffickers, formed a "triangle of terror" or narco-military alliance to hunt down guerrillas and their sympathizers. (Collett 1988: 132; and Bagley 1989-90: 161) In this case the traffickers provided the funding to hire the paramilitary *sicarios*, the Colombian Army supplied the weapons, and members of the local landowning elite gave the operations an air of legitimacy. (House 1990c: 86; and Gros 1992: 9-10)

In the case of the Magdalena Medio's Valley region, the FARC had established its presence as early as the late 1970s under the command of a respected if not popular guerrilla leader, Ricardo Franco. Although Franco's guerrillas collected taxes through extortion to sustain themselves and support their operations against the government, they treated the population, the farmers and cattle ranchers with considerable respect. The taxes were considered to be bearable and agro-industrial business of all types flourished. In the late 1980s all this changed as the

FARC headquarters ordered Franco to increase the taxes on the local population considerably. When he refused, he was replaced by other leaders and the taxes were then increased to a point where they were considered unbearable, causing farmers and cattle ranchers alike to seek other means to redress the situation. (Chernick: 1993)

Since the guerrillas wanted to overthrow the government and transform society, the traffickers, now landowners, ranchers and owners of industrial properties, tended to align themselves with the traditional Colombian power structure which sought to preserve the status quo in the face of the guerrilla-revolutionaries' threats. Traffickers caught up in this situation tended to perceive the guerrillas as mortal threats to their own enterprises and livelihood. Indeed, the FARC, while defending the right of the *campesino* farmers to grow coca, often threatened or actually attacked the narcotraffickers' drug industry as being immoral. To this end they extorted it for whatever money could be obtained. This increased considerably the traffickers' business overhead whereby they had to pay protection money to the guerrillas or spend considerable sums on arranging for the security of their own production-transhipment processes. (Lee 1989: 159; and Chernick: 1993)

As fate would have it, the trafficker land owners, finding themselves to be the victims of exorbitant guerrilla tax increases, struck back. Fortified with considerable money, weapons and British and Israeli mercenaries to train them, the traffickers formed self-defense groups which, in time, were converted into the paramilitary death squads similar to those of MAS. These groups unmercifully hunted down the FARC guerrillas, sympathizers, and even campesino peasant organizations and union leaders lobbying for land reform and higher wages, forcing most of them to abandon the Magdalena Medio region completely. (House 1990b: 84; Reyes Posada 1991: 37-39; and Chernick: 1993) This left the majority of the population in the region in relative peace without having to pay any taxes at all. Again, what the Army and police could not do, the narcotrafficker sponsored, paramilitary *sicarios* did.

The defeat of the FARC enhanced the image of the traffickers in the eyes of the local population and, although welcomed by the Army, was an embarrassment to the Colombian government. (Lee 1989: 118 and 163; and Arrieta 1990: 264) The *sicarios*, well armed and practiced in assassinations and guerrilla style combat, were now a lethal force unto themselves and could compete with the police and the Army on about even terms. As such, they were now dispersed throughout the country to provide security and carry out assassinations as desired by their employers. It was little wonder that President Barco was concerned about the magnitude of Colombia's now complex national security problem and the threat that the traffickers potentially posed to legitimate government throughout the nation. (Camacho: 1993)

The increase in violence which was taking place in the coca growing regions now attracted the attention of the government which throughout 1987 and into 1988 made a concerted effort to retake control of the coca growing areas. It was a largely futile effort as the vast size and remoteness of the regions were daunting factors. Nonetheless, with the then international market apparently saturated and coca paste earning less than a quarter of its former earnings during the boom days of the early 1980s, coca was now barely profitable for the growers. Precursors were also becoming more expensive and a number of farmers wanted to shift to some other alternate crop. While this was particularly true in the Guaviare Department, the lack of suitable alternate crops and efficient, cost effective farm to market transportation networks inhibited the farmers' efforts to shift away from the still relatively more profitable coca. (New York Review: 22 Dec 88)

As 1988 wore on, the US Congress took due note of the Colombian government's use of its military and approved an aid program of $15 million for the Colombian armed forces and an additional $5 million to help to protect judges and other key members of the judiciary. In short about 75 percent of the US aid programs for Colombia were now focused on the anti-drug effort. (Arrieta 1990: 340) Yet not helping the situation was the hasty Department of State's INM effort to develop a comprehensive anti-drug strategy for Colombia which would serve as a justification and instrument for further spending and allocation. On 29 August 1988 the Country Team's NAU in Bogota received a cable directive from INM in Washington, D.C. to develop an anti-drug strategy based on $47.5 million in funding. The suspense back to Washington for completion of the strategy and its supporting logistical requirements was 1 September or three working days later. This less than realistic attitude on the part of INM caused considerable resentment within the Country Team which could not possibly hope to develop an appropriate strategy without coordinating with the Colombian government. This took time. The resulting product submitted back to INM in Washington, D.C. in accordance with the deadline was in the end a jumble of operational concepts and ideas from the different Country Team agencies which, while in themselves targeting aspects of the narcotrafficking structure, had no coherency as a whole which logically lent itself to producing a decisive result. That the US would frequently act unilaterally without consulting or bringing the Colombian government into the planning phases of its strategy was all too often becoming the Country Team's operational norm. (Stickney: 1993; and Bagley 1988: 89)

To help solidify its anti-drug efforts in Colombia and insure the strongest Country Team leadership possible in support of the US anti-drug policy, in October of 1988 Thomas McNamara was appointed and confirmed as the new US Ambassador to Colombia. McNamara had only just previously served as the Director for Anti-Terrorism and Narcotics in the National Security Council in Washington, D.C. He was seen as just the right person with the right qualifications in terms of knowledge, experience and leadership to keep the US anti-drug policy for Colombia on track and stem the trafficker tide which was still reported as generating an annual income for the Colombian economy of between $900 million and $1.3 billion. (Arrieta 1990: 84) *Operation Snowcap*, then on-going in Bolivia and Peru was also extended to support Colombia. Violence was a serious issue which also had to be confronted as between 1985 and the end of 1988 the traffickers had reportedly murdered over 400 police and military officials, scores of judges, dozens of journalists and a number of government officials and politicians. (Washington Post: 8 Jan 89)

For 1989 US military aid for Colombia was allocated at a level of some $7 million. In addition there were $200 million in loans from the US Export-Import Bank to enable the Colombian military to purchase the equipment necessary to assist it in the fight against narcotrafficking. The Colombian government's own budget allocated some $220 million for the military in 1989 or some $50 million more than the previous year. These funds combined to eventually enhance the military's efforts to fight both the traffickers and the guerrillas. (House 1990b: 88; and Arrieta 1990: 343 and 369) The result of the dual US and Colombian emphasis on the anti-drug effort was seen in the significant successes recorded during the first half of 1989 when some 21.4 mts of cocaine base and HCl was captured (compared to 22 mts for all of 1988) and over 1.6 million gallons of precursor chemicals were captured (compared to 896,000 gallons for all of 1988). (Arrieta 1990: 342)

Despite the successes in capturing drugs, Colombia was having problems with drug usage among its own population. Marijuana usage rose from 6.1 percent in 1988 to 9.4 percent in 1989 and cocaine usage was noted as rising from 2.4 percent to 4 percent during the same period. For those drug users who could not afford refined cocaine HCl, *basuco*, a raw coca paste derivative, was available and the period saw its usage rise from 2.6 percent to 4.8 percent. These statistics reflected increases in Colombian domestic drug usage of from 50 percent to almost 100 percent in just one year. (Arrieta 1990: 15)

There were also problems with the Colombian economy which impacted on the anti-drug policy. In 1989 the US allowed the 27-year old International Coffee Agreement to expire. The coffee pact had served Colombia by instilling price stability and order in the world market, ensuring that adequate income levels were maintained for the producing nations and their farmers. With the collapse of the Agreement, coffee prices declined immediately and Colombia worried that it would lose between $400 and $500 million annually in export income earnings. With coffee exports now declining, the repatriation of narco-dollars became even more important to the government to enable it to meet its debt payment obligations. This placed the government in a quandary as to how strongly it should crack down on trafficking which now provided badly needed income. (House 1989-1990: 124; and House 1990b: 82) Another question confronting the Colombian government was how it could ask farmers to grow coffee instead of coca leaves when the international market price for coffee had now been slashed in half, with Colombia reportedly actually losing $118 million in export earnings (down from a 1988 level of $1,698 million). In fact the coffee growers share of the market earnings had dropped from 36 to 22 percent. (House 1989-1990: 113 and 123) Extracting the government from this dilemma was the distraction served by the traffickers' propensity to use violence.

The catalyst that propelled the Barco government more than anything else out of its quandary and full tilt into the drug war in Colombia was the Medellin cartel's instigated 18 August 1989 assassination of the popular and leading presidential candidate, Luis Carlos Galan. (Bagley 1989-90: 154) That same week the traffickers also issued a declaration that they would embark on a *guerra total* (total war) against both the government and society at large unless their demands for dialogue and eventual reincorporation into society were met. (House 1990c: 74) Gonzalo Rodriguez Gacha and Pablo Escobar assured the public of their good faith and intentions to terminate their terrorist acts if the government would come to terms and begin negotiations. If the government did not, then government officials, judges, businessmen, journalists and their respective families would become subject to attacks from the *sicarios*. To emphasize their intent, the traffickers executed a bombing campaign against airlines, banks, businesses, newspapers, the DAS, hotels and even schools. Casualties from these attacks numbered in the hundreds. (La Prensa: 25 Aug and 23 Sep 89; Miami Herald: 14 Aug 92; and Bagley 1990: 450) President Barco's response was to offer a reward of $250,000 for information which would lead to the capture of Escobar and Rodriguez Gacha. (Bagley 1990: 447)

The traffickers were a serious threat and their *plata o plomo* death threats were received by an estimated 1,000 of the some 4,800 serving judges through out Colombia. When they threatened to kill ten judges for every trafficker extradited to the US, over a hundred judges resigned and as many others staged short term walkouts, protesting the inadequate government security for themselves in general. (House 1990b: 85) Rodriguez Gacha, a one-time lieutenant of Pablo Escobar, carried out the narco-terrorist grudge-war against the government. (Gugliotta 1992: 113) No one was beyond the reach of his sicarios who attempted to disrupt the country's economic and social activities to the degree that both the people and the government would become not only demoralized but also convinced that accommodation with the traffickers was the only way to alleviate the crisis. To this end the narco-barons hoped to consolidate their economic position and win social acceptance, all the while isolating themselves from legal prosecution. (Bagley 1989-90: 157-158)

The public outcry in Colombia against the traffickers now was intense, reflecting a major change in public opinion which swung dramatically from 63 percent being opposed to extradition (March 1989) to 77 percent now favoring extradition (August 1989). (Bagley 1990: 449) With the death of Galan, Colombia's political elite now felt themselves and their status quo very much threatened. For the Barco administration from this point on, the militarization of the drug war became its primary focus. Included in the government's more aggressive posture toward trafficking was the extradition of key narco-kingpins by administrative means rather than the often prolonged judicial process. Decree 1860 was issued to this affect. (Arrieta 1990: 343) With the government now in crisis in the face of ever escalating narco-terrorism and the need for decisive action to enable it to reassert its control over the Colombian society, Barco sent his Minister of Justice, Monica de Greiff, to Washington, D.C. in late August 1989 to obtain additional funding with which to confront the narcotrafficker threat.

The results of the de Greiff trip were spectacular as the DOS provided some $14 million in additional aid monies for Colombia's counter-narcotics activities and the White House, using the President's 506A special funding rights, produced $65 million in emergency military aid funding. (House 1990b: 88) The US and Colombian anti-drug policies were now closely meshed in an all-out frontal assault on the traffickers as Barco himself then made a trip to Washington in September to lobby members of the US Congress and President Bush for even more aid. Nonetheless, Barco also insisted that the US address its own domestic narcotics user-demand problem, do something to control the export of precursor chemicals into Colombia, and deal with the laundering of drug-monies by international banks outside Colombia. (Bagley 1990: 453)

As part of the US effort, Bush authorized the formation of new rules of engagement whereby US military trainers such as the Special Forces (Green Berets) and Marines could accompany local forces on counter-narcotics training patrols. (House 1990b: 88-89; and Interview INM and ONDCP 2: 1993) To this effect on 18 September, Secretary of Defense Cheney issued a series of directives for the US military which stated that the "detection and countering of the production, trafficking, and use of illegal drugs is a high priority national security mission of the Department of Defense." (Cheney 1989: 86)

Accordingly, by October 1989 the JCS Operations Directorate (J3) began to spend up to 75 percent of its time on the drug war. (House 1990: 11) The Navy's and Coast Guard's anti-drug aerial surveillance capabilities in the form of E2C AWACs and P3 type aircraft were now to be provided for the counter-drug effort. Here it was hoped that the up to almost half a billion dollars allocated to DOD for the anti-drug effort would enable it to somehow gain control over the up to 18,000 unregistered or illegal flights and ship movements reportedly entering the US through its southern frontiers each year. (House 1989: 4, 13-14, 23, 27 and 33; and Interview ONDCP 2: 1933)

Colombia was in a position to exploit the US anti-drug policy support effort since it had now reestablished its credibility in the drug war. During the month after Galan's murder, the government's backlash in the form of intensive counter-drug activities saw both the police and military authorities arrest 535 suspected traffickers and confiscate 989 buildings, 32,773 farm animals, 367 airplanes, 72 boats, 710 vehicles 4.7 mt of coca and over 1,200 weapons as part of their operations. (Bagley 1989-90: 157) In the case of marijuana persistent aerial and manual eradication activity from late 1988 until the end of 1989 saw the crop under cultivation go from an officially acknowledged 13,085 ha down to 2,200 ha (about 3,000 mt of potential production) respectively. This was the result of an 18 month eradication effort of over 10,000 ha which now saw Colombia drop far behind Mexico as Latin America's leading marijuana producer. (House 1990c: 69-70) Unfortunately, there was another side to the eradication issue.

In the case of cocaine production, coca cultivation realized just the opposite trend to that of marijuana as it expanded significantly from 24,540 ha in 1987 to around 27,000 ha in 1988 and rose rapidly thereafter to a level of about 41,800 ha in 1989, contributing to Colombia's increased cocaine production potential (including imports of cocaine base from Bolivia and Peru) of some 566 mt of cocaine. (House 1990c: 69-70) One of the influential factors which helped to bring this about was that most of the expanding coca crop lands were located in territory generally dominated by the ubiquitous guerrillas, making it extremely hazardous for eradication teams to operate unless accompanied by a well armed military or police escort. For this reason the only coca eradication activity that took place (641 ha of coca during 1989 or 1.5 percent of the total Colombian crop then under cultivation) happened when coca plants were found growing in the vicinity of a laboratory which had just been raided by the police. Eradication in any event was generally carried out by laborious manual means. (House 1990c: 77)

At this point in time the US considered Colombia to be the most important country in the US anti-drug effort in the Americas. If nothing else, it was perceived as having the greatest national capacity of any country in the Andean Ridge to wage an anti-drug war. Demonstrating this was General Miguel Antonio Gomez Padilla, then Director General of the CNP, who carried out during 1989 Operation Primavera which captured about 38 mts of cocaine HCl and base, destroyed 452 laboratories of all types, and seized 50 aircraft, while arresting some 3,600 persons suspected of working in the cocaine production-trafficking process. In addition some two million gallons of precursor chemicals were also destroyed. (House 1990c: 73) US anti-drug policy objectives for Colombia remained:

1. Curb drug production and processing.
2. Immobilize and prosecute major traffickers.
3. Interdict or otherwise disrupt the flow of narcotics and processing chemicals. (House 1990b: 88; and 1990c: 76)

In addition to the anti-drug policy objectives, the US Ambassador's goals were:

1. Support democracy and democratic institutions.
2. Strengthen political will and institutional capability to confront the

cocaine trade.

3. Maintain the effectiveness of military and law enforcement agencies acting against the cocaine industry.
4. Inflict significant damage on narcotrafficking organizations. (SOUTHCOM 1991: 5-10)

These objectives reflected the 1988 presidential campaign speech of George Bush who had commented:

> The cheapest and safest way to eradicate narcotics is to destroy them at their source.... We need to wipe out drugs wherever they are grown and take out labs wherever they exist. (Andreas and Sharpe 1991: 108)

Bush's statements, once he formally became President in early 1989, became part and parcel of the now enhanced US national security imperative to eliminate the threat of drugs to American society by addressing the issue inside Colombia and the other Andean countries. Yet it had been recognized early on in 1989 that all was not going well with Operation Snowcap which, despite the spending of some $350 million in a supply-sided interdiction and eradication focus in the Andes, saw overall coca production increasing some 7,000 mt since 1987. In addition some 2,496 cocaine related deaths or about five times the number reported in 1985 had afflicted the US population. (Senate 1992b: 21-22; and DHHS 1991: 21) Bush intended to take action to alter this situation dramatically.

To expedite President Bush's agenda, the ONDCP and the NSC (Dennis Miller of NSC and John Walters of ONDCP) conducted a series of joint liaison visits to Colombia, Bolivia and Peru during March of 1989. Data was collected and over a period of a few months some studies were made as to how the traffickers were operating and where they were thought to be most vulnerable. By that Fall, National Security Advisor Brent Scowcroft, Bennet of ONDCP and Deputy Secretary of State Lawrence S. Eagleburger were meeting to formulate a new anti-drug policy and, as a calculated effort, to keep the drug issue on the NSC agenda as a national security issue in order to force a still reluctant DOD to continue to draw down equipment and personnel in support of the drug war. Despite this, the NSC was afraid of asserting itself more in an operational role due to the adverse domestic political repercussions that had taken place over this type of a modus operandi, stemming from the Iran-Contra scandal and the revelations concerning the activities of

Lieutenant-Colonel Oliver North in Central America. After several meetings a three-country Andean strategy was formulated. Miller wrote the implementing National Security Directive (NSD) 18, based on Walter's concepts for implementing the new strategy. So as to reduce the possibility of resistance on the part of elements within DOD, Secretary of Defense Richard Cheney was not immediately informed about the plan and only was read into it during its later stages of development. (Interviews ONDCP 1 and 2: 1993)

While an effort was initially made to keep the Andean Initiative a secret, the media began discussing it in August of 1989 or about a month before its official announcement and implementation took place that September. The positive results against the traffickers achieved by the Barco government's backlash impressed the ONDCP which became even more optimistic when it was realized that the price of cocaine on the street in the US had actually risen towards the end of 1989 (and on into 1990). The purity of the cocaine being sold was also reported as down. (House 1990: 7) Also favorably impacting on this situation was the December 1989 invasion of Panama by US forces which toppled the regime of Panamanian strongman Manuel Noriega and temporarily closed down Panama as a money laundering center and haven for narcotraffickers.

Ironically, in previous years despite the reported devastating effects that drug usage was having on the American population, the Reagan administration in its war on drugs had not wanted to decertify or otherwise confront Noriega's notorious, narcotrafficking-linked government which was both assisting in the trafficking of drugs through its territory from Colombia and serving as a convenient money laundering site for drug profits. The DEA, NSC and CIA for their own particular reasons all considered Noriega to be an "asset" whose importance to US intelligence operations reputedly outweighed any damage that his complicity and fostering of trafficking operations inside Panama might have on the US population, the war on drugs in general and the national security threat that narcotrafficking in cocaine allegedly represented for the US. (Callahan 1993) This policy continued despite the fact that Noriega had been indicted on criminal charges for trafficking by US legal authorities in Florida in 1987. Finally, on 5 February 1988 a twelve-count federal indictment was formally announced, charging Noriega with drug related crimes taking place as far back as 1982 and linking him to the Medellin cartel. (Miami Herald: 6 Feb 88) This action and its publicity over the extent of Noriega's activities tended to force the US government's here-to-fore protective hand. This initiated a process directed by President Bush which eventually culminated in the December 1989 invasion and the fall of Noriega from power in Panama. (Interviews ONDCP 1 and 2: 1993) The Andean Initiative and strategy (also called the *Bennet Plan*), as formulated by the NSC and the ONDCP, was still concentrated on interdiction and law enforcement, focusing primarily on Colombia, Peru and Bolivia. The reasoning of Miller and Walters was that, if Colombia could involve its own military against the traffickers as a model modus operandi, why shouldn't the other Andean countries do likewise? (Interview ONDCP 1: 1993) The long-term goal of the strategy was to effect "a major reduction in the supply of cocaine from these countries to the United States" through working "with the host governments to disrupt and destroy the growing, processing and transportation of coca and coca products." Specifically, the amount of illegal drugs entering the US was to be reduced by 15 percent within two years from the initial execution of the strategy and by 60 percent within ten years. (ONDCP 1990: 49-52 and 120-121)

A primary departure from previous narcotics control efforts was the Andean Initiative's deliberate incorporation of a host country's military forces into the counter-narcotics effort and an expanded role for the US military throughout the region. A phased approach that included a coca eradication program, crop substitution, and effective local military and law enforcement measures was also to be brought into play. Primary objectives for Colombia included the interdiction of air, road and riverine smuggling of drugs and the destruction of processing labs and infrastructure important to cocaine production and trafficking in general. (House 1990b: 10)

The several short-term goals of the Andean Initiative's strategy which were intended to impact on trafficking in Colombia were:

1. To strengthen the political will and institutional capability of Colombia, Peru and Bolivia to disrupt and ultimately dismantle the trafficking organizations by:

   a. providing military assistance, security training and equipment;
   b. strengthening the ability of the Andean governments to prosecute, extradite and punish narcotics traffickers; and
   c. providing economic assistance, beginning in fiscal year 1991.

2. To increase the effectiveness of law enforcement and military activities of the three countries against the cocaine trade by:

a. isolating key coca-growing areas;
b. blocking shipments of cocaine-producing chemicals; and
c. conducting eradication programs.

3. To inflict significant damage to the trafficking
   organizations which operate within the three countries
   by:

   a. targeting key traffickers for arrest and prosecution;
   b. impeding the transfer of drug-generated funds; and
   c. seizing the assets of traffickers. (ONDCP 1990: 49-51;
      and House 1990b: 10-11)

Thus, disruption of narcotrafficker activities and organizations as well as eradication would now carry equal weight. The Country Teams would carry out the strategy through their respective INM, DEA, DOD, AID and CIA offices as well as a host of other supporting agencies' personnel which included the Departments of Justice and Treasury, US Customs, the Border Partrol etc. (Perl 1992: 15; and author observations 1992-93)

Since all the programs and activities were to be executed largely by each government agency under the control of their respective host nation Country Teams and, as there was no designated mechanism or field operating office for actually directing a coordinated implementation of the strategy among the several countries, ONDCP concluded that it did not have sufficient operational control. To resolve this problem it attempted to influence the strategy's implementation through a series of study groups and the release in September 1989 of its own National Drug Control Strategy which represented the first integrated US national approach to narcotics control, consolidating the various separate agency and department policies for reducing both supply and demand. To accomplish this some $6.4 billion was requested from Congress to fight the drug war. Later budgets during the 1990s would double this amount. Although it could write a strategy, with inadequate staffing and lacking the trust of the other key US government agencies, ONDCP found it difficult to enforce its mandates and edicts. Only through NSC support was it able to keep its Colombian and Andean anti-drug policies on track. (ONDCP 1989: passim; and Interview NSC and ONDCP1: 1993)

As part of the US aid eventually allocated to Colombia by President Bush, the Andean Initiative (AI) was conceived as a five-year, $2.15

billion program to meet US perceptions of what was needed to win the drug war in the Andean Ridge. (House 1990b:17). Colombia received an important share of the AI allocation (Figure 4).

Under the Andean Initiative US aid continued to flow to Colombia as planned with an additional draw down of $20 million in US military aid provided in August 1990. When Peru's President Fujimori rejected a US military aid package of $30 million, $25 million of these funds were then reprogrammed and allocated to Colombia ($5 million went to Bolivia). Nonetheless, there were some discrepancies noted in the US funding policy in support of the anti-drug effort inside Colombia. Although the Colombian anti-narcotics police had been responsible for about 80 percent of the anti-drug operations conducted up to that time, only about 16 percent ($10.46 million) of the monies forthcoming from the US government were actually going to them. The Colombian Air Force was the single largest recipient of the aid (31.6 percent), even though it had at this time a minimal role. (House 1990b: 79-80) In general, 75 percent of these aid monies were allocated to the military and only 25 percent was ultimately designated for the anti-narcotics police effort.

### Andean Initiative - Assistance For Colombia
### (in millions of dollars)

|  | FY 89 | FY 90 | FY 91 | FY 92 | FY 93 | FY 94 | Total |
|---|---|---|---|---|---|---|---|
| Military | 8.6 | 40.3 | 60.5 | 60.5 | 60.5 | 60.5 | 282.3 |
| Economic | 0.0 | 3.6 | 50.0 | 50.0 | 50.0 | 50.0 | 203.6 |
| Law Enforcement | 10.0 | 20.0 | 20.0 | 20.0 | 20.0 | 20.0 | 100.0 |
| DEA Support | 4.2 | 4.4 | 4.4 | 4.4 | 4.4 | 4.4 | 22.0 |
| Total | 22.8 | 68.3 | 134.9 | 134.9 | 134.9 | 134.9 | 607.9 |

Source: Office of National Drug Control Policy: 20 June 1990 in House 1990b: 17.

Figure 4

Two items which were viewed by the Colombians as critical to their anti-drug operations against the cartels were secure radio communications equipment and radio signal intercept and locating equipment which would allow them to accurately pinpoint the location of trafficker radio transmitters. Despite the usefulness of this equipment, for national security reasons based on the Cold War defense policies of the US, the Colombian requests were refused. As a result the Colombian narcotrafficking detection capability lagged somewhat behind the generally state-of-the-art equipment used by the traffickers themselves to reduce their risks by monitoring government radio/telephone transmissions dealing with counter-drug plans and operations. (House 1990c: 81)

The US government attempted to take up the slack through the use of its own military means. This was reflected in the enhanced SOUTHCOM role for Colombia when President Bush signed a National Security Directive in August 1989, officially allowing US Army Special Forces training personnel to accompany local forces on counternarcotics training patrols. (House 1990b: 88 and 93) By early 1990 up to a hundred US military trainers, advisors and technicians were working in Colombia. (New York Times: 7 Jan 90) US Marines were reported working with their Colombian counterparts on practice anti-drug patrols along the Putumayo River in the vicinity of the Peruvian border. (Los Angeles Times: 2 Jul 90) In addition, US military intelligence collection platforms in the air and on the ground were increasingly brought into play on behalf of the Colombian focused anti-drug effort.

While the then Minister of Justice, Monica de Greiff, had asked the US for $19 million in emergency judicial aid, the US declined, substituting instead a $5 million package (originally allocated in 1988 but not yet spent) for judicial protection. This package involved the provision of some 30 armored vehicles, personal security training, communications security equipment and courses for judges, legislators, cabinet officials, and political candidates and their body guards. (House 1990c: 90). The logistics of the situation was confusing, with the US responding to the Colombian's needs by inadvertently sending Vietnam-era infantry flak vests, each weighing over twenty pounds for the judges to wear while on duty (These were later replaced with 398 commercial bullet proof vests). In short, the Colombian judicial system's security crisis was not reflected in the modest aid package it actually received. Under-funded and understaffed, while attempting to investigate some 4,200 cases of corruption by the police and another 1,700 cases involving the armed forces, the Colombian Attorney General and the judiciary was now essentially paralyzed by the escalating violence in terms of its ability to deal with the traffickers. (WOLA 1991: 5) Even Monica de Greiff resigned from her position out of fear for her son's life which had been threatened as part of the Medellin cartel's warning that it would kill ten judges for every Colombian extradited to the US to stand trial. (Insight: 2 Apr 90) Only very slowly had it been recognized by US (and Colombian) authorities that a functional and secure judiciary was essential in assisting the anti-drug effort inside Colombia. (House 1990b: 89-90)

As such, it had been found that Colombian judges who took up the anti-narcotics specialty often did so immediately after graduating from law school. In this case they lacked the investigative and practical knowledge of criminal justice procedures required to deal with the highly conspiratorial nature of narcotrafficking in Colombia. Unskilled in the use of physical and forensic evidence, they often relied on the testimony of victims, witnesses and a few captured traffickers in obtaining convictions. With Colombian citizens generally fearing to speak out and the state not allowed to use plea-bargaining in its judicial system, there was little or no incentive for a trafficker, let alone a criminal, to become an informant in support of the government. (House 1990c: 87; and Washington Post: 14 Apr 90)

It was also found that almost a third of the judges were unable to identify the elements of law required to obtain a drug-related conviction. If one took into consideration the relative lack of resources, low pay, hazardous working conditions (over a hundred judges had been murdered by this time during the 1980s), inefficient administration, and the lack of procedural knowledge, the judicial system was seriously undermined and was unable to guarantee the Colombian citizens the due process and protection the system should have provided. (House 1990c: 87-88) There were other problems too. Because the judiciary was not independent from the Colombian Executive, it could not provide impartial justice. Case congestion in the courts was such that about 75 percent of all criminal cases had not been tried. Likewise some two million cases remained unresolved. In short, the system lacked effective investigative and prosecution components. (GAO 1992c: 8 - 9)

With AID's AOJ-1 assistance effort having been completed in 1989, another iteration came into play in 1990 as AOJ-2. Although initially funded at $1.2 million, this program was projected as running for up to four years and eventually costing some $18 million. Reforms contemplated involved financial and administrative independence of the courts and the creation of distinct, elite groups of investigators, prosecutors and judges, trained and protected to such a degree that they could deal effectively with the traffickers' own legal tactics and highly coercive death threats. (House 1990c: 89) To this end AID again began to coordinate and bring into play a series of programs which attempted to modernize Colombian court administration, investigative research techniques and provide protection to the judges and other judicial officials. In addition a general national drug awareness and small business credit and training programs were promoted as adjuncts to the anti-drug effort. This last aspect affected some 13,000 businesses which were fostered and supported in the hopes that they would serve to bolster the overall economy and help wean away from the traffickers and guerrillas alike promising young Colombian entrepreneurs. (House 1989-1990: 162)

Despite the fact that US assistance was generally forthcoming, there were problems which surfaced and created some friction between the Country Team and its Colombian counterparts. Here the generally non-compatible frequencies of the antiquated Vietnam era radios of now obsolete US provided UH-1H helicopters with the CNP's own newer model Bell helicopter radios and those of the ground forces stood out. This meant that critical air to ground communications affecting the coordination of units and operations could not always be effected. While this compatibility defect was known to the US Department of Defense (DOD), the helicopters were turned over to Colombia anyway. (House 1990c: 83) Further aggravating the perspective of the CNP were the 30 new, late model Blackhawk assault helicopters purchased from the US by the Colombian government which then assigned them to the Air Force which was suffering from an acute pilot shortage. Meanwhile, the DAN, which had more than enough pilots, but not enough helicopters, felt itself the victim of an inefficient allocation system. (author observation)

The total US military aid for Colombia in 1989 was now $72 million or far beyond the level of 1985 ($0.8 million). Yet this was only a beginning as it was announced by President Bush on 5 September 1989 that $76.2 million in military assistance was now being proposed for 1990. (Arrieta 1990: 344) The US had opened the door for aid to Colombia which the former thought should allow it considerable leverage in the anti-drug effort with the latter. In addition Bush promised to reinitiate the International Coffee Agreement. As time went on the Washington community attempted to push its advantage to the maximum.

In early 1990 General Maxwell Thurman, then the Commander-in-Chief of the US Southern Command (SOUTHCOM) in Panama offered his own strategy for defeating the traffickers. The Thurman strategy conceptualized the raiding of trafficker operations and production facilities by US military forces throughout the Andes, as well as a plan whereby each country would provide a six battalion strike force (3,000 men) which the US would train and advise during its employment against trafficker strongholds. (House 1990b: 15; and SOUTHCOM J3: 1993)

Despite internal opposition in DOD to an increased physical role or direct contact by US forces with the traffickers, Thurman had enough influence within the US government to obtain authorization from DOD to begin a series of anti-drug intelligence support operations known as Support Justice. Interdiction was to take place in a series of defensive tiers or zones of operation, beginning with the source countries such as Colombia, followed by operations in the Caribbean and Central America, and finally along the US frontier. This *three tier strategy* was supposed to stop the now estimated 3,500 aircraft and over 15,000 boats all potentially smuggling illegal drugs into the US. (Senate 1990: 11, 22-25 and 56; and Newsweek: 6 Jan 92) Even so, the unexpected war in the Persian Gulf in early 1991 siphoned off considerable US military assets and disrupted somewhat the AWACs supported anti-drug intelligence effort in the Andes. Nonetheless, all other SOUTHCOM training and logistical efforts in support of the anti-drug war continued as planned by the various Country Teams. Narcotrafficking was still considered a national security threat since the drug traffickers were perceived as ultimately responsible for the drug-related deaths of some 2,500 Americans annually, as well as the undermining of American society and its values, all as part of a nefarious criminal enterprise. (Senate 1989a: 103; and Interviews NSC and Callahan: 1993)

Through all this the White House indicated that it was favorably disposed towards and would welcome the opportunity to send US troops to Colombia to help combat narcotrafficking. While the US aid was offered with good intentions, the Colombian government often saw it more as an example of potential Yankee meddling in the internal affairs of a Latin American nation. The Minister of Defense, Oscar Botero Restrepo, clearly indicated to the US that Colombia did not need foreign troops to resolve its internal problems. (Latin American Report: 5 Oct 89) By this time the DAN consisted of some 2,500 personnel and an air wing of 16 fixed wing and 27 helicopters which operated out of four dispersed bases. In addition, an elite paramilitary group (*F-2*), consisting of over 2,000 specially selected and trained policemen, had been established in April of 1989 to confront vigilante groups. More often than not F-2 personnel found themselves pitted against the traffickers, investigating and raiding laboratories and the offices of the cocaine production industry. (House 1990c: 72)

Also not helping the US image in Colombian eyes was the US

invasion of Panama which, while eliminating General Manuel Noriega as a protective narcotrafficking link to the Colombian cartels, money laundering and trafficking in Panama, was roundly denounced by the Colombian government as an act in contravention of international law. (Arrieta 1990: 345) Fears within Colombia that the US might be secretly planning a Panama-style, anti-drug invasion of that nation appeared to be vindicated when the US announced in January of 1990 that the US Navy's aircraft carrier John F. Kennedy and an accompanying frigate would be taking up stations off Colombia's Caribbean coast as part of an anti-drug *blockade*. The Colombian Ministry of Foreign Relations declared that the stationing of US naval forces in Colombian waters was unacceptable to the government. In its ire it also stated that any plan to install anti-drug radars on Colombian territory would also be considered unacceptable. (El Espectador: 8 Jan 90) That the US had not previously coordinated its intent with the Colombian government before making a public announcement concerning its operations, tended to prejudice somewhat the US in its anti-drug efforts inside Colombia. (El Espectador 11 Jan 90) During March, the US Navy, without approval from the government in Bogota, seized two Colombian freighters within the country's two-hundred mile maritime limits further agravating the relationship. (Bagley 1991: 17) This was the backdrop against which the Andean Initiative began to be initiated in earnest.

# Chapter 4

## Confronting The Traffickers

To emphasize the importance of the Andean Initiative and underscore the US interest in promoting hemispheric cooperation in the drug war, an Andean anti-drug summit, involving the countries of Colombia, Bolivia, Peru and the US was convened in Cartagena, Colombia in mid-February 1990. While President Bush did emphasize interdiction and the use of the military in an anti-drug role, for the first time a US president acknowledged that *demand* was an important factor in the narcotrafficking phenomenon. In addition, a nation's economic development was recognized as an important component of the anti-drug effort as a way to assist the transition away from coca cultivation into more legitimate crops. To support US policy, the Andean governments agreed to consult and collaborate with each other in the war on drugs and to take concerned action against the traffickers who were formally recognized as a serious, mutual international threat to the existing economic and social order of all four countries. (Bagley 1991: 16-17; New York Times: 14 and 16 Feb 90; and Walker 1992: 265) In short, the US had set the stage for the implementation of the $2.2 billion anti-drug effort which would take place over the next five years throughout the Andes.

In early 1990 some of the leading traffickers suggested to Colombian authorities that they would now be favorably disposed towards suspending their operations, turning over to the government all aircraft, explosives, weapons, laboratories, clandestine airfields, as well as stopping the assassination of political leaders, government officials, judges, journalists, police and members of the armed forces in exchange for their formal reincorporation into Colombian society without prejudice by the government. The Barco government remained unmoved in its original position of not tolerating the traffickers or their operations and rejected their offer. (Semana: 23 Jan 90)

Since Barco had rejected their offer and continued to apply the extradition agreement with the US (extraditing some 28 traffickers throughout the period of his administration), as a reprisal, the traffickers now extended their terrorists acts throughout the country. Over a period of about half a year during 1990 some 1,700 Colombians were murdered, including several judges, scores of judicial assistants, and several presidential candidates and journalists. Two hundred bombs were exploded in Bogota alone. In addition over 400 police officers were killed in the line of duty; some 200 of which were killed in the city of Medellin. Encouraging the high police murder rate for 1989-90 were the trafficker sponsored bounties of $4,000 for each police officer killed in Medellin and $8,000 for each F-2 member assassinated. That the police were willing to persevere in the face of their high losses was an indication of their dedication to duty and a belief in the government's anti-drug policy. (House 1990b: 85 and 1990c: 75; and Washington Post: 30 Mar 90) Despite the violence and intimidation tactics on the part of the narco-mafia, some 844 persons involved in trafficking were apprehended as the government fought back tenaciously. (Bagley 1990: 471)

Fearing extradition to the US above all, the traffickers' objective was to avoid capture and cause the government to abandon its campaign against them by cowing the Colombian legislature and weakening the resolve of the Executive, all the while offering to negotiate a "solution" to the problem. (House 1990c: 91) The government, however, remained firm in its position and the policy of no negotiation, extradition, and militant confrontation continued as the 27 May presidential elections approached. This did not mean that the government was totally inflexible in terms of negotiating. A dialogue and negotiation process did take place with such insurgent groups as the M-19, but not the drug traffickers.

On 9 March 1990 the M-19 turned over its weapons, agreeing to a formal peace settlement with the Barco government and the termination of its revolutionary effort in exchange for being reincorporated into society and insuring its participation in the democratic process. (Bejarano 1990: 57 and 59) Barco was far less successful with the FARC which, in conjunction with the ELN and EPL (and the former M-19), had founded the *Coordinadora Guerrillera Simon Bolivar*

(CGSB - Simon Bolivar Guerrilla Coordinator) in an effort to unify all elements at war with the government. The intransigence of the CGSB in accepting the government's overtures for a negotiated peace was based on its perception that the government was not trying to redress the still very dire socio-economic problems affecting a full third of the population. This malady served as a basic, motivating raison d'etre and catalyst for the guerrillas' revolutionary cause. (Bejarano 1990: 88 and 122-123)

In terms of the drug war the government was in a strong position as its anti-drug policy and related operations were seemingly having considerable effect on the traffickers. The ferocity and extent of the government's determined backlash over the death of Luis Carlos Galan had taken many of the trafficking groups and cartels by surprise and for the first time in the drug war the government felt it was beginning to call the tune. At this time numerous drug-traffickers denounced the violent tactics of the Escobar group and attempted to make their position clear publicly in the hopes that this would somehow lessen the intensity of the government's interests in eventually bringing them to justice. (Washington Post: 17 Apr 90) On 15 December 1989 Gonzalo Rodriguez Gacha and his son were killed in a confrontation with a joint Army-police force at a ranch near Cartagena. Shortly thereafter the nation-wide bombings came to a halt, ending the four month duel in which Rodriguez Gacha's sicarios had generally fought the government to a standstill. (Senate 1992a: 123; and Gugliotta 1992: 113)

Nonetheless, as time went on, other traffickers, thought to be led by Pablo Escobar himself, began to use terrorist/extortion tactics to intimidate the goverment, involving the kidnapping of prominent Colombians, including the son of one of Barco's closest advisors. The idea was to use the hostages to blackmail the government into negotiating a peaceful settlement favorable to the traffickers' interests. (Gugliotta 1992: 113) When negotiations lagged and the traffickers perceived that all was not going well, Escobar's cartel took retribution in the only form it knew - violence. To this end they murdered Diana Turbay, the daughter of the former President, who had been kidnapped some months earlier. (Lee 1992: 110)

An indicator of the success garnered by the military and police operations was evident in the levels of reported labor earnings by the Banco de la Republica which stated that their earnings had dropped off by as much as 50 percent from September of 1989 to about March of 1990. The serious cash flow shortages on the part of the traffickers also crippled the Bolivian and Peruvian coca markets, plunging them into virtual depressions during the early months of 1990. With no readily available cash on hand on the part of the traffickers to pay the campesinos for their coca leaves and paste, the Andean Ridge coca growers began to worry, if not panic, some making the decision to turn to alternate crops. (Gugliotta 1992: 119) During the first five months of 1990, 38 mt of cocaine base and HCl were seized in Colombia, surpassing the total for 1989. (House 1990b: 86; And Arrieta 1990: 79-80) While this reflected the impact that the US-Colombian repression strategy had, the traffickers were otherwise able to rebound, readjusting their marketing systems and operations to accommodate the intensified anti-drug effort on the part of the government.

Indicative of the truth of the situation in Colombia was the report that cocaine output was still rated as being about 80 percent of the pre-August 1989 levels. (Washington Post: 13 May 90; and Lee 1992: 108) In part this was due to the almost total focus and exclusive targeting of the Medellin cartel by the government's forces. While the Medellin groups saw their operations disrupted to a considerable degree, the Cali cartel was left largely intact and was generally able to continue its operations, picking up the slack in meeting the continuing and steady international demand for cocaine. As a result of the government's operations, the Cali cartel and the trafficker independents throughout Colombia increased their share of the international cocaine market, all the while maximizing their legitimate commercial holdings both inside and outside Colombia, producing and transshipping up to 600 mt of cocaine during the year. (House 1990b: 86-88; Insight: 2 Apr 90; and Gugliotta 1992: 115) This created a situation in which the Medellin cartel groups now became convinced that the Cali groups were betraying the former to the police by turning over information which led to the arrest of the infamous sicario Dandeny Munoz Mosquera. A mysterious letter surfaced in the Colombian press to this effect and, while he discounted it as a disinformation effort on someone's part, Pablo Escobar and his cohorts bitterly denounced the Cali group and even declared war on it. (El Nuevo Herald: 7 and 8 Jan 92)

Another result of the government's repression was the influx of Colombians into Bolivia and Peru to ensure that the cocaine processing laboratories continued to function and that a steady flow of cocaine base and HCl was maintained. The depressed prices resulting from the Barco backlash and heightened anti-drug repression, which had disrupted significant portions of the refining process, had duly created a glut of coca leaves on both the Bolivian and Peruvian coca markets. (House 1990c: 74 and 92) To react to the situation Bolivian and Peruvian laboratories in many cases were upgraded by the Colombians as part of a vertical integration process where the complete production cycle from coca paste to refined cocaine was now carried out outside of Colombia. Colombians were also noted in increasingly large numbers in Brazil, Ecuador, Argentina and Chile, working to develop suitable infrastructures for their cocaine production-transshipping industry. (House 1990b: 37)

Additional shipping and smuggling networks were also found to have been established and expanded in both Ecuador and Brazil, with the Ecuadoran port city of Guayaquil being noted as a primary export route out of Colombia. Here too, Colombians were reported as having purchased large tracts of land throughout Ecuador, paying in US dollars up to double the local market value. These operations were not just limited to the Americas as cocaine-refining and investments were also taking place in Spain, Italy and France in response to the Barco crackdown. Finally, chemical precursors, in the form of acetone and ether continued to flow into Colombia from both the US and Europe. (Washington Post: 4 Sep 90) In the meantime, the US and other countries were attempting to initiate counter-money laundering operations in an effort to disrupt the traffickers' operations by diminishing their profits.

Money laundering by the traffickers throughout the Americas and Europe had reached unprecedented levels by 1989-90. At the same time, the US and other United Nations (UN) countries, were attempting to deal with this situation through a UN sponsored Financial Action Task Force (FATF). The purpose of the FATF was to try and disrupt the bank transfer process throughout some fifty countries, involving the roughly $3 billion in proceeds estimated as being yielded to the narco-kingpins by the international drug trade. Disclosure of beneficial owners of accounts and the use of selected recording data and accounting measures were to open the door for the DEA and US Treasury Department money laundering investigations. Also caught up in the effort were the non-bank financial systems or *casas de cambio* (exchange houses) operating throughout the Americas. (House 1991a: 57)

As part of the anti-money laundering effort, the DEA initiated its Green Ice campaign which had as part of its focus, Panamanian strongman Manuel Noriega. In exchange for his generally permissive attitude concerning cocaine transhipment operations and money laundering inside Panama throughout the 1980s, Noriega had received numerous kickbacks amounting to scores of millions of dollars from the

Medellin cartel. When things did not go well for the cartel inside Panama (Noriega had raided a major cocaine refining laboratory complex in the Darian province to appease US interests, even though he had accepted $5 million to protect it.) and Noriega became ever more greedy while demanding ever higher rates of compensation in exchange for his permissiveness towards narcotrafficking, the cartel decided to have him murdered. Only through the actual intervention of Fidel Castro of Cuba and former Colombian President (1970s), Alfonso Lopez Michelsen, was the dispute mediated and resolved in favor of sparing Noriega's life. (Senate 1988a: 66 and 81-88; New York Times: 27 Sep 91; and Miami Herald: 15 Dec 91) Panamanian based banks such as the Bank of Credit and Commerce International, Banco Occidental of Colombia, Chase City Bank, and Continental of Illinois all secretly provided evidence to the US government on the Noriega money laundering operations then going on. (Senate 1989: 102) This formed part of the confirming evidence for the Bush administration's actions which, when confronted with the fact that Noriega was facilitating Colombian narcotrafficking in Panama, eventually culminated in the US invasion of 1989, toppling the Panamanian strongman from power.

Narcotraffickers typically laundered their funds in such diverse operations as disbursement by couriers to cartel managers throughout the Americas, fictitious accounts in stock exchange-securities companies, real and dummy trading corporations, over and under-invoicing on imports and international sales, and the use of off shore banking and wire-transfers to a myriad of distant bank accounts. Separate lots of money of up to $10 million each were frequently disbursed to some 14,000 corporations throughout the Caribbean using a variety of false import/export transactions whereby the funds were eventually deposited into legitimate bank accounts and then held for future use. The schemes involved to this end were infinite. (House 1991a: 58-59; and Maingot 1988: 181)

By under-invoicing an export, a Colombian resident could direct the unreported difference between the invoice amount and the actual receipts to a foreign bank account. In over-invoicing an import, an unreported deposit outside the country could be hidden as part of the cost of the imports which were actually lower than those reported. (Gunter 1991: 129) In the end the traffickers were merely exploiting systems and techniques of illegal contraband which had already been in place in Colombia and elsewhere for decades. Bank secrecy laws permitting shell corporations and bearer shares, "grey" markets and other methods had been created over the years to help individuals and corporations avoid government sponsored tax collections and restrictions on foreign exchange controls. (House 1991a: 60) All these were now exploited by the various cartels to further their own ends.

In an effort to undermine money laundering by the trafficking organizations, the US initiated Operation Polar Cap which was a two-year money laundering investigation, targeting the Medellin cartel's activities in jewelry exchanges, gold brokerages and liquor companies in Los Angeles, Houston, Miami and San Francisco. Working through Atlanta based banks, the Banco de Occidente in Panama was also found to be involved in the laundering process. Over time, US Treasury agents seized $105 million and arrested 111 individuals involved in the scheme. As this operation and others like it took place, considerable information was obtained concerning cartel accounts and money laundering processes. Despite the complex nature of money laundering, DEA and US Treasury investigators were able to achieve a number of successes and infamous money launderers such as Eduardo Martinez were captured in Colombia and then extradited to the US as part of the Green Ice effort. (House 1991a: 69 and 72)

In 1990 the newly elected Liberal Party President, Cesar Gaviria, drew the distinction between the narco-terrorism which generally characterized the Medellin cartel and the more benign trafficking activities of the Cali and other lesser cartels and independents then operating. The Medellin group was seen as the most serious threat to the government's security. Nonetheless, in a significant departure from the Barco policy, Gaviria announced on 5 September 1990 (Decree 2047) that any trafficker who voluntarily surrendered and confessed to a crime would not only receive reduced sentencing by at least one-third, but would also not be extradited to the US. In addition traffickers would have to identify or turn over all their assets (laboratories and aircraft etc) and any related proceeds (stashed cocaine, cash and bank accounts). The extradition policy was being deemphasized, if not overturned, and a form of plea-bargaining strategy was now brought into play. (House 1990b: 86; and Washington Post: 18 Jan 91)

About two months later the *Extraditables* responded with a counter-proposal. They were willing to surrender themselves (up to 300 individuals) to the Colombian authorities and cease all trafficking and the use of violence, provided there would be no extraditions made and that trials would be held by Colombian courts only. In addition they rejected the concept of confessing to crimes or the denouncement of fellow traffickers and instead demanded that they be given special protection and detention privileges to prevent any form of revenge or reprisals against them or their families. (Lee 1992: 115) To this end they promised to release any and all hostages, if their demands were met. The government, acquiescing somewhat in the trafficker's position, now responded in turn and suggested that the cartel members had to stand trial for a crime of some sort (illegal enrichment, delinquency, etc.) in order for the process to retain a form of legitimacy and be accepted by the public. (Lee 1992: 115) On this basis an understanding was forged which enabled the Gaviria strategy to begin to bear fruit, seeing the Ochoa clan brothers (Fabio, Jorge and Juan) voluntarily surrender to the government over a period of the next half year (The brothers, for example, served jail sentences of roughly five and a half years, being released from prison in mid-1996). (El Nuevo Herald: 17 Sep 1996)

At this time the Colombian public was reported as being exhausted by the continuous violence and the related pressures generated by the drug war. The situation in Medellin alone during 1990 was a case in point. Crime had gotten out of hand both within the city and its surrounding area and some 7,400 murders were reported. Surgeons reported up to 150 gunshot cases a night being treated in city hospitals. With the police unable to stem the tide of violence let alone provide for the safety of the people (a person walking no more than three blocks in the Medellin inner city or slum areas was said to have a 50 percent chance of being killed by gunfire), local people's militia and vigilante groups were formed to protect the residents. Medellin was in a virtual state of war. While often led by left-wing guerrillas, the vigilante groups were tolerated by the police, and numerous summary executions of drug-gang leaders, pushers and other persons considered undesirable by the local communities were carried out. (Independent: 28 Nov 91; and Washington Post: 7 Dec 91) While terrorism and violence were at the top of the list of the public's worries, unemployment ranked second and narcotrafficking in general was a far distant third, indicating the generally ambivalent attitude on the part of the population towards the government's anti-drug campaign. So intense was the situation, the vast majority of the people favored amnesty for the traffickers if that would bring peace to Colombia. (Semana: 8 Jan 91; and New York Times: 12 Aug 90)

Helping Colombia in this time of crisis was the 27 June announcement by President Bush of his Enterprise for the Americas Initiative, which, in addition to free trade agreements, also forgave up to $7 billion in foreign debt. Gaviria looked at the Bush proposal as an adjunct to the previously implemented Andean Initiative. (Bagley 1991:

18) Here was another helping hand being extended to Colombia. Later, in December, the DOS directed the Country Team to develop specific ground, air and riverine counter-narcotics operations plans for the Colombian military and police forces. Nonetheless, since no specific counter-narcotics program effectiveness indicators could be agreed upon to measure progress made, the US General Accounting Office (GAO) called into question the viability of the anti-drug program being pursued in Colombia. (GAO 1991f: 4 - 6)

A key US anti-drug policy focus now being fostered by the DEA was on the directors and principal leaders of the trafficking cartels. This was known as the "kingpin strategy." As such, there was now a somewhat lower priority focus on confronting the coca farmers throughout the Andes and bringing about eradication as an end in itself. (Callahan 1993) The primary objective now was to disarticulate as much as possible entire trafficking organizations in the hopes that this would reduce the flow of drugs into the US. At this time federal cocaine seizures inside the continental US were reaching almost 100 mt per year. (Interview INM 1993)

The government's FY 1990 budget submission of some $8 billion for general anti-drug related programs and activities proposed by Bush allocated about 70 percent of the monies for enforcement and about 30 percent for education and treatment. The Senate, not satisfied with this emphasis, added another billion dollars towards education, treatment and local law enforcement. (Bagley 1991: 26) This was understandable considering the domestic situation involving cocaine usage then facing the US.

During 1990 the gross annual profits from illegal drug sales world-wide were estimated to be as high as $110 billion, or more than all the profits enjoyed by all the Fortune 500 companies combined. (Seyler 1991: 1) While the bank accounts and assets of the traffickers were potentially highly vulnerable to seizure and other government measures to curtail their use, the Financial Action Task Force within the US was only able to seize or force the forfeiture of some $650 million in trafficker assets, a relatively small amount compared to the gross profits realized up to that time. (USIA 1991: passim) In Congress it was being reported that cocaine had the potential of contributing up to $4 billion in earnings to the economies of the Andean countries. Here cocaine was reported in Congressional hearings as supplying "10 percent of the export earnings of Colombia, 25 percent of the export income of Peru, and 50 percent of Bolivia." Some 1.5 million Andean farmers were reported as being involved in coca cultivation. (Senate 1991: 124; and

Gamarra: 1993)

As an indicator of the continued intense drug demand in the US, there were now being reported some 80,000 cocaine related emergency room mentions and as well as 33,800 mentions for heroin, indicating that the intensity of drug usage had increased some 25 percent over that of 1988. (DHHS 1991a: 56) This intensified demand by certain elements of the US population was offset by the National Institute on Drug Abuse's contrasting surveys which showed that the use of cocaine among the general population had fallen off some 72 percent, reflecting an overall downward trend in drug usage. (NIDA 1990-1991: 21) Despite these conflicting statistics, it was found that drug use had intensified among a core of about six million adults who purchased the drug in sufficient quantity to stimulate a strong market demand. (DHHS 1991b: 25)

The US anti-drug policy still figured prominently as a basic national interest deliberately linked to the NSC's 1990s national security strategy and the "survival of the United States as a free and independent nation, with its fundamental values intact and its institutions and people secure." Reiterated was the perception that the international drug trade was a major threat to US national security. (White House 1991: 3 and 17) To meet this perceived threat the NSC's anti-drug policy objective was: "Reduce the flow of illegal drugs into the United States by encouraging reduction in foreign production, combatting international traffickers and reducing demand at home." (White House 1991: 3) The goals of the Andean Initiative were now modified to reflect a 20 percent reduction by 1993 and a 65 percent reduction by the year 2001 of the amount of drugs entering the US. (ONDCP 1991: 15)

By the end of 1990 DEA's own Operation Snowcap was showing some results as the Colombian government had captured over 53 metric tons of cocaine, arrested some 7,000 suspected traffickers and destroyed over 300 processing laboratories of which 29 were major cocaine refining facilities. The police had spearheaded these operations, although the Army itself had accounted for 19 mt of the cocaine seizures. In the case of the Army's operation, it was assisted by Air Force helicopters, enabling it to conduct a series of raids on transhipment sites in the Meta Department. Besides capturing the cocaine, six trafficker aircraft were seized and 24 airstrips were rendered unusable. In all, over 50 major traffickers had been captured or killed during Operation Snowcap and of these, 24 had been extradited to the US. In addition some 700,000 gallons of precursor chemicals had been seized. The DEA found that its working relationships with the Colombian law enforcement agencies were highly effective as intelligence information was routinely exchanged on suspected cocaine HCl, base and paste refining laboratories, clandestine airstrips, narcotrafficker kingpins and operators, and the infrastructure and marketing operations in general. (House 1991d: 14 and 34-35) Yet all this came at a significant cost, as the CNP and the DAN suffered losses of 420 officers killed and 537 wounded over the period of a year. (USE-CO 1991: Cable 6299)

A major DEA focus during this time inside Colombia was the traffickers' own financial and precursor chemical operations. Investigations by the DEA and Colombian authorities concerning the actual monies involved in tracing the purchase of cocaine, the transfer of proceeds from illegal cocaine sales, and the conversion of the drug monies into tangible assets ensued. Before he was killed, Jose Gonzalo Rodriguez Gacha in particular had become the subject of a worldwide law enforcement effort to trace his assets. Over time, the painstaking research provided enough information to enable the DAN to eventually locate him. This was greatly facilitated by an asset sharing agreement which Colombia signed with the US in 1990. To this end some $203 million in illegal cash profits were confiscated from Rodriguez Gacha and other cartel king pins. (House 1991d: 36-37)

In terms of precursor control, the US Chemical Diversion and Trafficking Act of 1988 was more strictly enforced in 1990 making it more difficult for the traffickers to obtain the essential chemicals or precursors required to mass produce cocaine inside Colombia. The legislation enabled DEA and US Customs officials to monitor, control and verify the movement of shipments not only out of the US but also through Colombian ports of entry. In addition chemical control conferences were held in Brussels in 1990 (and in La Paz in 1991) to emphasize the problem and formulate appropriate solutions. The end result was that by early 1991 some 1,436 foreign companies had been submitted by US chemical export companies to the DEA for approval for export. Of these, some 84 (64 of which were located in Latin America) were denied approval due to their known or suspected links to narcotrafficking in Colombia. (House 1991d: 37-38)

An indicator of some success of the US supported anti-drug effort in Colombia was the fact that during 1990, for the first time since the early 1980s, the price for a gram of cocaine HCl on the street in the US had temporarily increased from $50 to as high as $175 and its purity had declined to an average of 54 percent of its former level. (House 1991d: 39; and Senate 1992a: 43) Nonetheless, the DEA reported the US wholesale price level for a kilogram of cocaine during the first quarter of 1991, while rising as high as $25,000, had again dropped down to a range of $14,000 to $23,000 towards the end of the year, indicating that cocaine was not only cheap but also still available in abundance in the US. (Senate: 1992a: 43) Purity was also again reported to have risen to 84 percent or about the average level sustained during the late 1980s. (House 1992: 120-121) In addition, the DEA was reported as estimating that, despite the disruption of cocaine production inside Colombia, the balloon effect had come into play and overall cocaine production in the Americas had steadily increased to as much as around 900 mts by 1990. (Washington Post: 24 Feb 90)

At this time the US anti-drug policy goals for 1991 and extending into the mid-1990s in support of the Colombian government were:

1. Destroy or disrupt major trafficking organizations;

2. Seize assets of and disrupt money laundering by major traffickers;

3. Destroy cocaine processing laboratories, disrupt major traffickers and eliminate trafficking organizations;

4. Prosecute and punish major traffickers by strengthening the judicial system to overcome corruption and intimidation;

5. Increase operational effectiveness of the National Police Anti-Narcotics Directorate; and

6. Increase the level of public awareness regarding the severity of the narcotics problem in Colombia. (DOS 1991: 27)

In short, the overall US objective for Colombia was to "reestablish the rule of law and destroy the illicit narcotics industry." (Levitsky 1991: 7)

As 1991 progressed, by late June the US supported multi-service Colombian anti-narcotics effort increased its momentum against both the Medellin and Cali cartel groups, capturing 53 mt of cocaine products alone during the first half of the year as well as destroying 40 cocaine HCl laboratories, 58 clandestine airstrips and arresting some 1,500 suspected narcotraffickers. (House 1991d: 14 and 35) The end result was that, while most of the Medellin cartel's known senior leadership found itself in jail, the Cali, North Coast and other cartel groups remained largely in tact. Feeling the pressure from the government's counter-drug activities, the traffickers attempted to fight back using their traditional methods of indiscriminate bombings and assassinations which, while generally targeting public officials, also produced thousands of casualties among innocent bystanders. (House 1991d: 15) From 1989 to 1991 the Medellin cartel had sponsored more than 600 assasinations, including the 1989 sabotage bombing of a commercial airliner (107 deaths) and a car bomb in front of the national intelligence service headquarters (60 deaths). (El Tiempo: 16 Apr 94)

A highlight of the year was the negotiated 19 June surrender of Pablo Escobar and other major Medellin cartel traffickers under President Gaviria's plea bargaining decree. The President's strategy of using unrelenting police pressure as a stick and plea bargaining with reduced sentences and no extradition to the US as the carrot appeared to be working. (Washington Post: 20 Jun 91) With Escobar in jail the US became very optimistic and AID planned to authorize $36 million under the President's NSD-18 Economic Support Funds to further support a comprehensive strengthening of the Colombian judicial system with a continued focus on improving its administration, operations, security and overall effectiveness. (House 1991d: 15-16; and AID 1992: 43)

Although Escobar had turned himself over to the government, it was reported by the DEA that he was continuing to run his cartel operations out of his jail cell at the Bureau of Prison's Envigado municipal facility. That Escobar had not turned over any of his laboratories or airplanes indicated that the Medellin cartel's trafficking structure was still very much intact. This was particularly frustrating to the US government which felt that Gaviria's plea bargaining policy was merely acquiescing to trafficking interests, allowing the cartel leaders to continue operating out of their prison cells. (Washington Post: 21 Jun 91; and Toft: 1993) When informed of this situation, President Gaviria pledged on 30 June 1991 that this would not be allowed to happen. (House 1991d: 45 and 59)

Despite governmental denials to the contrary, reports continued to flow in indicating that Escobar was exploiting the national prison system against the government. The government had badly overestimated its ability to control the narco-kingpin. (Silva Lujan: 1993) Escobar had established an entire network of his cohorts and even armed *sicarios* inside the prison so that he could continue his operations while protecting himself at close quarters. (House 1992: 189) From prison Escobar even ordered the assassinations of some 40 members of the Medellin cartel itself, including members of the Mocada and

Galliano families, who were perceived as now working against him (not paying a $2,000 per month stipend to his war chest) or gaining undue influence over the cartel's operations. (El Nuevo Herald: 25 Jan 93; and Interview DEA:CO 1993) Gaviria's own orders to circumscribe Escobar's activities in early 1992 were ignored by prison officials who themselves had succumbed to the corruptive and intimidating influences of *plata o plomo*. As a result, Escobar lived in relative luxury, operating out of a suite of offices which served as his prison quarters. (Semana: 24 Nov 92 and Tiempo: 2 Sep 92)

Throughout this time the US-Colombian anti-drug effort continued in concert, with the DEA supporting some 275 separate investigations now targeting members from all levels of the Cali cartel. (House 1991d: 47) Led by the Rodriguez Orejuela brothers (Gilberto and Miguel) and Jose Santa Cruz Londono, the cartel began to feel the pressure of the government's anti-drug efforts and it accordingly began to look more and more towards Europe as a market for its cocaine products. Included in this new effort was the Italian Mafia which now saw an opportunity to receive major shares of the lucrative profits to be made in the cocaine trade. (El Espectador: 18 Oct 91) In part, the Colombian traffickers were anticipating the fact that by 1992 the European community would be deepening its relationships among its member nations to the degree that most customs barriers would be eliminated, facilitating the movement of goods across borders. The traffickers viewed Holland, Spain and Portugal as particularly lucrative for smuggling operations, exploiting the thousands of containers moving through their commercial ports every month. (House 1991d: 55; and White 1989: 45-46) In addition, significant portions of the cartel's refining and smuggling operations were now taking place under the auspices of front companies operating out of Ecuador, Brazil, Argentina and Venezuela. (Independent: 21 Jun 91)

At this same time, Ecuador, while actively operating to circumscribe narcotrafficking activities, found itself the focus of large quantities of cocaine and precursor chemicals transiting its territory. During 1990 and 1991 law enforcement officials seized an annual average of over one metric ton of cocaine paste and base. Even though coca cultivation in the country had expanded since the 1980s, some eradication on the part of Ecuadoran authorities had also taken place. Nonetheless, the endemic corruption of the cocaine business also afflicted the Ecuadoran government, undermining its efforts. (DOS-INM 1992: 38) Colombian traffickers also exploited Ecuador to launder money in a plethora of exchange houses located in the vicinity of both of Ecuador's Peruvian and Colombian borders. In addition, as both a cover for drug trafficking and a method of laundering money, traffickers also invested in Ecuadoran real-estate, farms and other commercial enterprises through which they were able to purchase large quantities of readily available precursor chemicals. (DOS INM 1992: 431)

Brazil was another bordering country which was being exploited as a cocaine transshipping and money laundering haven. Over time it became more and more significant as a transshipment route through the Amazon region for cocaine being exported out of Colombia and precursor chemicals being shipped in. Since Brazil produced vast quantities of ether and acetone for its own legitimate commercial enterprises, smuggling through the Amazon region, as well as Colombia's Caribbean Sea and Pacific Ocean ports enabled the traffickers to obtain much of the precursors needed in the production of cocaine. The sheer vastness and extent of the Amazon River and its tributary systems made it extremely difficult for the government to control let alone restrain the shipment or actual production of cocaine within Brazil. (DOS INM 1992: 99) At this time the Colombian military and police met with their counterparts from Brazil to discuss various ways and means of dealing with the cross-border operations being engaged in by the traffickers. (La Prensa: 6 aug 92) The Brazilian Federal Police did attempt to monitor and interdict narcotrafficking activities, but only achieved limited success. While not thought to be suitable for the production of high quality coca, Brazil was nevertheless found to be cultivating coca to a notable degree in the Amazon region during 1991. (DOS INM 1992: 101) In addition, money laundering, involving millions of dollars, was reported as taking place in Rio de Janeiro and Sao Paulo. (DOS INM 1992: 428-429)

Panama too remained a major transshipment point for Colombian cocaine destined for the US and Europe and local authorities there arrested 914 persons for involvement in trafficking operations. In addition, at US government behest, some 300 Panama City bank accounts belonging to various traffickers were frozen.(DOS INM 1992: 183-184) Still, during this time Panama's 120 banks and financial institutions were reported as having laundered between $1.2 and $2.2 billion over a period of a year. (El Nuevo Herald: 29 May 91)

To the east of Colombia, Venezuela had become not only a major transit country for marijuana, cocaine and heroin, but also served as a trafficker safe haven and center for money laundering activities. (DOS INM 1992: 132) In itself, Venezuela was becoming ever more important to the Colombian traffickers and reflected the balloon effect of their cross border operations, as well as the *plata o plomo* modus operandi in which Venezuelan judges now found themselves being threatened unless they complied with Colombian trafficking interests. Local Venezuelan authorities confiscated almost double the amount of cocaine products, compared to the previous year, being smuggled through the country via San Antonio del Tachira, San Cristobal, Barinas and Caracas, as well as in the Orinoco River region where cocaine refining laboratories were also reported as operating. (Claudio 1991: 75)

Nonetheless, significant amounts of cocaine were stored, repackaged and then shipped from Venezuela to the international markets via air and surface means, including containerized cargo and individual couriers. Notorious for their lax controls, the Venezuelan ports at Maracaibo, Maracay, and Puerto Caballo were ideal for the transshipment of cocaine. In addition to Venezuela's geographic location, its often uneven and sometimes depressed economy contributed to the smuggling of cocaine and precursors as well as money laundering. Scandals implicated public figures in narcotrafficking, including politicians and high ranking members of the military, and were indicative of the corruption which was frequently taking place and facilitating trafficking operations. (DOS INM 1992: 131-132; and New York Times: 1 Sep 91) The US anti-drug effort worked around this by helping the government to improve its intelligence collection effort against the narcotraffickers. Information passed to the DEA and US Customs enabled the US to intercept and confiscate major shipments of cocaine after they had left Venezuelan territory en route to the US. As a result, federal authorities in Florida captured 19 mt of cocaine hidden in shipments of concrete and broccoli and the Cali cartel found its regional distribution system in southern Florida partially dismantled. (DOS INM 1992: 135; and El Tiempo: 31 Oct 92) Offsetting the US interdiction efforts somewhat were the weak controls of the Venezuelan government over precursor chemicals which continued to flow into the country and were then reexported or smuggled into Colombia. (DOS INM 1992: 383)

In a major gain for the US anti-drug policy effort, the Colombian Banking Association reached an agreement with member banks and financial institutions whereby all transactions exceeding $10,000 would require a declaration of origin and be subject to police investigation. (El Tiempo: 30 Oct 92) This was opportune as the DEA's Green Ice operations could now be intensified in a less secretive banking atmosphere. Its objectives were:

1. The arrest of all major money launderers;

2. The destruction of money laundering cells;

3. The seizure of cash and assets; and

4. The infliction of economic disruption on the cartels' operations. (DEA 1991: passim)

As part of its kingpin strategy being implemented throughout the Andean Ridge, the DEA initiated Operation Royal Flush which was a financial component of the strategy. With counter-money laundering operations now becoming a major focus of the US anti-drug policy in Colombia, the US government now established the Multi-Agency Financial Intelligence Center (MAFIC) which included DEA, Customs, Federal Bureau of Investigation (FBI) and Internal Revenue Service (IRS), as well as Colombian police personnel. Here the money managers for the various cartels were targeted and the information essential to conducting raids was assembled and processed into useful intelligence data. Targeted was the narcotrafficker money manager who could usually launder between $30 and $50 million per month. Nonetheless, while numerous money managers were arrested, they were merely replaced by others. (DOS INM 1992: 403-404)

Where the trafficker cash accounts could not be confiscated, they were frozen as happened to the Cali cartel which found that roughly 150 of its bank accounts in five countries (Colombia, Britain, Germany, Hong Kong and the US) had been frozen through the actions of the FATF. (Senate 1992a: 6 and 9; and Washington Post: 31 Dec 92) This had taken place as a result of 32 simultaneous raids in Cali, Bogota and Barranquilla in which a reported 500 floppy disks and some 20,000 key financial documents were confiscated and evaluated. (El Tiempo: 11 Dec 91) Still, the Cali raids indicated that the traffickers were now also reacting to the DEA's Green Ice activities.

To counter the US-Colombian efforts, the traffickers were found to be employing former bankers, stockbrokers and other professional and commercial money managers. The sophistication of the money laundering schemes increased over time and a labyrinth of nominee accounts, front companies, wire transfers and the like were combined with loan and credit systems, involving development and life insurance projects, contraband construction equipment imports and exchange houses throughout Latin America. (DOS INM 1992: 395-400)

Nonetheless, the traditional trafficker route for flowing money into Colombia remained in Panama with its 130 banks, trading companies and the Colon Free Zone. During this time at least $1.5 billion entered Colombia in the form of repatriated foreign-held funds, much of which were actually narcotrafficker profits. (DOS INM 1992: 424-425 and 429)

Trafficker investment inside Colombia was estimated to be about $1 billion annually over a period of a decade. By the mid-1990s Colombian authorities were reporting that 45 percent of this money was invested in urban and rural realestate, 20 percent in cattle ranching, 15 percent in commerce, 10 percent in construction and the remainder in services and recreation activities. Around 60 percent of the most fertile and productive agrarian lands (about 1 million ha) were now owned by the traffickers. (El Nuevo Herald: 11 Apr 94)

There was no doubt that during 1991 Colombia was now spearheading the US anti-drug policy effort in the Andean Ridge. The seizure of approximately 87 mt of cocaine base and HCl, half of which was reported to belong to the Cali cartel (about double the total amount captured the previous year), was the best the US-Colombian effort had produced up to this point. The Colombian judiciary's counter-narcotics program was functioning and noted for its 60 percent conviction rate of traffickers compared to only 12 percent in the regular courts. In addition, some Cali cartel king pins who had received acquittals in local courts now found the Colombian government overturning the decisions and reprosecuting the cases. (Senate 1992a: 10; and Washington Post: 21 Jun 91) With the Medellin cartel seemingly very much fragmented, the government had shifted its attention more towards the Cali groups where raids against their offices had enabled the DAN to seize thousands of incriminating documents which showed the extent of the trafficking effort as well as the money laundering that was also taking place.

Quite clearly the Medellin cartel groups had been displaced to a considerable degree by the Cali cartel which not only had taken over much of the former's trafficking efforts but was now also becoming a priority government target by virtue of this expansion. (El Tiempo: 19 Apr 91) This had its affects on the cartel's operations within the US in 1991 where the DEA arrested over a thousand members of both the Cali and Medellin cartels, seizing over $200 million in assets and decommissioning 172 mt of cocaine base and HCl. (House 1992: 47) Even clandestine trafficking routes, such as those through Cuba, with the complicity of high ranking members of the Fidel Castro government were now exposed. (Miami Herald: 21 Nov 91) An eminently pleased US President George Bush congratulated his Colombian counterpart, saying in a letter that Colombia and President Gaviria were "truly making a difference in the war against drugs." (La Prensa: 11 Dec 91) If nothing else the Colombian government's efforts were raising the cost of the traffickers commercial operations inside the country which was a primary objective of the Gaviria government. (Silva Lujan: 1993)

In addition to the successes that were taking place in dismantling some of the major cartels and the relatively successful parallel anti-marijuana campaign, a major focus was made by the Colombian government on the fledgling opium production in which some 1,000 ha of poppies were manually eradicated and two heroin laboratories were destroyed. (DOS INM 1992: 37) While not readily noticeable, the apparent saturation of the international cocaine market had caused some traffickers at the end of the 1980s to begin to look for other drugs which could be exploited in terms of profits equal to or greater than cocaine. Heroin appeared to meet this requirement. Given the Colombian technical experience in producing cocaine, heroin was relatively easy to produce. In addition, if a kilo of cocaine was selling on the Bogota market for some $1,200, high quality heroin was earning at least ten times that amount. (Miami Herald: 10 Apr 93; and Independent: 21 Aug 91)

Conducive to the growing of gum opium poppies from which heroin was made was the wet, cold climate of the highlands (6,000 feet above sea level) found in the Huila, Caldas, Cauca and Tolima Departments' mountains. While US and Colombian authorities had estimated poppy hectarage at about 2,500 ha, other reports indicated that some 10,000 ha were more likely under cultivation in the Huila area alone. The plantations were often guarded by FARC guerrillas, which frequently led to vicious fighting between the guerrillas and the Army and other government officials intent on eradicating the plants. Although first brought to Colombia as early as 1978 and grown in the Cauca Department, poppy cultivation was now enjoying a real boom, despite the devastating effects of its slash and burn farming techniques on the countryside. Working in conjunction with the Cali cartel for production purposes, poppy farmers in the Huila Department were reported as able to produce up to a full ton of pure heroin per year. (DOS INM 1992: 6 and 107; Miami Herald: 10 Apr 93; and Independent: 17 Aug 91 and 27 Feb 92)

The average poppy worker was able to collect about an ounce of pure opium (worth $70) per day, earning in the process roughly $7.00 or the equivalent of the Colombian industrial wage and up to several times higher than daily worker earnings from agricultural crops. To promote the production of poppy farming, the traffickers frequently offered interest-free loans from $5,000 to $8,000 for the new farmers to clear the steep mountain slopes and plant poppy crops which could be harvested two to three times a year. (Miami Herald: 10 Apr 93; and Washington Post: 3 Feb 92) In addition, Indians, Pakistanis and Sri Lankans were hired by the Colombian cartels to train indigenous personnel in the production techniques of high quality heroin. Besides the US, Japan, Australia and Europe were viewed as potentially lucrative markets for the Latin American heroin supply. As a result, Brazil, Surinam and Venezuela became more and more involved in the transshipment of not only cocaine but also heroin to the US and Europe. (Independent: 27 Feb 92; and USE-CO 1992d: Cable 4009) While a kilogram of cocaine might bring $30,000 to a drug wholesaler, a similar amount of heroin could sell for up to $200,000. (New York Times: 27 Oct 91; and Miami Herald: 2 Apr 92)

With the potentially lucrative profits now verging on the astronomical, independent Colombian traffickers who had previously dealt in cocaine, now expanded into heroin. A new cocaine-heroin cartel called the "North Valley" group, because of its focus on the northern portion of the Valle Del Cauca Department and led by the infamous Urdinola brothers (Ivan, Julio and Alberto), began its operations. Expanding rapidly it became known to Colombian authorities as the first narcotics *conglomerate* inside the country. To this end it specialized in preparing and shipping mixed loads of tons of cocaine and heroin to the US and Europe. Noted for his extreme violence and cruelty, Ivan ("the terrible") Urdinola and his cohorts organized a reign of terror over the small agricultural farmers throughout the region, often murdering them with chain saws if they refused to sell off their land to the cartel or attempted to inform the Colombian authorities as to what was going on. That some members of the local Army detachments were also involved only compounded the problem for the farmers who did not know where to turn and, out of desperation, looked to the guerrillas for help. (Washington Times: 12 May 92) The Urdinola brothers' operations and terrorism were so effective that, even when Ivan was captured, the clan's activities never slackened. (Washington Post: 3 Feb and 27 Jul 92)

Needless to say, elements of the Cali cartel were also interested in the heroin trade to the degree that a major disagreement took place within the cartel's hierarchy in which younger cartel members vehemently argued for a more aggressive marketing operation which would encompass both cocaine and heroin. To this end the younger group was able to influence the cartel interests in favor of exploiting the heroin market with the result that resisting Paez Indians in the Cauca Valley region were massacred by the scores and run off their lands by Cali *sicarios* who offered the traditional *plata o plomo* as a business choice. (La Prensa: 18 Dec 91; and Miami Herald: 2 Sep 91)

By this time the Cali cartel was reported by the CNP as consisting of up to ten smaller, but now more independent groups or mini-cartels spread throughout the Valle, Cauca, Narino, Risaralda and Caldas regions. These reportedly still controlled up to 80 percent of the distribution of the cocaine and heroin on the international market. At this point in time hundreds of independent traffickers were now coordinating and working together on a temporary basis, making the Cali cartel far more amorphous and therefore that much more difficult to detect and deal with. There was no longer one center of gravity consisting of a few key leaders on which the US and Colombian authorities could focus to achieve decisive results, but a multitude of independent and semi-independent operators all seeking to make their profits while avoiding capture. (La Prensa: 30 Jun 91) To fight back against the heroin problem, the US and Colombia formulated plans to use herbicides in an aerial eradication campaign against the poppy fields. (Senate 1992a: 10)

Ironically, despite the government's successes against the narcotraffickers, Ambassador McNamara's Country Team in Bogota became quite concerned that the bureaucracy and myriad of routine administrative matters had become so burdensome that the US approach in supporting the Colombian anti-drug effort was now "inflexible and unresponsive." Cited as an example were the delays of up to a year in providing judges with sidearms to protect themselves against trafficker reprisals, all the while encouraging them to get tough with the Medellin and Cali cartels which merely placed them at ever greater risk. (USE-CO 1991: Cable 6299) In addition, the Country Team itself came in for criticism from the GAO which commented tersely on its anti-drug operations, saying: "U.S. officials had not established program plans and controls to ensure that aid would be used efficiently and effectively to meet the intended objectives." (GAO 1991b: 3)

Part of the 1991 counter-narcotics campaigns being conducted by the Colombian government included an aerial interdiction component. Here the Colombian Air Force, working in response to information provided by SOUTHCOM radars and aerial surveillance platforms, was carrying out enough interception operations so that the traffickers actually began to feel the pressure. As a result, it was found that in the major north-south air corridors for trafficker infiltration into and out of Colombian airspace drug flights had tapered off. A number of the traffickers began to place emphasis on maritime smuggling routes rather than risk aerial harassment and even interdiction by the visibly enhanced targeting capability of the Colombian Air Force. (Senate 1992a: 11)

At this time SOUTHCOM considered Colombia to be the priority target country in its own strategy for supporting the war on drugs in the Andean Ridge. That national security considerations were the driving force in this effort there was no doubt as reconnaissance, 26 military training teams, logistics, medical support, command and control support, operational planning and civic action all played their part and were merged into the play of the SOUTHCOM strategy's operations. Stopping the narcotraffickers not only at the source but also in transit were considered complimentary objectives. (Senate 1992a: 31; Harmon 1993: 28; and SOUTHCOM J3 1993)

Colombia's mix of coca growers, cocaine refining and shipping operations - all on-going simultaneously - made the country an attractive target. To this end the US government had allocated $37.1 million in military assistance and an additional $1.6 million in equipment to support the Colombian military's joint anti-narcotics operations with the police, as well as its own operations against the guerrillas. During one operation Colombian Army forces parachuted into their target areas, seizing some 12 mt of cocaine from the narcotraffickers. (DOS INM 1992: 108)

The NAS-DEA sponsored naval riverine training and operations program was an effort which constantly harassed the traffickers in the eastern half of the country and received considerable SOUTHCOM support. Often requiring complex multi-service coordination in order to carry out the operations, the riverine forces were pitted against both the narcotraffickers and the guerrillas in the Putumayo River region. The Colombian Marine Infantry riverine forces obtained relatively good results, successfully attacking and destroying 22 cocaine processing laboratories over the period of a year. (DOS INM 1992: 106; and USE-CO 1991: Cable 11260) US Navy Sea-Bees constructed a riverine operations base at San Jose del Guaviare on the Guaviare River from which the Colombian Navy and Marines could conduct further counter-narcotics operations. (El Tiempo: 23-24 Dec 92)

The Navy and its Marine infantry contingent were configured into ten riverine assault units which, using a combination of ocean going coastal patrol vessels, fast moving assault boats, and even helicopters from time to time, sought to gain control of the 26 major river arteries which coursed through most parts of Colombia. Albeit over 10,000 strong, the force could only focus for relatively short periods of time on one or more sectors before having to refit and move on to another zone. While intermittent, the raiding and ambush operations attacked portions of the narcotraffickers' laboratories located along the Putumayo and Orinoco Rivers to the south and east respectively, to the Atrato River in the north-west, and the Arauca River to the northeast, as well as the Caribbean and Pacific coast regions where a fledgling Coast Guard was only just beginning operations. Trained by US Navy special operations forces (SEALs), the riverine forces also found themselves engaging the FARC guerrillas which themselves were attempting to attack oil tankers and other shipping plying the inland waterways. (USE-CO 1993: Cable 1749; and Interview USN:CO 1993)

Perhaps SOUTHCOM's most important role in Colombia during this period was in the provision of timely and accurate intelligence on the traffickers' production and transshipping operations. Detection and monitoring support provided a relatively complete picture of the aerial patterns of the trafficking networks. The several month surge operations of Operation Support Justice II was a case in point where over 60 intelligence collection missions were flown in support of refining the US-Colombian counter-drug target data, detecting up to 250 distinct aircraft entering and exiting Colombian airspace each day. Of these, between 50 and 75 were considered suspect narcotrafficker aircraft. The overarching technical problem was to determine which of these aircraft were narcotraffickers. Only two or three aircraft could be successfully tracked at any given time which further compounded the problem. (Interview USAF:CO 1993; Washington Post: 24 Feb 91; and SOUTHCOM J3 1993) Once a decision was made as to the most likely narco-aircraft suspects, the Colombian air force and/or police were notified to carry out the intercept mission. One result of the effort was the capture of some 42 trafficker aircraft. This effort, combined with the disruptive efforts of the DAN against the cartels, helped to produce the glut of coca paste and cocaine products which the traffickers then attempted to store in warehouses to await further shipment. Towards the end of 1991, Support Justice III came into play as another iteration of this SOUTHCOM effort. (Senate 1992a: 32-33)

Support Justice III saw A-37, Mirage, and KFIR intercepter aircraft of the Colombian Air Force continue to react to the reports generated by the several ground radar sites in the vicinity of the Colombia-Peru border which, along with Colombian air controllers and US Customs' P-3 aircraft, served as the backbone of the aerial surveillance effort. The traffickers responded accordingly and altered their transhipping patterns which reflected a steady increase in night flights from December 1991 on. During the day trafficker aircraft were reported as flying at treetop levels to avoid radar detection. During the period of a year, over 6,000 distinct aircraft tracks were reported, of which some 1,700 were evaluated and identified as probable traffickers. Nonetheless, only between six and ten trafficker aircraft were reported as having been actually forced down by the Colombian Air Force. Most of the 42 aircraft reported captured had been intercepted after they landed and were surprised in the process of carrying out their trafficking activities. (DOS INM 1992: 105; and Senate 1992a: 33)

An inhibiting factor to the overall success of the aerial interdiction campaign was the fact that throughout the 1980s and into the 1990s Colombia had subscribed to the international aviation Chicago Agreement, whereby the subscribing countries agreed not to shoot down any aircraft overflying their respective national airspace. Only in the case of a provocative attack could an aircraft be shot down. This contrasted to Peru which was not a subscriber and which freely shot down any and all suspected trafficking aircraft encountered. This meant that, despite the application of hundreds of millions of dollars in ground based radars, static balloons and airborne radar and support systems to identify, monitor and intercept narcotrafficker aircraft, there was no comprehensive consensus on shooting down or forcing down identified trafficking aircraft. As Colombia opted to hold to the Chicago Agreement, its air force could only attempt to force down a suspected trafficking aircraft through non-lethal means (signalling or flying in close proximity). (USE-CO 1991: Cable 6299; and Silva Lujan: 1993) Despite complaints from the Country Team in Bogota, the situation remained largely unchanged until March 1994 when President Gaviria directed certain modifications to Colombia's adherence to the Chicago Agreement, authorizing the Air Force to shoot down suspected aircraft which did not meet specific criteria involving a certified flight plan, failure to respond to radio communications and ignoring instructions to land for inspection purposes. (El Nuevo Herald: 3 Mar 94)

SOUTHCOM's effectiveness in terms of aerial interdiction was brought into question by the GAO, which saw the former's operations generally failing to reduce the flow of cocaine supplies in a significant way. This was important since defense anti-drug spending had now increased to over $1 billion for FY 1991. The returns for the US anti-drug policy's efforts in detection, monitoring and interdiction appeared to be relatively insignificant compared to the ever increasing expenditures being made on their behalf. (GAO 1991c: 5 and 13; and 1991d: passim; and House 1990: 12 and 25) Adding fuel to these antagonistic fires within the government was the media, which conducted its own investigation and evaluation of the progress of the US anti-drug effort in the Andes, concluding that the situation was a "quagmire" of deceit and corruption. (Newsweek: 27 Jan 92)

# Chapter 5

## Thrust And Counter-Thrust

While the seizing of cocaine, advanced production laboratories, and money and aircraft by the Colombian government did attack the cocaine trade at vulnerable points, most traffickers, both independents as well as the cartels, were able to adjust to their setbacks and frequently changing situations. The loss of a certain amount of cocaine and money was now factored into the business-loss equation of the drug trade in general. Generally made up of Americans and other third-country nationals or Colombians with no special status in the cartel hierarchies, cocaine smuggling pilots, ship captains and couriers generally worked in some of the most dangerous jobs relating to the transhipment phases of the marketing process. They were as individuals well paid but also considered expendable as part of normal business operations. (Gugliotta 1992: 117)

The US supported the Colombian Customs officials at all ports of entry as part of a port police project which had as its goal the prevention of the smuggling of cocaine out of Colombia. Nonetheless, corruption remained an effective barrier to effective narcotics control at most ports. (DOS 1991: 28-29) In addition, it was found that, while the government had seized some hundreds of buildings, ranches and other properties belonging to the traffickers as part of its campaign to confiscate the latters' ill-gotten wealth, some 230 farms, 192 houses and 92 airplanes, albeit linked to the narcotraffickers, were returned by the government to their actual owners since they specifically did not have a criminal record. Even if the properties were registered in the name of a known trafficker, they were returned by the government if they could not be proven to have been directly purchased by actual drug-related monies. (Washington Post: 24 Mar 91)

To give the anti-drug policy more credibility during 1991, the US attempted by its own example to demonstrate for the Andean source countries how eradication operations should be conducted. To this end, an eradication attempt, using Army, National Guard, DEA, and state and local law enforcement personnel, was made in California's Humboldt County. There the marijuana cash crops were producing up to $500 million in profits annually (marijuana was the number one US cash crop, earning an estinmated $13 billion per year nationwide). Washington's objective was to quash the production of marijuana through eradication, coupled with the destruction or seizure of the production equipment. Called Operation Green Sweep the effort lasted ten days (30 July to 9 August) and was an abject failure in the face of an irate local population which saw its livelihood threatened. (Mendel 1992: 81-85) There was no getting around the similarities between the marijuana farmer's situation in the US and the coca farmers' predicament in Colombia and the rest of the Andes. In addition at this time, the Mayor of Washington, D.C., Marion Barry, went to trial for using cocaine, further tainting the US's anti-drug image. These events were not lost on Colombia. (Callahan 1993)

Not helping in the execution of the US anti-drug policy was the Persian Gulf War in early 1991. In this situation DOD withdrew for a period of about half a year virtually all of its AWACs aerial surveillance platforms which were involved in supporting US anti-drug efforts throughout the Andean region and sent them to the Middle East. At this time in late-April another anti-drug summit was held in Cartagena (sometimes referred to as Cartagena II). Robert Bonner, then Director of the DEA, defended the use of interdiction and repressive law enforcement measures, as well as extradition, as priority counter-drug measures, arguing that through these means it had been possible to raise the price of cocaine in the US. In contrast, unimpressed representatives from Colombia, Bolivia and Peru demanded more economic assistance for their battered economies and complained that the war on drugs was an economic drain on their respective countries. Colombia's President Cesar Gaviria also argued that more international cooperation was needed to combat the drug problem. On this somewhat confrontational note the conference ended. (Tiempo: 28 April 91)

Responding to interests expressed at Cartagena II and to assist the Andean economies, at the behest of President Bush, the Congress passed a November 1991 Andean Trade Preference Act which reduced US tariffs on some $325 million worth of imports from the region. In addition, Bush's Enterprise for the Americas Initiative offered debt relief and the promotion of trade and investment for the region. All these were seen as economic components of the Andean Initiative. As a whole they were well received throughout the Andes, including Colombia which began to feel that the US was now promoting initiatives in favor of its interests. (Perl 1992: 16; and Interview ONDCP 2: 1993) The drug war continued on.

There were times when the DEA and the DAN were able to penetrate a portion of a cartel infrastructure through an informant in the form of a pilot or aircraft dispatcher. Nonetheless, this did not happen with any great frequency. In any event, if one could spot and then follow a trafficker pilot, there was an excellent chance of locating a laboratory. Arresting an unsuspecting narco-pilot could produce dividends in the form of finding out the approximate locations of the laboratories being serviced and when they could expect to be functioning and otherwise stocked with refined cocaine ready for pickup and shipment out of the country. These were the lucrative targets which the DEA and the DAN hoped to hit, as one not only eliminated the laboratory but also captured that much more cocaine which would otherwise have entered the international drug market. (Gugliotta 1992: 117-118) To assist in this effort, the DOS's Bureau of International Narcotics Matters (INM) spent most of its $20 million allocation on upgrading the CNP's air wing which saw extensive employment, exploiting information and intelligence leads to target the various cartel infrastructures and leadership. (DOS INM 1992: 108) An offsetting factor was the interminable insurgency situation afflicting Colombia.

The guerrillas remained a serious threat not only in the southern part of Colombia, but also in other parts to the north. When President Gaviria sponsored a special assembly in 1991 to rewrite the 1886 version of the Constitution then in effect to modernize the government and broaden political participation, recognizing the human and political rights of each and every Colombian citizen, he was trying to resolve a serious problem plaguing the nation. Included in the revision was the provision to make the Upper House of the Colombian Congress elected by proportional representation. Also incorporated in the new version was the guarantee for some representation for all social and political movements. The idea was to eliminate the stereotyped perception that the Liberal-Conservative party monopoly had abrogated any possibility for meaningful, peaceful participation in Colombian politics by outside groups. In addition, at the local municipal level all mayors were to be elected and not appointed as frequently had been the case. (Bushnell 1993: 251)

For his efforts, Gaviria was denounced by the FARC and the ELN. The guerrillas contended that the assembly was not representative of Colombian society and for that reason was not legitimate. While the FARC with some 6,000 armed guerrillas and the ELN with another 4,500 adherents had been offered Congressional assembly seats and full participation in Colombia's political process if they demobilized, they had refused the offer. Their rejection of the process took place despite Gaviria's efforts to improve the reporting of human rights violations through an ombundsman program at the grass-roots levels of society which sought to hear complaints of arbitrary arrest, homicide and torture. (Gallegos: 1993)

Claiming to represent a broad spectrum of society, the guerrillas, having now joined forces in a coalition effort (the CGSB) began to attack the government in a nation-wide effort. Particularly damaging to the Colombian economy at this time was the demolition by the insurgents of several pumping stations and segments of the highly vulnerable Cano Limon-Covenas oil pipe-line in Colombia's north-central region. Overall, the Colombian petroleum industry suffered $700 million in damages from guerrilla attacks, which caused exports to fall off some 25 percent ($1.5 billion of a total Colombian remittance of about $9 billion). (Washington Post: 9 Feb 91; and Economics Section 1992: 1, 6 and 7)

With most of the coca growing in the Caqueta, Putumayo, Vaupes, Guaviare and Bolivar Departments, it was estimated by US and Colombian authorities that the entire Colombian coca crop could produce but 54 mt of cocaine HCl. (DOS INM 1992: 107; and NAS 1991a: 1) This production in itself was now more than offset by the almost 90 mt of cocaine seized during the year by Colombian authorities. Marijuana production was now estimated at a low of 2,000 ha, although 307 mt of marijuana, some of which was hidden in cartons of Marlboro and Kent cigarettes, had been seized during the year. This production appeared to be coming from a newly discovered area in the vicinity of the Perija Mountains along the Venezuelan frontier. (DOS INM 1992: 109; and PNC 1992a: passim)

While coca production may have been played down somewhat by the Country Team in terms of its importance, the traffickers continued to process Colombian coca paste and cocaine base, using dozens of microwave ovens powered by mobile 50 kilowatt generators at their laboratory sites to speed up the drying cycles of the production process.

(PNC 1992d-f: passim; and Interview DEA:CO 1993) In addition, re-oxidation techniques were employed to improve the quality of the base as well as insure a form of quality control for cocaine base arriving from laboratories located in Peru and Bolivia. (Lupsha 1993)

The end of 1991 did show other promising results for the US anti-drug policy in Colombia. The Colombian government, besides capturing almost 90 mt of cocaine base and HCl, destroyed some 239 cocaine-producing laboratories and arrested over 1,100 persons involved in trafficking. The public order courts convicted 60 percent of the roughly 700 persons formally charged with narcotics-related crimes (487 convicted and 209 acquitted). This indicated that the AID funded, newly trained investigators, prosecutors and judges implementing the new prosecution style judicial system had been relatively successful. (DOS INM 1992: 104-105) In addition coca hectarage saw a 7 percent reduction from an estimated level of 40,100 ha in 1990 down to 37,500 ha for 1991. While the CNP seized the vast majority of the refined cocaine interdicted (about 74 mt), the Colombian military was now formally participating in the anti-drug effort and was achieving some successes. (DOS INM 1992: 105) Worldwide, about 27 Colombians per day were being arrested for smuggling drugs (9,714 Colombians charged in 24 countries in 1991). (Miami Herald: 6 Jan 92) Nonetheless, smuggling was on-going and about 500 mt of cocaine were transhipped by the Colombian based traffickers to the US and Europe.

Whereas drugs had been the primary issue of concern to 60 percent of all Americans immediately following President Bush's prime-time television and radio speech to the nation in September 1989, by January 1992 some 55 percent considered the economy and unemployment as their primary concern, while only 5 percent rated drugs in the same category. (New York Times: 27 Jan 92) Obviously at this time there were more important things on people's minds besides drugs. This was not so with President Bush, who, at San Antonio, Texas, on 26 and 27 February brought about another presidential-level, international anti-drug summit, involving the the countries of not only Colombia, Peru and Bolivia but also Mexico, Venezuela and Ecuador. Bush was able to get the participating countries to declare formally that drugs were a threat to their respective national securities. Emphasis was placed on developing regional mechanisms to help coordinate the anti-drug effort. Likewise, interdiction and law enforcement, followed by alternate development, demand reduction, money laundering and multilateral cooperation were the ordered priorities of the summit's agenda. Economic issues involving investment, trade and debrt resolution were also discussed in the context of the drug situation. Nonetheless, as the US was to learn, the Andean countries had gone through a learning process. They now bargained with the US, adapting their positions to achieve the "best deal" for themselves as a way of making progress. (DOS 1992: passim; Interview DOS 1993; and Bagley 1992: 9)

At San Antonio President Gaviria reaffirmed his country's commitment to the international anti-drug struggle and helping to coordinate additional multi-lateral measures for combatting the narcotraffickers. He expressed his feelings on the trafficking situation, commenting that it was demand sustained, multinational in nature and difficult to control inside Colombia as a result. He maintained that the solution involved controlling and depressing demand, money laundering and arms trafficking. In addition, enhancing the Colombian economy was seen by him as a key element in undermining both the guerrillas as well as the traffickers who drew most of their recruits and labor respectively from the economically depressed sectors of the Colombian society. Nonetheless, as President Gaviria perceived it, it was the factor of international market demand over which Colombia had no control that was the primary motivating cause of Colombia's narcotrafficking problems. (Camacho and Tokatlian: 1993)

That January the ONDCP had issued its National Drug Control Strategy. Four near-term anti-drug goals involving Colombia, Peru and Bolivia were now established by the strategy:

1. Strengthen the political commitment and institutional capability of the governments of Colombia, Peru and Bolivia to confront the cocaine trade.

2. Increase the effectiveness of law enforcement and military activities against the cocaine industry, including planning law enforcement, paramilitary and military operations against trafficking organizations, and coordinating them with other countries.

3. Inflict significant damage on the trafficking organizations by disrupting the operations and elements of greatest value to them.

4. Strengthen and diversify the legitimate economies of the Andean countries to enable them to overcome the destabilizing effects of eliminating cocaine, a major source of income. (ONDCP 1992: 81-82)

The 1992 US drug control strategy still emphasized a supply side anti-drug focus through the dismantling of drug trafficking organizations, disrupting the flow of drugs, chemicals and money, and reducing the growth, production and distribution of cocaine products in the Andean source nations. Nonethelsess, by mid-1992 the ONDCP was evaluating the stark reality of its anti-drug policy and strategy in play in the Andes. Things were simply not going that well with the US anti-drug policy and that previous January it was forced, as part of its national drug strategy, for a third time to again modify the Andean Initiative's goals. Eliminated now were the two and ten-year fixed percentage reduction goals for the amount of drugs entering into the US. (ONDCP 1992: 26; and Interview ONDCP 2: 1993)

Measured by the original goal of a 15 percent reduction in the imports of illicit drugs into the US, the ONDCP was now facing an estimated 13 percent increase (84 mt!) in cocaine and other drugs entering the past year or the exact opposite of what its policy was intended to achieve. (Senate 1992a: 52) After an expenditure of about $1 billion under the Andean Initiative, there was now a net increase of some 39,000 mt in coca leaf production throughout the Andes. For Congress, which more often than not used eradication as its principal means of measuring anti-drug policy progress in the Andes, this was an even more serious situation, implying that the anti-drug policy in the region was not working well at all. (Senate 1992b: 22)

The ONDCP reevaluation of its anti-drug strategy reflected criticisms emanating from various governemnt agencies which had the purpose of evaluating the government's programs and policies. The GAO had reported on Peru that it was unlikely that the US anti-drug effort there would ever be effective unless factors involving corruption, political instability and a weak economy were overcome. (GAO 1991a: 4-6 and 18-28) Similarly, the counter-narcotics' effort in Bolivia was challenged by the Department of State's own Inspector General (IG) who saw insufficient progress in reducing the cocaine industry and a lack of will on the part of government officials to deal with narcotrafficking in a serious manner as obstacles to the success of the US policy there. (DOS-IG 1991: 1-4) In terms of Colombia, while acknowledging the dramatic intensity of the host nation's efforts and achievements against the traffickers and their organizations, the GAO questioned the Bogota Country Team's ability to evaluate the effectiveness of the US aid in achieving the Andean Initiative's goals.

Despite the administrative problems involved in implementing the US anti-drug policy, during 1992 the US-Colombian efforts had forged ahead and on 28 February President George Bush, in his Presidential Determination 92-18, again certified Colombia as deserving of US support. Nonetheless, the US government expressed concerns that the Colombian traffickers were still able to continue to transship large quantities of cocaine through the country. (House 1992: 251 and 258) This situation was further complicated by the insurgency situation facing the Colombian government.

As peace talks ground to a standstill between the Colombian government and the insurgent Simon Bolivar Guerrilla Coordinator group, the guerrillas attempted to pressure Gaviria throughout 1992 into resuming peace talks by continuing to carry out attacks throughout the nation. These operations involved some 1,285 armed activities and generally tended to take place in a swath running from the Choco to the Arauca Departments, affecting in part mines, oil pumping installations and related pipelines, government offices and banks. (El Espectador: 15 and 19 Nov 92) That the guerrillas were able to extort the Colombian Petroleum Company (ECOPETROL) for about 10 percent of its earnings (40 billion pesos), rob a bank of some $600,000, successfully kidnap and hold for ransom ($500,000) the President of the Colombian House of Representatives and were now reportedly involved in growing coca and poppies as relatively lucrative cash crops (called the "third drug cartel" by President Gaviria), now became a major concern to the military which felt that, as long as the guerrillas had an independent source of financing, they would be very difficult to defeat, if at all. (El Tiempo: 29 Nov 92; and El Nuevo Herald: 24 May, 21 Oct and 26 Nov 92) Guerrilla extortion activities in the Barrancabermeja area of north-central Colombia were noted as fairly extensive, as were the reported 171 politically motivated assassinations in support of the guerrilla efforts in the region. (El Espectador: 14 Feb 93)

An incident which served as another catalyst and galvanized the government to further action against the guerrillas involved the ELN massacre of 26 policemen guarding a petroleum facility at Orito, Putumayo. (Pais: 10 Nov 92) In an effort to stem the extortion and violence, in which up to 450 local officials were secretly paying off the guerrillas in exchange for not being harassed, Gaviria declared on 8 November a state of emergency which was to last into 1993 as part of a total war on Colombia's guerrillas and organized crime. (Miami Herald: 15 Nov 92) In an attempt to attack the guerrillas' financial base, Gaviria directed that all banks, oil and even mining companies, regardless of national origin, would be severely sanctioned, possibly losing their contracts if they paid ransom and extortion fees to the guerrillas. (USE-CO 1993: Cable 1749; and Christian Science Monitor: 8 Dec 92) The guerrillas fought back organizing protest marches, road blocks and burning buses along the Pan American and other key highways throughout Colombia. (El Nuevo Herald: 8 and 23 Oct 92) SOUTHCOM detection and monitoring efforts for 1992 were showing that narcotrafficking smuggling and transhipment operations out of Colombia were taking place at a rate of some 1,300 to 3,000 aircraft and some 3,000 to 5,000 ship movements annually. (House 1992d: 34) These movements were carried out by narco-contracted pilots from a group of about 1,500 persons who flew or piloted the roughly one thousand privately owned aircraft and as many boats which were considered to be potentially available to the traffickers (At Guaymaral, half of the 217 registered commercial aircraft were said to be flying on behalf of the traffickers). Despite this information interdiction was relatively infrequent and by the end of 1992 only 38 aircraft and 43 boats were positively identified and detained or confiscated because of their involvement in trafficking operations. (El Tiempo: 3 Feb 93; and El Espectador: 3 Nov 92)

The aerial interdiction operations, using a combination of ground based radars positioned at Araracuara and Leticia in southern Colombia and US Customs and Navy reconnaissance aircraft, monitored suspected narcotrafficker aircraft flying from Bolivia, Peru, Ecuador and Brazil into Colombia, but were only able to force down or capture about a dozen planes during the year. (DOS INM 1993a: 107; and USE-CO 1993: Cable 1749) Corruption may have been a significant factor in the low interdiction rate as Colombian air controllers at the 497 authorized airports were frequently noted as alerting the trafficker pilots as to when and where the Support Justice aerial interdiction operations were taking place. (DOS INM 1993a: 107; Interview DEA-CO: 1993; and El Nuevo Herald: 16 Jun 93)

The smuggling of cocaine and other drugs out of Colombia by surface means was pervasive at the port of Baranquilla where sealed cargo containers were loaded aboard ships docked at privately controlled wharfs. In this situation search warrants had to specify the exact container (among hundreds) to be inspected and be approved by a local, certifying judge in order for it to be approached and opened. This complicated the search process, often allowing contraband cargos and drugs to be dispatched without being inspected. At the government controlled or public wharfs the police were generally more successful and even found cocaine hidden inside the anchor chains of some cargo vessels. (USE-CO 1993: 1749) In other ports such as Cartagena, cocaine filled containers allegedly carrying bags of sugar to the Middle East were also seized as part of the Customs intercept campaign. (PNC 1992b: 1) The DEA's office in Puerto Rico even reported that traffickers, using non-metallic or fiber glass and wood submarines constructed in Colombia, were making drug shipment runs into the island. Operating at sea level and below, the blue and white painted submersibles were difficult to detect and were often confused for waves on Coast Guard radars. (El Nuevo Herald: 7 Oct 93)

A major coup for the US and its DEA directed Operation Green Ice campaign against Colombian money laundering in 1992 involved the Trans Americas Ventures Associates in San Diego, California. Trans Americas typified how money laundering was often carried out by the traffickers. Supposedly an importer and distributor of hides with branches in New York, Chicago, Houston, Miami and Fort Lauderdale, Florida, the company camouflaged its activities on behalf of the Cali cartel by over-invoicing its imports, claiming 30 tons of hides imported instead of the actual one ton actually involved. Unknown to the Cali group was the fact that Trans Americas was a DEA sting operation, established for the purposes of tracing money laundering operations within the US and overseas. Over a period of about two years, the DEA identified some 525 Cali cartel bank accounts in the US and Colombia involving some $70 million in narcotrafficker earnings which it was then able to freeze. In addition, over 160 cartel related traffickers and contacts in Costa Rica, United Kingdom, Canada, Spain, Italy, the Cayman Islands and the US were apprehended. As part of this operation, 634 kg of cocaine was seized along with trafficker assets valued at $47.7 million. Assisting the operations, was the Kerry Agreement in which the Colombian government agreed in February 1992 to exchange currency transaction information on all accounts recording transfers of $10,000 or more. (DOS-INM 1993: 510; USE-CO 1992a: Cable 19022; and El Mundo: 18 Oct 92)

While President Gaviria had committed Colombia to agreeing to the 1988 UN Convention Against Illicit Traffic in Narcotics, Drugs and Psychotropic Substances (also referred to as the Vienna Convention) as a demonstration of national will to confront narcotrafficking, he found that trying to get the Colombian Congress to ratify the Convention was not so easy. While Colombian Law 30 enacted in 1988 did provide adequate sanctions against trafficking activities, the UN Convention did oblige signatory countries to agree to enact laws criminalizing all drug related money laundering, which meant that bank secrecy laws had to be modified so that they could no longer serve as barriers to criminal investigations. (DOS-INM 1993a: 411) Having come into force in November of 1990 with some twenty governments agreeing to ratification or accession, Colombia was under pressure from the US to follow suit. Nonetheless, opposition mounted over legal and sovereignty concerns which caused the Colombian Senate's Committee on International Relations to approve with reservations the UN Convention. Factors, such as fear of trafficker retribution in the form of *plata o plomo* were intimidating and considered by Gaviria and his staff as influential in the slow Congressional decision making process. While this was aggravating to both Gaviria and the US Country Team, Colombia continued to attempt to meet all its basic US policy goals and objectives. (DOS-INM 1993a: 105; and Silva Lujan: 1993)

President Gaviria's problems with the Colombian prison system reached an apex in mid-1992. Pablo Escobar, in response to well founded fears that the new Prosecutor General, Gustavo de Greiff, and other government officials were planning to move him to another prison where he would have far less freedom of action to run his cartel or even possibly extradite him (a June 1992 US Supreme Court ruling had been publicly announced supporting the seizing of criminals overseas for trial in the US), escaped on 22 July with the complicity of some of the Envigado prison authorities. (Semana: 11 Aug 92) The former director of national prisons, Colonel Hernando Navas, received 28 months in prison for his complicity in Escobar's escape. (El Nuevo Herald: 24 Apr 94) That Escobar was able to negotiate his own surrender, live in luxurious prison conditions, continue to run his cartel operations from his jail cell, and then escape at will, indicated that he was a formidable opponent for both the US and Colombian governments. While the visibly embarrassed Colombian government and President Gaviria initiated a massive manhunt for Escobar and his followers, that following September a Medellin judge, then presiding over a murder case against the now escaped Escobar, too was murdered. (Christian Science Monitor: 23 Sep 92; and El Nuevo Herald: 2 and 7 Aug 93) In addition, Colombian Senate investigative records relating to Escobar mysteriously disappeared before they could be presented at a suitable legal hearing. (El Nuevo Herald: 14 Nov 92)

To force the government to bend to his will and begin a process of negotiations, Escobar, using his *sicarios* and other hired killers to include guerrillas, began a vicious campaign based on continuous waves of indiscriminate car bombings and assassinations. In Medellin, during a three month period, over a hundred policemen died as Escobar reaped his vengeance, offering $2,100 for each policeman assassinated. (New

York Times: 14 Feb 93; and El Nuevo Herald: 8 Nov 92) Gaviria, now viewing the priority problem facing the government as narco-terrorism, reacted by enacting new laws against paying ransom and failing to report extortion attempts. As time went on it became more and more difficult to distinguish between the guerrillas and the traffickers in terms of who was perpetrating the on-going violence. People began to perceive them both as equal threats to society. (Semana: 19 Jan 93; Economist: 30 Jan 93; and Silva Lujan: 1993)

The situation became so serious that Gaviria placed Medellin under martial law and declared Colombia under a state of siege which allowed him to rule by decree. (El Nuevo Herald: 10 Nov 92 and 21 Jan 93) Besides soldiers and police, some 10,000 high school students were also mobilized in Medellin in an attempt to try and control the city's streets which were convulsed with violence. In some of the poorer barrio sections of the city up to 75 percent of all males between the ages of 15 and 25 were now reported as dead from the violence. Serving this end, death cults abounded whereby newly initiated members had to "prove" themselves through murder to gain acceptance among their peers. (Excelsior: 29 Jan 93; and Ross: 1993) In December de Greiff formally charged Escobar with the 1989 murder of Luis Carlos Galan and two others. It was now the third Colombian murder indictment against Escobar since the new Prosecutor General's office had been opened in July as part of the 1991 Constitutional reform. (Miami Herald: 19 Jan 93; and DOS-INM 1993a: 106)

Escobar's tactics began to work against him as the murder of innocent people and even former cartel members and trafficking associates caused others to organize vigilante groups to track him down. One group, made up of former Medellin and Cali cartel members who Escobar had turned against and even tried to have murdered, known as the *Perseguidos por Pablo Escobar* (PEPES - People Persecuted by Pablo Escobar), reaped their own vengeance against Escobar's family and his properties. (Semana: 2 Mar 93; and El Nuevo Herald: 5 and 31 Mar and 26 Sep 93) Other public spirited groups likewise joined in, in their own efforts to kill or capture Escobar and collect the government's $7 million reward on his head. ( El Espectador: 2 Feb 93; and Miami Herald: 17 Feb 93) The pressure was so trying for some cartel fugitives that a dozen of Escobar's closest cartel cohorts decided to return to prison rather than face possible death at the hands of the vigilante groups. (El Nuevo Herald: 10 Oct 92 and 23 Feb 93) Despite the rewards for his capture and the massive efforts to find him, Escobar evidently had enough loyal friends willing to hide and protect him so that he was able to evade the government's efforts to find him for about 18 months. His civic action activities of previous years were now paying off. (Semana: 26 Jan and 2 Feb 93)

While evading the government's manhunt, Escobar continued to engage the Colombian authorities in his form of guerrilla-terrorism, using car bombings to intimidate the people and persuade the government to enter into negotiations once again. (El Nuevo Herald: 14-15 Aug 92 and 19-20 Jan 93) Gaviria's own popularity among the people was now at an all time low (22 percent approval rating) and some 57 points below the rating from the year before, as the relentless narco-bombings continued on into 1993. (Semana: 19 Jan 93; and El Nuevo Herald: 23 Jan 93) It was only with Escobar's death in a shootout with police and military forces on 2 December 1993 and the resultant cessation of the terror bombings that Gaviria himself was able to regain some of his former popularity.

To combat the international, cross-border "balloon effect" of narcotrafficking, the Colombian government attempted to coordinate some of its anti-drug activities as part of a series of mutual efforts with the various countries on its periphery. To this end, SOUTHCOM, as part of its Support Justice III and IV operations, attempted to synchronize air, land and riverine efforts to exploit the available intelligence to inflict the maximum amount of damage on the trafficking infrastructure. Peruvian, Ecuadoran and Colombian liaison officers routinely flew in the SOUTHCOM sponsored monitoring and detection aircraft on station along the border regions. Nonetheless, the lack of a night intercept capability was admitted by SOUTHCOM's General George A. Joulwan as a significant inhibiting factor to the success of the aerial interdiction effort. (Joulwan 1993: 16 and 18) DOD's surveillance missions in Colombia were also called into question by the US General Accounting Office (GAO). The GAO assessment stated that despite an increase in operational monies (from $212 million in FY 1989 to $962 million in FY 1992 and $844 million in FY 1993) in support of aircraft and ship operations, "Estimated cocaine flow has not appreciably declined and most drug smugglers were not interdicted." (GAO 1993b: 3 and 15)

Ecuador was cooperating with the Colombian government and attempted to take action against Ecuadoran based trafficking networks linked to the Cali cartel, as well as some of the FARC guerrillas. The guerrillas and traffickers who frequented the border areas attacked Colombian oil pumping stations in the Putumayo River region, as well as military and police patrols attempting to deter such activities. About

3,000 persons were arrested by the Ecuadoran government, continuing a similar policy begun in the late 1980s. (DOS-INM 1993a: 116; DOS 1994: Cable 87397; and Interview NAS:CO 1993) In addition, the national police attempted to stem the spread of opium poppies over the border from Colombia which, in conjunction with cocaine, were being transshipped by Ecuador's Pacific coast Manta cartel through the nation's aerial and sea ports. (El Nuevo Herald: 8 Jul 93) To assist the anti-drug effort, Ecuador allowed SOUTHCOM to position and operate radars along its Amazon frontier. Nonetheless, despite numerous seizures in excess of a metric ton each year (INCR 1994: 113), these activities did not stem the flow of drugs and Ecuador saw its ports exploited as the traffickers made considerable use of the containerized shipping taking place to transship over 30 mt of cocaine through the country. (DOS-INM 1993: 112-113 and 1994: 37; Miami Herald: 8 Nov 92 and El Nuevo Herald: 13 Nov 92)

Brazil also remained as a major cocaine transshipping and money laundering country, as well as being important to the traffickers for the production of precursor chemicals. The ready availability of precursor chemicals and the relative inability of the Brazilian government to patrol its vast border areas continued to give the traffickers the upper hand and a virtual carte blanche to conduct their operations with relative impunity. (DOS-INM 1993a: 97-99) SOUTHCOM's Support Justice operations and the pressures exerted by the Colombian authorities had merely caused the traffickers to continue to establish branch cocaine refining and transshipment operations inside Brazil. As such, the local authorities more and more frequently came into contact with the trafficking operations and were able to seize ever increasing amounts of cocaine with some 7.7 mt captured in 1993 alone. (INCSR 1994:99) Despite creating an anti-drug secretariat within the Ministry of Justice, the lack of a comprehensive national anti-drug strategy, along with the means and the will to carry it out inhibited Brazil's ability to have any significant impact on narcotrafficking within its territory. (DOS 1994: Cable 87397)

In early August of 1992 the Colombian and Venezuelan presidents signed a bilateral cooperation agreement which included a commitment to combat trafficking along their mutual border regions. (El Tiempo: 7 Aug 92) As a result their first joint counter-drug interdiction operation took place later that month and accounted for one metric ton of cocaine and one aircraft captured. (DOS-INM 1993a: 107) Later operations over a period of a year also accounted for some 7 mt of marijuana captured in the border region. (El Nuevo Herald: 7 Aug 93)

While the US sought to incorporate the Venezuelan government more and more into its anti-drug policy effort in order to stem the trafficking taking place in that country, effective narcotics control measures were significantly impeded. Control measures announced by President Carlos Andres Perez in 1991 never came to fruition. The continuous scandals over corruption rocked the government's leaders and resulted in a number of military coup attempts which diverted the national focus away from the anti-drug effort to attempting to restore internal domestic order. As a result, up to 2,500 Air Force pilots and aircraft technicians found themselves in prison as part of the government's counter-coup backlash. In short, the Air Force's counter-drug reconnaissance activities were significantly reduced as an entire OV-10 squadron was grounded. In addition, SOUTHCOM saw several of its radars working inside Venezuela malfunction for periods lasting up to several weeks which lessened further the interdiction capability of the Venezuelan authorities. (DOS-INM 1993a: 130-131; and SOUTHCOM J3 1993) General officers within the Venezuelan military were also found to have been involved in trafficking operations, indicating the extent of the corruption now taking place within that country. (DOS-INM 1993a: 132; and El Nuevo Herald: 15 Sep 93)

In short Venezuela had become a hub of Colombian trafficking in cocaine, marijuana and even heroin. Indicative of the extent of the trafficking going on, some 200 mt of Colombian produced cocaine were reported to have transited the country during the period of a year. (DOS-INM 1993a: 130 and 1994: 127; and El Nuevo Herald: 14 Jul 93) Also reflecting the state of affairs within Venezuela was the number of arrests of suspected traffickers which fell off by as much as 60 percent (1,022 persons arrested in 1992 compared to 2,908 in 1991). As a result of the political instability, the amounts of cocaine products intercepted by the Venezuelan authorities fell off significantly, only 3.3 mt for 1993 compared to almost 10 mt in 1991. (INCSR 1994:132)

Also captured in Venezuela during this period were 68 mt of essential chemical precursors in the form of methyl-ethyl-ketone (MEK) as it was being transshipped overland towards its Colombian destinations. (DOS-INM 1993a: 135 and 483) Beginning back in March 1992, the US-chaired Chemical Action Task Force (CATF), supported by the Group of Seven Industrialized Nations (G-7) was generally successful in regulating international transactions in chemicals and their export from the US and Europe into Colombia. Covering some 22 specific chemicals, including those used as precursor chemicals in the production of cocaine, an attempt was made to gain control of this aspect of trafficking operations. Unfortunately, regulations to this effect were neither universal nor always stringently enforced. As a result the traffickers were able to obtain their required chemicals through legal importation and then by subsequent diversion or smuggling into Colombia from nearby countries such as Venezuela. (DOS-INM 1993a: 473-478)

While the extent of money laundering inside Venezuela was not fully clear, there was extensive evidence that Colombian cartel members and Italian mafia and other criminal groups were closely linked and up to $3 billion was being laundered annually. (DOS-INM 1993a: 514; and Miami Herald: 14 Feb 93) Although a Colombian government policy allowed its citizens to hold US dollar accounts, a new tax law concerning the conversion of US dollars into pesos had precipitated the traffickers to launder their dollars in Venezuela to avoid the new tariff. To this end US dollars were converted into Venezuelan or other foreign currency and then transferred back into Colombia by wire or courier without paying any tariffs. Venezuelan banks, some of which were owned or heavily influenced by the cartels, were now found to have opened their own branch banks and offices inside Colombia, further facilitating these transactions. (DOS-INM 1993a: 510) In addition, coca was now reported as being cultivated inside Venezuela in the vicinity of the Sierra de Perija region where some cocaine refining operations were also reported to have been initiated. (DOS-INM 1993a: 133)

The balloon affect was also in evidence in Panama where major cocaine refining complexes and coca growing farms were found to have been operating in the Darien region adjacent to Colombia. Despite the fall of dictator Manuel Noreiga in 1989 and the ensuing improved anti-drug cooperation between the US and Panamanian governments, corruption continued apace with narcotrafficking still taking place and major drug shipments transiting Panama's Colon Free Zone. Multi-ton cocaine seizures increased considerably, but still had little or no effort on trafficking in general. (DOS INM 1992: 187; Prensa: 16 Feb 93; DOS 1994: Cable 87397 and INCSR 1994:172) In sum, the balloon effect was now very much an inhibiting factor to the success of the US anti-drug policy and, to the degree that the US and Colombian anti-drug efforts could harass and even close down the traffickers, the latter had merely shifted their operations over the frontier to adjacent countries. (Interview CT:CO 1993)

Ironically, in a twist of fate, Colombian traffickers also began to make arrangements to exploit the North American Free Trade Agreement. In this case Colombians working with Mexican smugglers began establishing front companies to exploit the future open borders between Mexico and the US. Using legitimate businesses such as *maquiladora* manufacturing and assembly plants (over 2,000 currently functioning) as cover, it was anticipated that the warehousing and trucking industries would serve as convenient conduits to the more accessible entry points into the US, allowing the some 1,700 rigs which crossed the Rio Grande River each day to potentially move drugs freely throughout the US and Canada. (Miami Herald: 24 May 93)

Heroin production at this time was still perceived as a significant and rising threat to the US anti-drug policy in Colombia and the Country Team encouraged the Colombian government to take action accordingly. Although initially thought in 1991 to be on a level of production equivalent to that of marijuana (approximately 2,000 ha), later analysis in 1992 indicated that actual poppy hectarage had been badly underestimated and was actually well over 30,000 ha, growing in a gigantic swath from the Magdalena Department in the north, through the Colombian highland region to the Narino and Putumayo Departments on the Ecuadoran frontier. (DOS-INM 1993a: 110; PNC 1992: 19; and Kalmanovitz: 1993) Tests of the opium gum indicated that each cultivated hectare of poppies had a potential yield of up to 8 kg of gum opium or about one kilogram of heroin per hectare. (DOS-INM 1993a: 108) Each kilogram was reported as earning on a wholesale basis from $80,000 to $180,000 inside the US (compared to about $2,000 for a similar amount of marijuana or $14,000 to $42,000 for cocaine HCl). (DEA 1992: 3 and 6-7) In short, the roughly 30,000 ha being cultivated had the potential of producing up to 30 mt of heroin and was growing or being refined in 14 of Colombia's 25 departments, as well as Bogota itself! (Miami Herald: 10 Apr 93; PNC 1992c: passim; and USE-CO 1993: Cable 1749) Trafficking in heroin was a temptation to all elements of society as the apprehension of a Colombian judge from Cali and his daughter by New York City police in late 1992 would indicate. Posing as tourists they were trying to sell 2.2 kg of processed cocaine on the New York drug market. (La Prensa: 8 Nov 92)

To enhance the Colombian poppy eradication effort the US provided $15 million in additional monies over those previously allocated for 1992. The Colombian authorities responded with an aerial crop suppression campaign which sprayed the *Glifosate* herbicide, neutralizing some 9,400 ha of opium poppies by the end of 1992. (DOS-INM 1993a: 105-106; and PNC 1992: 25) In addition some 3,319 ha of poppies were eradicated by hand, producing an overall reduction effort of 12,715 ha which reduced the total poppy hectarage to about 20,000 ha (equivalent to about 20 mt) still under cultivation. (USE-CO 1993: Cable 1749; DOS-INM 1993a: 109-110; and Interview DEA:CO 1993) Nonetheless, reflecting an increasing guerrilla interest in poppy cultivation and heroin production as a highly lucrative source of revenues, in the Santander Department and others, the ELN guerrillas were reported as having begun the cultivation of opium poppies. (El Nuevo Herald: 4 Sep 92 and 9 May 93; El Tiempo: 16 Nov 92; and Tokatlian: 1993) The FARC, in turn, was now reported as charging poppy growers and traffickers up to 30 percent of the drug's value as a tax surcharge. (Nacional: 25 Jul 92)

In an effort to gain popular support, isolate the coca-poppy growing regions, and attack the traffickers' production infrastructure, the US and Colombian governments hoped to offer an economic support package for all displaced persons and farmers without legitimate employment. (Stickney: 1993) To this end the Colombian government attempted to engage the Guambiano, Paez and Yanacona Indian tribes (63,000 population) of the Cauca Department in a manual eradication project to eliminate the poppy crops growing on their respective reservations. In exchange for not spraying the Indian lands with the deadly glifosate herbicide, and offering alternate development projects as a substitute, the tribes were to use *mingas* (communal labor) to eradicate the poppy crops. As time went on and the eradication took place, the tribal leaders found themselves harassed by both irate Indian farmers who had lost their cash crops and some of the guerrillas who found themselves without their lucrative tax base. As alternate development opportunities and material resources did not appear to be readily forthcoming, the Colombian government found itself being accused of reneging on its promises. (Miami Herald: 10 Apr 93; and Tokatlian: 1993) Poppy production thus continued apace and by 1994 was rated at a sustained level of 20,000 ha despite the almost 10,000 ha eradicated throughout 1993. The poppy farmers were merely increasing their production in the anticipation that significant amounts of the plant would be subject to the government's eradication measures. (DOS-INM 1994: 108)

Since 1992, the ONDCP more and more considered Colombia to be its first priority country for implementing the Andean Initiative's anti-drug policy. That Pablo Escobar had successfully escaped from his Colombian prison in mid-1992 was more than offset by the boost this event had given the US anti-drug policy inside Colombia. A visibly embarrassed President Gaviria had acknowledged that his government was badly corrupted and compromised and, as a result, a comprehensive crackdown had taken took place, seeking out and apprehending the traffickers wherever they could be found. (Interview ONDCP 1: 1993) The Medellin cartel had responded with waves of violence in the form of bombings and assassinations, which only further incited the government to intensify its anti-drug operations. Nonetheless, while the Colombian government initiated its crackdown on the Medellin cartel, the Cali and other major trafficking cartels continued to operate. In the meantime the costs of maintaining the US controlled AWACs and P-3 aerial surveillance platforms, ground radars and offshore picket ships was considered by ONDCP as using up too much of the approximately $12 billion drug budget in terms of the relatively small return that was being achieved. Disruption of Colombian supply was still having little or no impact on the streets of metropolitan USA where an estimated 25 percent of the heavy user population was consuming some 75 percent of the drugs flowing in from South America. (Senate 1992a: 31; and SOUTHCOM J3 1993)

At this time Colombia was now recognized by INM as being potentially the third largest producer of heroin after Burma and Afghanistan. With heroin having a rated market potential of up to five times the amount of profits that cocaine could earn, the reports of gum opium poppy production in Colombia caused considerable concern within the Washington community. (Interview DEA 1993) While it was noted that the Gaviria crackdown was a hinderance to trafficking operations inside Colombia, lesser organizations were continuously stepping into the interntional drug market to fill the production gaps. While cocaine production had slackened off somewhat, this appeared to be due in part to the increased trafficker interest in cultivating gum opium poppies whose product was then refined into heroin. (Interview GAO 1993) As such, with the Andean regions total cocaine production running between 900 and 1,100 mt, all the while being smuggled on the 4,300 to 8,000 air and ship movements extending out from the north Andes worldwide, the chances for a decisive US anti-drug policy success appeared to be even further away than ever. (DEA 1992: 15; Joulwan 1992: 33-34; and Interview DOS 1993)

During 1992 Robert Nieves, the new Director of the DEA, replacing Robert Bonner, had realigned his agency's focus to one of giving the highest priority to dismantling trafficker groups and leaders throughout the Andean Ridge with a special emphasis on the Medellin and Cali cartel groups. This was a continuation of the ONDCP national strategy thrust released in January 1992 whereby a primary focus was to be made on the source countries' trafficking organizations and their respective commercial structures as key centers of gravity. If the trafficker infrastructure (production, processing and shipping facilities) was destroyed, drug traffickers and money launderers were prosecuted and punished, and drugs and assets seized, advocates of this supply approach   contended that trafficking operations would be sharply curtailed in general. Operations Green Ice, Ghost Zone and Safe Haven were all crafted to this end as part of the "kingpin strategy" being implemented by DEA. (ONDCP 1992: 79-81; US News and World Report: 11 Jan 93)

Despite attempts by the ONDCP to manage the anti-drug policy during the early 1990s, it was found that even though individual departments and agencies could be programmed and funded, they still would have to be left alone to manage their portions of the anti-drug effort. As a result of the decentralized nature of the programs, the US ambassador was held responsible in each Andean country for ensuring that his Country Team accomplished its designated anti-drug goals. The Deputy Chief of Mission for each embassy, as a primary duty, was to oversee and direct their respective Country Team efforts. In short, aircraft, equipment, communications, intelligence, training and US and host nation anti-drug police and counter-narcotics personnel, as well as other activities, were now being directed entirely or in part by US the embassies which were not always fully prepared or formally staffed for these types of operations. (Interview ONDCP 2: 1993; and author observation 1992-93)

Sensing the frustration among the several Country Teams over the issue of policy implementation and beginning with General Maxwell Thurman's efforts in 1990, SOUTHCOM had asserted itself by attempting to create operational order and bring about some coherence among the myriad of anti-drug activities taking place in Colombia and other parts of the Andes. To a certain degree it was successful and a steady series of liaison visits and training and operations teams rotated through the US embassies, advising and otherwise assisting in the implementation of the anti-drug policy. War games took place at both SOUTHCOM's headquarters in Panama as well as in the Washington, D.C. area to highlight operational problems and assist those agencies principally involved in the supply side anti-drug effort to better coordinate and integrate their efforts. It was part of SOUTHCOM's intent to demonstrate that the image of "no one in charge" of the anti-drug effort had some validity and it was necessary for the anti-drug community to work in unison to enable a higher degree of execution to be achieved. (SOUTHCOM J3 1993; and Interview SOUTHCOM LNO:

1993)

A debate over which supply side focus should have priority took place. SOUTHCOM, DOS and the Secretary of Defense all wanted to attack the trafficking organizations and laboratory complexes as part of a source oriented focus. The question was when and how to do so. The JCS and the several military services including the Army, Navy and Air Force, as well as the Navy's Atlantic Command (LANTCOM) advocated focusing on the traffickers while they were in transit. In the end some of both focuses were engaged in. By fixing narco-production in place, it was thought by SOUTHCOM planners that it would be easier to dismantle the traffckers' organizatins. Colombia was now considered by the US military as the first priority country for the US anti-drug effort. (SOUTHCOM J3 1993; and Miami Herald: 29 Oct 93)

Wrangling among the various anti-drug actors took place over which aerial intelligence platform was best to use. The armed forces advocated the E2C AWACs, the CIA wanted to use its Schweitzers and the Customs its P3s. National Guard F-16s operating from Howard Air Force Base in Panama were brought into play and with their powerful radars were able to track some of the trafficking aircraft. Over time, the flexibility of the traffickers became apparent as they entered and left Colombian airspace at will, guiding their aircraft along US radar beams or avoiding US radar coverage by flying over Brazilian territory to escape the interdiction efforts. There was also the factor of corruption through bribes by which traffickers were often able to buy their way out of capture by Colombian authorities, permitting them to continue to ply their trade. These became daunting problems for the US anti-drug effort which was never able to resolve the problem to any great satisfaction. In addition, unexpected political problems confronted the anti-drug community such as occurred in Venezuela where failed military coup attempts in 1992 resulted in dozens of key pilots, otherwise involved in flying anti-drug intelligence missions, to be relieved or put in prison, disrupting the anti-drug detection and monitoring efforts there. Of concern to DOD, was the use of aerial platforms for SOUTHCOM's Support Justice operations which were costing about $3 million per month, detracting from other important intelligence gathering missions worldwide. (Interview DOD 1993; and SOUTHCOM J3 1993)

SOUTHCOM officials acknowledged that the roughly 100 mt of cocaine being seized annually in the Andes, while impressive, was not enough to impact significantly on the overall supply flowing into the US. (SOUTHCOM 1993: 44) At the end of 1992, GAO investigators were concluding that the US supply side anti-drug policy for the Andes was having little or no impact on the availability of cocaine and heroin in the US drug market. Complicating the situation was the fact that each government agency was invariably preparing its own agenda which might or might not be in concert with long-term US intersts or anti-drug strategy. (GAO 1992: 16; and Interview GAO 1993) The INM in its 1993 INCSR commented: "Despite stepped-up programs, hundreds of tons of cocaine and heroin contine to flow to the United States and Europe." (DOS INM 1993: 1)

# Chapter 6

# Colombian Reality

One statistic which was very disconcerting to the US-Colombian effort was the fact that, whereas narcotrafficking land holdings in 1987 were reported to be about one million hectares, by the end of 1992 the holdings were reported as considerably higher and amounting to a third of the total lands being used for raising cattle. To this end the traffickers had exploited their propensity to use *plata o plomo* against the local peasant farmers to enhance their own personal and business investments. These farmers formed part of the 250,000 families which had legally obtained land during the agrarian reform programs of 1962-1979, overseen by the Colombian Institute of Agrarian Reform (INCORA - Instituto Colombiano de Reforma Agraria). Many of these peasant farm families had previously been squatters who now had land titles. Despite this the farmers were often displaced or driven off their land by large scale commercial agricultural enterprises. This was a factor of ever increasing significance as to why two-thirds of rural Colombia lived in poverty and exacerbated the unequal distribution of income. The rural or generally poorest half of the population now earned but 16 percent of the nation's income compared to the richest 10 percent which earned about 43 percent. (Bushnell 1993: 234) In short, the narcotraffickers were undermining the government's agrarian reform movement, all the while establishing their own ranches and laboratories and further conducting their trafficking operations. This, ironically, played into the hands of the guerrillas who also wanted to undermine the agrarian reform movement, demonstrating to the rural poor and campesino farmers alike that the government could not be trusted and was indeed not worthy of their support. In addition, the guerrillas continued to tax both the government's experimental crop development projects (INCORA), farmers and landowners alike. (El Tiempo 31 Jan 93; Interview NAS:CO 1993; and Gros 1992: 10)

During this time US AID was attempting to influence coca and opium poppy farmers to desist and shift to alternate crops. While this multi-million dollar effort was financed by both the US (60 percent) and Colombia (40 percent), it was the UN which had made the largest commitment ($31.6 million) in support of a three year, 21 project implementation effort. Crop substitution and alternative development, as well as treatment and prevention were the major focuses. (USE-CO 1993: Cable 1749) Another parallel effort at influencing the Colombian population involved the Country Team's demand reduction project which was spending up to half a million dollars in an attempt to make Colombians aware that drug abuse was not just a US problem but a serious domestic one for them as well. (NAS 1993: 2) It was estimated at this time that about half a million persons living in Bogota or about 10 percent of the city's population smoked *basucos*. (Insight: 2 Apr 92; and Ross: 1993)

During 1992 counter-insurgency operations continued and Colombian military authorities reported that during their *Operation Eagle* the FARC and ELN combined had lost up to 12 percent of their combat personnel, losing in the process some 951 guerrilla fighters killed and over 1,500 captured. In part this success reflected the government's attempts to promote constitutional reform and assure greater respect for human rights which tended to undermine the guerrillas' various causes. As a result the Colombian intellectual left became less and less supportive. (El Nuevo Herald: 12 Nov 92; El Espectador: 9 Dec 92; and Ejercito Nacional 1992: 1) The Gaviria administration had allocated $210 million to its military to fight the Simon Bolivar Guerrilla coalition. (Christian Science Monitor: 3 Jun 92; and Martz 1994: 135)

Still, unless legendary guerrilla leaders such as the FARC's 35-year veteran Manuel Marulanda Velez (alias *Tirofijo* or "Sureshot") and the ELN's Father Manuel Perez for whose capture among others the government was offering over a million dollars in rewards could be brought down, in the eyes of the people the government would lose credibility and even be seen as a failure. (Semana: 12 Jan 93; and Rutledge and Chernick 1993) Although the 76 year old Marulanda Velez was reported as having died of cancer and old age in August of 1993, he continued to surface from time throughout the mid-1990s. (El

Nuevo Herald: 19 Aug 93) Over time Perez did offer to enter into a truce with the government but the negotiating process broke down and the guerrilla's revolutionary campaigns continued on. Despite the Army's reorganization and the formation of nine specially equipped counter-guerrilla battalions (over 6,000 men), the guerrillas continued to inflict considerable damage to the economy, all the while extorting over a million dollars anually in ransom from their kidnapping activities. (USE-CO 1993: Cable 1749; Semana: 7 Jul 92; and El Nuevo Herald: 8 Aug 93)

Despite Army and Marine operations to the contrary, the guerrillas continued to dominate significant portions of rural Colombia, controlling their zones through some 70 "fronts" or guerrilla groups. Touting their ideals and ideologies, extorting taxes from government and private parties alike, imposing their own defacto rule and will over much of the population, and intervening in everything from labor disputes to disagreements over property, the guerrillas carried on a bandolero type of survival existence. (Miami Herald: 10 Jan 93) To this end they protected and even fostered the coca and heroin producing areas to a significant degree and remained a formidable obstacle to the government's anti-drug efforts. (Chernick: 1993; and Miami Herald: 10 Jan 93; and El Espectador: 6 Nov 92) The army did its best to strike back at the guerrillas, inflicting heavy losses on FARC fronts 24 and 36 in eastern Meta while destroying one of the latter's well-equipped secret redoubts. (El Nuevo Herald: 3 May 94) During this time President Gaviria declared a temporary state of emergency to prevent the release of about 700 imprisoned guerrillas and drug traffickers whose court cases were still pending. The required six month legal time limit for prosecuting these cases was about to expire and would have freed the prisoners had it not been for Gaviria's intervention. (Miami Herald: 2 May 94)

The 1994 election campaign was marred by the threat of violence to virtually all of the candidates, both national and local. The threats generally came from left-wing guerrillas, paramilitary groups, some drug traffickers and common criminals. Most candidates were afraid of being kidnapped for ransom or killed outright. Many used bullet proof vests and traveled in armored cars, escorted by body guards, limiting their campaigns to televised indoor appearances rather than run the risk of attracting a bullet or bomb at an outdoor rally. (Miami Herald: 25 Jan 94) Guerrillas even targeted their former rebel comrades-in-arms and supporters as "deserters" who had laid down their arms and entered into the now democratic political process. In the Uruba banana growing region of northwestern Colombia along the Panamanian frontier, in an effort to prevent the electoral process from taking place, the EPL gunned down some 35 persons celebrating at a politically motivated street party. This incident typified the ongoing intra-guerrilla struggles that sometimes took place between the FARC and the EPL. In this region in 1991, the EPL had accepted the Government's offer of amnesty and peaceful involvement in the political process. Since that time about 300 former guerrillas and their supporters in the Uruba Department had been assassinated by the FARC. The former guerrillas, in turn, formed their own paramilitary groups which then carried out assassinations of Communist Party members. (El Nuevo Herald: 23 Nov 93 and 6 Jan 94; Miami Herald: 24-25 Jan 94)

Guerrilla threats to some of the candidates were particularly severe. In November 1993 after unsuccessfully having warned the Colombian Congress not to vote for a bill widening the president's counter-insurgency powers, insurgents gunned down the Senate Vice-Chairman Dario Londono Cardona, the bill's sponsor. In addition a number of small-town mayors met a similar fate. Pressures on the  town of Codazzi near the Venezuelan border became so intense that the mayor and the entire city council resigned after receiving guerrilla death-threats. Nonetheless, the Congress went ahead and approved laws which prohibited radio and television interviews with guerrilla leaders, transmission of insurgent actions and communications and the locally sponsored initiation of dialogues with guerrilla groups. Still, the guerrilla power and influence in its own way did force some municipal governments to initiate public works projects. This form of lobbying on behalf of their constituents remained one of the insurgents' tools for redeeming themselves in the eyes of the poor rural peasant population. (Miami Herald: 25 Jan 95)

The guerrillas threatened to disrupt the municipal, congressional and national presidential elections scheduled for mid-1994 and took measures to that end. Despite using political violence tactics in the form of bombings and shootings to intimidate and coerce voters and candidates into not participating, the attempts at destabilizing the electoral process largely failed. Both the ELN and the FARC kidnapped, extorted, and often murdered mayors and other candidates to no avail. (El Nuevo Herald: 21 Feb, 19 Apr and 5 May 94; and Miami Herald: 14 Mar 94) Not all rebels agreed with the guerrilla tactics and a splinter ELN group, the Social Renewal Movement of some 400 fighters, took advantage of the government's amnesty laws under the 1991 Constitution to surrender and reincorporate itself into society, receiving small land grants and political representation within the government. (Miami Herald: 10 Apr 94) This was not always easy to do since both the FARC and the ELN took revenge by murdering dozens of repatriated former guerrillas who had chosen to live in peace. (El Nuevo Herald: 6 Jan, 21 Feb, and 19 Apr 94; and Miami Herald: 24 Jan and 14 Mar 94)

Despite government sponsored community development projects involving the construction of schools, health centers and sewage systems, rural populations in areas such as Remedios and Segovia in north-central Colombia still very much feared the Army and its operations and offered the guerrillas some sympathy and support. (Miami Herald: 4 Jan 93; and Tokatlian: 1993) That police and military forces were frequently the subject of media reported human rights violations against the civilian population, undoubtedly reinforced the guerrillas' position that the government was not worthy of the people's support or trust. This enabled the guerrillas to maintain considerable *campesino* support. (Human Rights 1993: passim; and Chernick: 1993)

The guerrillas could not be taken lightly by the government and during December 1992 rebel units coordinated their attacks, destroying navigational aids and communications equipment at the Medellin, Pereira, Cucuta, Buenaventura and Bucaramanga airports. The success of these attacks, in conjunction with trafficker bribes offered to air controllers at selected airports, facilitated the successful infiltration of trafficking aircraft which sought to avoid detection while entering and leaving Colombia. (USE-CO 1993: Cable 1749; and Falino: 1993) The Cano Limon-Puerto Covenas petroleum pipeline running through north central Colombia was a primary focus for guerrilla sabotage attacks, with the government estimating the resultant oil revenue losses at approximately $3 billion. (Martz 1994: 135) By the mid-1990s guerrilla power in rural Colombia was still acknowledged as a fact of life as politicians, ranchers, businessmen and contractors working on government projects continued to make routine payoffs to the guerrilla comandantes. (Miami Herald: 25 Jan 94)

In Washington, the ONDCP itself was looked upon by the new administration of President Bill Clinton as an agency with merely a one issue agenda. With the appointment of a new drug czar, Lee Brown, the former Police Commissioner of New York City, as its Director and the elevation of the position to cabinet level status, the ONDCP should have been in a position to improve its efficiency and ability to coordinate all national anti-drug policies in general. Nonetheless, early in the year the office was reduced from an authorized manning level of about 125 personnel to about 25. This massive reduction in personnel curtailed its capabilities for detailed policy making worldwide and limited its operational focus to only a few fronts. While it could now only cover about 50 percent of its former portfolio of anti-drug issues and countries, it did remain firmly focused on the Andean region. (Clinton 1993a: and Interview ONDCP 1: 1993) Despite the emasculation of the ONDCP, it officially remained the lead government agency for establishing policy, priorities and objectives for national drug control purposes. (Clinton 1993b)

The roughly $13 billion anti-drug budget for 1993 was slightly less than the NASA budget of some $15 billion. Nonetheless, Andean source country anti-drug funding under the Andean Initiative was reduced about 28 percent to a level of $78 million for the year. In addition, DOD announced that it was cutting some $200 million from its $1.1 billion anti-drug budget. In part this reflected the government's belt tightening process for all its offices. (Interview ONDCP 2: 1993; and Miami Herald: 29 Oct and 15 Dec 93)

After having spent some $50 billion in anti-drug funding over a ten-year period, the majority of which had been consumed in the supply-side strategy effort, in terms of reducing the flow of cocaine supplies into the US, the government's Colombian anti-drug policy was not much better off than when it had started. From 1988 to 1992 cocaine supplies for the world market had actually increased about 165 percent, going from 400 mt to nearly 1,100 mt. In short, after twelve years of effort, the policy was achieving far less than the anticipated success it was expected to be. (ONDCP 1994: 15, 17 and 103) That the US government had intercepted and seized 108 mt during the period of a year inside the US proper and a further 163 mt of cocaine in Mexico, Central America and the Caribbean transit zones appeared to have no impact at all on the availability of cocaine HCl on the street. (DOS INM 1994: 3 and 71) The ONDCP estimated that Americans were spending $49 billion annually on illegal drugs and that 5 percent of the population (15 million people) remained in the drug user category. (ONDCP 1994: 100 and 105)

Ironically, US efforts in late 1993 to ameliorate its military presence which involved naval base construction at Puerto Lopez in central Colombia and radar site construction in southern and northern Colombia became the subject of considerable controversy. At issue were the 156 US Army engineers working on civic action projects involving road, school and medical service center construction projects on the Colombian west coast in the vicinity of Juanchaco. The *Fuertes*

*Caminos* civic action-public relations work in support of the US military's anti-drug efforts in Colombia had not been properly coordinated with the Colombian legislature and overnight became a national polemic. Both the traffickers and guerrillas saw the enhanced US presence as potentially threatening. The traffickers worked against the US effort through the legislature stressing the issue of national sovereignty and the guerrillas set off a series of bombs in Medellin and Bucaramanga to indicate their displeasure over the US military presence, as well as foreign commercial enterprises in the form of oil and mining interests which were said to be exploiting Colombia. Now under considerable pressure, the US withdrew its highly visible civic action engineers, leaving the more remote radar and base constuction personnel in place. (El Nuevo Herald: 25 Jan and 5, 23 and 25 Feb 94)

While the Colombian economy reportedly grew some 3.3 percent in 1992 (the narco-assisted construction industry growing by 9.8 percent), guerrilla attacks (over 38) on petroleum pipelines cost Colombia an estimated 29,400 barrels of daily production (out of a total of 240,000 barrels per day) and actually retarded overall economic growth by a full half percent. (Economist: 14 Nov 92; El Nuevo Herald: 4, 14 and 27 Nov 92 and 22 Aug 93; and El Espectador 29 Dec 92) Another 39 attacks during 1993 caused the loss of some 80,000 barrels which was now considered to be having an adverse ecological impact, the oil spillages contaminating the nearby countryside. (El Nuevo Herald: 3 Jan 94) All this was particularly noteworthy in light of the still relatively depressed coffee export economy (15 percent of total exports) which continued to suffer under a plague (*la broca*) which was estimated to have destroyed some 10 percent of the crop. Unemployment in areas such as Quindio remained at 20 percent with wage levels for those employed at not much more than about $100 per month, offering the traffickers and guerrillas alike a lucrative source of labor and recruits respectively. (Miami Herald: 26 Sep 93; Cassman and Chernick: 1993) Nonetheless, the discovery of major new oil reserves in the Eastern Plains region in the vicinity of Cusiana, increasing by at least another third the 1.5 billion barrels already in reserve, appeared to be a long term salvation of sorts for the Colombian economy which was relying on petroleum for up to 25 percent of its exports. By the late 1990s, Colombia was expected to surpass Mexico as a regional oil source and become the second-largest oil producer in Latin America after Venezuela. (Miami Herald: 31 Oct 92; Cassman: 1993; and Martz 1994: 136)

The US anti-drug policy's training and support efforts saw the

Colombian government in 1992 seize or destroy some 39 mt of cocaine base and HCl, over 200 laboratories (including 18 cocaine refineries), some 391,000 gallons of ether, acetone and other precursor chemicals, 110 airstrips and 37 aircraft. (USE-CO 1993: Cable 1749; and DOS INM 1993: 107) In 1993 about 32 mt of cocaine base and HCl was seized while some 400 laboratories were destroyed. (DOS-INM 1994: 104) In addition, minor progress had been made in eradicating coca so that total coca crop hectarage was now reported at 37,100 ha or only a 400 ha drop from 1991. The relatively small eradication effort (959 ha) was said by INM to be due in part to the DEA estimate that the Colombian coca crop was perceived as not particularly threatening to the US and, in part, to the fact that many of the cultivated coca-poppy growing areas still remained in guerrilla contested zones. (DOS-INM 1993a: 108; and USE-CO 1993: Cable 1749) Nonetheless the price of cocaine HCl on the street inside Colombia was recorded as having risen from $500 per kg to as much as $1,200 per kg. (DOS 1992: 8) By 1994 the coca hectarage under cultivation rebounded and was reported at about 40,000 ha, indicating a gradual increase to a level comparable with production levels achieved during the late 1980s. (DOS-INM 1994: 103 and 108)

While the national police could raid a "mom-pop" laboratory complex or even a major cocaine refining laboratory, they could not stay more than about two days without risking a serious guerrilla counter-attack. In the Putumayo River region alone there were over a thousand mom-pop coca paste and gum opium (500,000 poppy plants) production complexes which, whenever they were attacked and destroyed, merely recapitalized and reconstituted themselves over a period of not more than several months, continuing to produce their small, three kilogram batches of paste or gum. South of the Putumayo, inside Peru, the situation was very much the same with almost an equal number of similar, small-scale production operations underway. (Interview NAS:CO 1993; and USE-CO 1992b: Cable 17638) While not all coca plots and production facilities operated in a synchronized manner, narcotrafficker buyers could pass through the zone every six weeks and purchase up to a metric ton of paste for further conversion at advanced laboratories. The 1,500 airfields located throughout the southern border regions of Colombia greatly facilitated these operations. Under these conditions the coca farmers were able to sustain a level of roughly 40,000 ha of harvestable crops. Even the cocaine refining processes had become more sophisticated as the Cali cartel and other independents now recycled their precursor chemicals up to five times in the production of cocaine base and HCl. (Interview NAS:CO 1993; and DOS-INM 1994: 108) In turn, marijuana was making a comeback and, despite government eradication successes during the 1980s, had doubled its harvestable cultivation levels to some 5,000 ha. (DOS-INM 1994: 103 and 108)

Through all this on the one hand, the Medellin cartel had been badly decimated, losing over 110 key members and another 2,000 captured due to the government's backlash and reaction to Pablo Escobar's use of terrorism. (El Nuevo Herald: 22 Mar 93) This trend continued throughout 1993 with an additional 145 members and sicarios killed, including Pablo Escobar himself in December 1993. (El Nuevo Herald: 19 Jul 93; and Miami Herald: 3 Dec 93) On the other hand, the Cali cartel and the myriad of other lesser groups had now, by default, captured the Colombian cocaine production market, as well as more of the distribution operations inside the US. (El Nuevo Herald 28 Aug 93; and DOS-INM 1994: 103) Despite over 400 laboratories having been destroyed during 1993 (about double the rate of 224 labs destroyed during 1992), the cartel continued to move some 500 mt of cocaine through Colombia to its markets in the US and Europe. (El Nuevo Herald: 5 Dec 93 and 3 May 94; and DOS-INM 1994: 107) Nonetheless, life was not easy for the Cali cartel at this time as some 150 members offered to negotiate their surrender to the DAN rather than face the vengeance of the paramilitary death squads and 2,000 police special forces who ranged over the country in their fleet of 61 helicopters and other aircraft. (El Nuevo Herald: 2 and 7 May 93; and NAS 1993: passim) For Julio Fabio Urdinola the pressure became so great that he surrendered to Colombian authorities after months of negotiations between his lawyers and the Attorney General's office. (Miami Herald: 13 Mar 94)

Operation Green Ice had also made an impact in 1992 on the cartels' fortunes as $4.6 million in 525 narcotrafficker bank accounts were frozen inside Colombia (Bogota, Medellin, Cali, Barranquilla and Pereira) and another $54 million frozen in the exterior (an additional $1.4 billion involving the Medellin cartel would be frozen in 1993 alone). In one FATF operation 197 members of the Cali and Pereira cartels as well as others were arrested in the US and Italy and $44 million in cartel assets were also seized. (USE-CO 1992c: Cable 16357; UPI: 28 Sep 92; and El Nuevo Herald: 7 Oct 92 and 19 Jul 93) Colombian economist Salomon Kalmanovitz estimated that trafficker net earnings had fallen from a high of nearly $5.3 billion in 1987 to about $3.4 billion. (El Espectador: 13 Dec 92)

While impressive, these seizures by Green Ice would pale in comparison to the $150 million seized from the seventeen Julio Cesar Nasser (North Coast cartel) accounts in Switzerland. Nasser, wanted at this time by US authorities for illegally importing 25 tons of cocaine into the US since the late 1970s, had begun his extensive trafficking empire through smuggling cigarettes, liquor and blue jeans into Colombia as a young man. Eventually he moved on to marijuana and cocaine where he learned the trade well enough under the tutelage of the Medellin traffickers to establish his own family based cartel. Although frequently purchasing cocaine from the other cartel groups, he carried out his own transportation, distribution and money laundering. In time he was moving three tons of cocaine a month into the US during the decade starting in the mid-1980s. A US Coast Guard intercept of a shipment near the Bahamas in 1989 eventually enabled US and Swiss authorities to capture Nasser's wife. In time Nasser became a fugitive in his own country. (Miami Herald: 16 Apr 94)

Over time, the Colombian judiciary began to profit from the reforms of the 1991 Constitution where it had been established as an independent body. In addition to the significant change from being an inquisitory to an accusatorial system, it was having more positive results as a network of prosecutors were dispersed throughout Colombia in 21 local offices and Public Order Courts. The new Constitution had constituted the courts as a separate and accountable branch of the government with a separate budget and distinct organizational structure. Also established was a distinct public prosecutor's office which would handle all investigations and case prosecution activities. (GAO 1992: 9; and Miami Herald: 2 Feb 92) To support the US objective of strengthening the judicial system, USAID provided training in Colombia and the US to 641 federal judges and prosecutors and 921 investigators, forensic technicians and other officials. (DOS-INM 1994: 107)

Plea bargaining as a new Colombian policy did have an effect which could be seen in the 1993 settlement with Medellin cartel kingpin Jorge Luis Ochoa who, in exchange for an eight year, four-month prison sentence, agreed to turn over to the government some $2.5 million in property. (USE-CO 1993b: Cable 9015) Ivan ("the terrible") Urdinola likewise was able to negotiate a 17 year sentence down to four and a half. A 1993 penal code modification enabled traffickers, who surrendered and turned over their illicit gains and otherwise disclosed their operations to state authorities, to obtain leniency. Other traffickers, such as the Cali cartel's Gilberto and Miguel Rodriguez and Jose Santa Cruz Londono, opted to wait and see how Urdinola fared before submitting themselves to the new Colombian justice. (Maimi Herald: 13 Mar and 4 Apr 94) As time went on the new *Fiscal General* (Prosecutor General), Gustavo de Greiff, began to take on a heroic stature in the eyes of the Colombian public, as he and his 10,000 member prosecuting authority openly defied trafficker violence and corruption. (Miami Herald: 13 Aug 92) Over a two year period (1992-93) de Greiff's office indicted and convicted 15 major traffickers with sentences ranging from three and a half to twelve years in prison. Nonetheless, the US government considered the sentences imposed on the traffickers as not commensurate with the seriousness of their criminal activities. The five federal prosecution courts and their prosecuting units of lawyers, as well as de Greiff, began to receive US criticism in terms of not producing the decisive results that the multimillion-dollar US Congressional investment was looking for. (DOS INM 1994: 106)

Corruption as a deeply rooted societal factor in Colombia continued to remain a major obstacle to the success of the judiciary. The fundamental cynicism and distrust of the government on the part of the population, combined with salaries of not much more than $100 a month, contributed to a general lack of civic consciousness, making public officials highly susceptible to the corrupting influence of the traffickers. (Falino, Tokatlian, and Chernick: 1993) Reflecting this situation was the revelation that one of the Attorney General's top aides, Guillermo Villa Alzate, had been coopted as an informant by the Cali cartel's Gilberto and Miguel Rodriguez Orejuela. The Cali cartel had been able to infiltrate the highest levels of the newly reformed judiciary and were privy to many of its most confidential activities until a police intercept of a telephone conversation eventually revealed what was transpiring. This corruption had taken place despite the increase in salaries for judges who now earned up to $2,800 per month, compared to their pre-1991 earnings of about $200 per month. Within the Congress and the government at this time some 136 other persons were also under investigation for corruption. (USE-CO 1992b: Cable 17638; El Nuevo Herald: 1 Oct 93; and Tokatlian 1993) Getting elected or appointed to public office was more often than not looked upon as an opportunity to enrich oneself at the expense of the nation and for this reason the concept or ethic of uncorrupted public service on behalf of society was for many virtually non-existent. To this end trafficker monies were said to have supported the election of up to half of the members of the Colombian Congress. (Interview DEA:CO and Ross: 1993) Indicative of the problem was the former chief of the Colombian National Police, General Jose Guillermo Medina, who was prosecuted for unexplained enrichment during the period of 1986 and 1987 when he amassed a small fortune ($250,000) while earning a salary of little more than $500 per month. ((El Nuevo Herald: 13 Apr 94)

The issue of corruption came to a head in April 1994 when the Assistant US Attorney General, Jo Ann Harris, accused Gustavo de Greiff of engaging in plea bargaining negotiations with the traffickers without first consulting with US officials. In addition, de Greiff's efforts were said to be producing minimum sentences for some of the world's major traffickers, permitting the trafficking organizations to essentially remain intact and their illicit gains untouched. That the US had provided Colombian authorities with evidence for some 50 cases involving 124 suspects, including 37 Colombian traffickers of the Medellin and Cali cartels, many of whom received relatively light sentences or were never prosecuted, raised considerable ire in US Senate hearings on the subject. (Miami Herald: 21 Apr 94) De Greiff's activities were feared to be undermining the joint US-Colombian efforts against cocaine smuggling. Despite the lenient terms being offered to selected drug kingpins, there was considerable hesitancy on the part of the traffickers to submit to de Greiff's justice since actual prison treatment was not clearly portrayed in advance. (Miami Herald: 15 Apr 94)

Adding to the controversy was the fact that Attorney General de Greiff had openly contended that the war on drugs was unrealistic and a "failed fight" (*lucha fallida*). From his perspecteve, since a kilogram of cocaine cost only about $50 in the source countries and between $5,000 and $10,000 in the consuming countries, there would always be someone willing to run the risks of illegal drug trafficking. To take away the profit incentives, de Greiff suggested that legalization should be considered seriously as an appropriate solution. That Colombian Nobel Prize winner for literature, Gabriel Garcia Marquez, also contended that drugs ought to be legalized, only added fuel to the controversy and galled the Country Team in Bogota. President Cesar Gaviria chastized de Greiff, declaring that legalization was not a solution for his administration. (El Nuevo Herald: 29 Nov 93 and 24 Feb and 5 May 94) De Greiff's position concerning the legalization of drugs was reinforced when the high level Constitutional Court (*Corte Constitucional*) issued a controversial ruling in May 1994 declaring that it was legal to possess small amounts of drugs for personal use. Now a person could legally have in their possession one gram of cocaine and up to 20 grams of marijuana (28 grams are equal to one ounce). Apart from this, narcotrafficking itself still remained outlawed. (Miami Herald: 7 May 94) With the US government castigating the Colombian judiciary for its perceived indulgence of the traffickers with inordinately light sentences and the Colombian president irate over de Greiff's remarks, the Prosecutor General's value to the anti-drug effort was now being seriously questioned. (El Nuevo Herald: 24 Apr and 4 May 94; and DOS-INM 1994: 104) The situation came to a head through a national plebiscite sponsored by President Gaviria himself to determine if the government could obtain sufficient popular authority to overturn the Constitutional Court's ruling. (Miami Herald: 8 May 94)

Despite the criticism, de Greiff stood his ground, expressing himself publicly and contending that the major cartels such as the Cali group did not offer the cohesive, monolithic, readily targetable center of gravity that the media often supposed. Instead, there was a myriad of different groups and persons involved in the commercial exercise of drug trafficking which made the effort to repress it as an illegal activity almost futile. De Greiff argued that despite efforts to the contrary, coca, marijuana and poppy crops had increased from 13,000 to 50,000 hectares (over 100,000 acres). (El Nuevo Herald: 5 May 94) In sum, de Greiff contended that despite the expenditure of $52 billion by the US government, the steady market demand in the US and Europe permitted no more than 10 percent of the cocaine product to be intercepted each year while the traffickers continued undaunted. The only solution from de Greiff's perspective was to somehow eliminate the profit incentive which, alone, drove the cocaine production market forward! He maintained that the drug war was a failure and other alternatives needed to be entertained to achieve a reasonable solution. (Greiff 1994; and El Nuevo Herald: 23 and 24 May) The debate over repression, legalization and/or education in Colombia intensified considerably. In Washington, John P. Walters, the former acting Director for Supply Reduction and Chief of Staff for the ONDCP under the Bush administration concluded that the reduction in domestic drug usage that had taken place inside the US was mainly due to the work of concerned parents and the mobilization of entire communities, schools and work places. It was education and not supply reduction that was having an impact in reducing somewhat the use of drugs and its potential for demand inside the US. (House 1993a: 39; and Washington Post: 16 Apr 93) Yet, as 1994 approached even the educational focus was being criticized as drug usage trends were reported as rising in many of the nation's high schools. (Miami Herald: 10 Feb 94)

Yet it was not until mid-October 1993 that the Clinton administration began to release what was to become its Western Hemisphere anti-drug strategy. Upon the completion of a NSC review of the drug situation in the Americas, it sought to play down the drug issue as a top priority of the foreign policy agenda. There was to be less emphasis on interdiction and more on seeking host-nation cooperation and the demonstration of proper "political will" in combatting narcotrafficking. The fomentation of democracy, economic stability and growth, human rights and the rule of law were all to be given the highest priority, but still comparatively evaluated in terms of the corrupting influence of the illegal drug trade on the nation's authorities. Both cocaine and heroin were to be emphasized as the main threats to the US from Colombia. US resources and attention were to be duly focused on counter-drug enforcement operations in Colombia, Bolivia and Peru. In short, it was the demonstrated political will and genuine commitment to combat the drug trade on the part of the Andean countries that would be the defining element to the provision of US aid. (ONDCP 1994: 50-51; and Perl 1994: 143-145)

Having reviewed the situation in Colombia, Bill Clinton, in his Presidential Determinations (No. 93-18 and 94-22) reaffirmed that Colombia had "cooperated fully" in complying with US counter-narcotics interests throughout 1992 and 1993. (DOS-INM 1993a: vi; and DOS 1994: Cable 87397) For this, Colombia was rewarded in fiscal year 1994 with of US funding of $25 million for narcotics control operations. This stemmed in part from the implementation of the Clinton administration's Western Hemisphere Drug Strategy shift in emphasis which focused most of the US anti-drug support for the Americas on the Bush initiated Andean Initiative focus. (DOS 1993: 106 and DOS-INM 1994: 106) This new strategy was to gradually make a transition from a policy which primarily emphasized interdiction to one of increasing US cooperation for Colombia, provided that it demonstrated the will to deal with narcotrafficking. Other foreign policy goals were now emphasized and were to be addressed on an equal footing. These included fomenting and strengthening democracy (democratic institution building), economic stability and growth (diversification), human rights, the rule of law and a clean environment. (Perl 1994: 144-145) The US government's ONDCP and INM specific narcotics control goals for Colombia remained "the arrest, prosecution and imprisonment of key narcotics traffickers and the dismantlement of their organizations, the aerial and manual eradication of opium poppy, coca and marijuana crops, denying necessary chemicals to traffickers and the strengthening of Colombian institutions to pursue these objectives within a legal and constitutional framework that respects human rights." (DOS-INM 1994: 106)

For the US Country Team in Colombia this translated into a "new" program in which a first and primary objective was "to strengthen the political will of the government and its institutions to pursue drug activities." In turn, strengthening "the counternarcotics capabilities of the Colombian law enforcement and military organizations and to disrupt drug-trafficking organizations" became second and third objectives. The last objective was to strengthen, as well as diversify the Colombian economy (Beginning in April, 1992 the US provided $41 million in Economic Support Funds to Colombia to reduce its debt to the former.). (GAO 1993a: 17) Gaviria's support of the US policy emphasis and shift was apparently rewarded by his receipt of a full endorsement by the US government in his quest to become the president of the Organization of American States (OAS) in 1994. (El Nuevo Herald: 15 Apr 94) Nonetheless, the Colombian narcotraffickers, reacting to a leveling off and even decreasing demand interest from a saturated cocaine market in the US, were now increasing heroin production in response to a relatively higher heroin demand, thus compensating for the lower net cocaine profits. (USE-CO: Cable 17638; El Espectador: 13 Dec 92; and Kalmanovitz 1993)

Although DOD through its SOUTHCOM directed activities did disrupt and diminish to some extent aerial transshipment of illegal drugs into the US, a GAO study found that: "Since 1989, estimated cocaine production had increased, most shipments are still not interdicted, and the estimated cocaine flow into the United States has not appreciably declined." (GAO 1993b: 17) This devastating conclusion was further buttressed by the observation that DOD anti-drug surveillance activity was not producing the "drug war benefits that are commensurate with its cost" (DOD expenditures were $976 million from 1989 to 1993). (GAO 1993b: 17, 35 and 37) The GAO report went so far as to recommend Congressional cuts in the DOD counter-drug budget. In fact, DOD did take a cut in its drug control monies for FY 94 and FY 95 which reduced its operating capital for this mission to $868 and $874 million respectively or well under the FY 93 allocation of $1.1 billion.

Ironically, the aerial interdiction issue came to a head in early May 1994 when the Pentagon and other government legal authorities persuaded the NSC and the president to stop sharing US radar anti-drug aerial intercept information with the Andean governments. There was an evolving, yet sincere fear, on the part of the government that it was inadvertently making itself a party to human rights violations. The issue of the possibility of shooting down of innocent civilians by the Andean militaries, using US provided intercept data with the US thereby becoming an accomplice, cast an ominous shadow over the aerial interdiction portions of the US anti-drug policy. That this change in the policy was made abruptly with little or no coordination with the governments of Bolivia, Peru and Colombia added considerably to the increased tensions arising from the apparent lack of confidence by the US in its dealings with its Andean allies. (Miami Herald: 31 May 1994) This was especially galling for Gaviria whose government just that past March had authorized, for the first time in Colombian history, the Air Force to intercept and shoot down suspected trafficking aircraft or all those who refused to identify themselves, refused to submit to an inspection, or did not have a formally registered flight plan. (El Nuevo Herald: 3 Mar 94)

The US Congress also reduced appropriations for the State Department's international narcotics control program for FY 94, scaling it down from about $147.8 million to $100 million. In addition, the Congressional Foreign Operations Appropriations Act (HR-2295 of 30 September 1993) withheld all ESF and Foreign Military Funding (FMF) for the Andean Initiative until the administration revealed its "new" version of the Andean strategy. (Perl 1994: 147-148) The US Congress was evidently disenchanted with the results of the Andean Initiative and held little confidence in the ability of the Clinton administration to improve the former. The reduction of the ONDCP staff was just one indicator of President Clinton's own dissatisfaction with the way the drug war was being waged. Yet it was not until February 1994 when the ONDCP released its new strategy (the classified version was produced as Presidential Decision Directive 14) for fighting the drug war that the administration's position became clear. In terms of Colombia, interdiction would remain as an essential element of the US foreign policy agenda. (ONDCP 1994: 1 and 3) Crop control, the arrest and imprisonment of drug kingpins and the strengthening of host nation counter-narcotics institutions remained key ONDCP strategy objectives. (ONDCP 1994: 4)

While a myriad of operations of all sorts were constantly taking place in Colombia during the early to mid-1990s, hurting the US anti-drug effort there was the lack of a clear, defining strategy with operational objectives (ends), an operational campaign plan (ways) and sufficient and timely resources (means) by which the Country Team and the Colombian government could pull all their efforts together in a coordinated manner. As a result there appeared to be no continuity or coherent manner in which the activities underway were leading to a decisive finish and accomplishing the goals that the US anti-drug policy desired to achieve. In sum, the lack of a unity of effort had now resulted in often competing plans, institutions, agencies and resources. (Senate 1992d: 171; Joulwan 1993: 18; and Interviews: CT:CO, DEA:CO, and Camacho: 1993) Perhaps this was inevitable since Colombia was such a complex environment in which to wage a drug war.

Nonetheless, the Colombian government, reacting as never before to the dual threats of trafficker and guerrilla violence, was implementing its counter-measures at maximum intensity. In the case of the anti-drug effort, the major focus was now on the Cali cartel whose groups were being gradually apprehended along with those remnants of the Medellin cartel. Despite the aggressive and highly disruptive US and Colombian anti-drug counter-measures, the strong international demand for cocaine and heroin continued to provide sufficient incentives to cause numerous other traffickers to either enter into the trade or take up the slack from the decimated cartels by expanding their efforts either inside Colombia or in neighboring countries. While the Medellin cartel's senior leadership was out of commission and losing control of its trafficking empire, the Cali cartel now attempted to assume the lead trafficking role, using its generally non-confrontational style of business operations. Despite government threats and operations to force it to surrender and cooperate, it was able to dominate the trafficking structure inside Colombia for the time being, controlling an estimated 70 to 80 percent of the cocaine being transshipped to the US market. (Miami Herald: 22 Jan, 20 Feb and 4 Apr 94; and DOS-INM 1994: 103)

Cali cartel leaders Gilberto Rodriguez Orejuela, Miguel Jose Santa Cruz Londono and Helmar Herrera retained overall control of the group's operations. Nonetheless, the killing of Pablo Escobar by Colombian police did make a profound impression on these and other narco-barons in terms of indicating the seriousness of the government's anti-drug efforts. This ultimately led to the surrender of Julio Fabio Urdinola and other lesser Cali cartel traffickers. Urdinola, whose brother was already serving a 4-year sentence for trafficking, had succumbed to the carrot and stick plea bargaining strategy which the Attorney General had introduced to influence traffickers to turn themselves in voluntarily.

US authorities feared that the traffickers who surrendered in Colombia were actually doing so so that they could avoid the fate of Pablo Escobar by receiving short prison sentences, all the while preserving their ill-gotten wealth and continuing their operations from jail. Upon release they could then continue their operations under a veneer of legitimacy, having already served their sentences. (Miami

Herald: 13 Mar 94). Attorney General Gustavo de Greiff's attempts at achieving a mass narcotrafficker surrender came to naught when President Gaviria, under pressure from the US not to allow lenient prison terms or treatment, objected to the former's strategy. (Miami Hearld: 15 Apr 94) At this time the DEA was estimating that the Cali cartel alone was still moving about 500 tons of cocaine through Colombia. With Americans reportedly spending up to $50 billion per year on illegal drugs, the market demand inside the US still remained commensurately strong. (El Nuevo Herald: 11 Apr 94 and 3 May 95)

The policy of leniency or amnesty by the government towards its adversaries did have some positive consequences. Some 500 guerrillas of a dissident element (*Corriente de Renovacion Socialista*) of the ELN in the Flor del Monte area of the Colombian north coast formally turned over their weapons as part of a reincorporation process into the mainstream of society. (El Nuevo Herald: 9 Apr 94) A few weeks later another group consisting of some 650 guerrillas from both the FARC and ELN turned themselves in to the government in exchange for the opportunity to reincorporate. (El Nuevo Herald: 27 May 94) Despite these setbacks, the surviving FARC and ELN insurgent diehards could continue to point to the 46 percent of the population which still lived in poverty. Adding to the problem was the fact that millions of people still lacked potable water and one-half of the nation's youth never finished high school. This condition continued despite the effort by Gaviria to slash tariffs and subsidies, privatize state owned companies and ease restrictions on foreign investments inside Colombia, contributing to enhanced economic growth. Tariffs for example dropped from 53 percent to 12 percent, while imports jumped 68 percent and foreign investment doubled over the period of two years. (Miami Herald: 28 May 94)

The 1994 electoral process, with the national presidential election taking place in May, was indicative of Colombia's violence-prone society which was convulsed by the politics of narcotrafficking. One of the two leading candidates, Andres Pastrana (Conservative) had been kidnapped for a week by the *Extraditables* in 1989 and Ernesto Samper (Liberal) had survived a narco-assassination attempt in which he was struck some ten times by bullets. (Miami Herald: 2 Feb 94) Pastrana stated that, in addition to narcotrafficking, base poverty and a lack of education (Only one elementary student out of a hundred ever graduated from college!), as well as kidnapping, corruption, violence and contraband activities were grave societal problems which still had to be addressed. (El Nuevo Herald: 30 Mar 94) It is interesting to note that the US GAO also reflected on and commented about corruption, violence ("insurgency and narcoterrorism activities") and the expansion of the cartels into heroin as "major obstacles" hindering the US counternarcotics efforts in Colombia. (GAO 1993a: 16)

Despite guerrilla plans to terrorize and otherwise disrupt the electoral process in Bogota and elsewhere through a series of bombings, the election results once again favored the Liberal Party with Ernesto Samper, a former minister of economics and senator, having been elected by a slight margin. The Liberals strengthened their hold on the Senate while the Conservative and M-19 Parties lost ground respectively. The M-19's Democratic Alliance saw is Senatorial representation shrink from nine seats to two. (El Nuevo Herald: 5 May 94 and Miami Herald: 14 Mar 94) Possibly indicative of Colombians' disenchantment with their socioeconomic and political processes was the up to 70 percent abstention rate noted among the voting population. (El Nuevo Herald 16 Mar 94)

# Chapter 7

# The Quagmire

Newly elected President Ernesto Samper inherited the societal problems of violence, corruption, contraband and trafficking which perennially had faced Colombian governments for decades. Despite trying to work toward a peaceful solution to the now more than thirty-year guerrilla insurgency, Samper almost immediately found his efforts undermined by Right-wing paramilitary death squads, one of which was responsible for the August 1994 assassination of a left-leaning senator of the Patriotic Union (UP) and Communist Party coalition. Although the Attorney General's office was aware of an alleged plot on the part of some elements within the Colombian military to assassinate the senator, the government remained helpless to adequately defend the democratic process. That some two-thousand UP Party members had been murdered since the end of the 1980s without a single apprehension and conviction of a perpetrator underscored the situation and caught the attention of human rights groups such as the Andean Commission of Jurists. (Miami Herald: 10 Aug 94) The situation also reflected attitudes among traditional leaders, some of whom wanted to see the innovative reforms of the 1991 Constitution (civil liberties, human rights, expanded political participation and greater public accountability) rescinded. (Chernick 1996: 79)

As part of its efforts to cooperate with US anti-drug policy, the Samper administration made a commitment to thwart money laundering operations. Narco-dollars were generally known to have flooded Colombia over the past several years which, with the liberalization of the country's exchange laws, were gradually pushing up the value of the peso and hurting the nation's exports. The situation was not easy to resolve, and its complexity was illustrated in one case where a money launderer's office, raided by Colombian anti-drug police, was found to have bank accounts in some 40 other countries. Often coalitions of criminal groups, such as the Russian and Italian Mafias, joined hands with trafficking groups operating out of Brazil, Colombia and Israel to launder an incredible $30 billion worldwide each year. Within Colombia itself an estimated up to $2 billion was being laundered each year. To meet this situation Samper promised legislation to make money laundering a crime and increase penalties accordingly. (Miami Herald: 6 Sep 94) Julio and Sheila Nasser of the Barranquilla (North Coast) trafficking cartel, over a period of fifteen years, amassed a fortune of some $200 million which was later confiscated in Switzerland as part of a counter-money laundering effort by the Swiss and US governments. (El Nuevo Herald: 11 Aug 96)

At about the same time a major purge of the national police took place. Major General Rosso Jose Serrano began attacking corruption throughout police ranks (90,000 members) in earnest and a total of 174 officers were fired for illegal enrichment and taking bribes from the traffickers. This was the result of an investigation of 2,685 police officers thought to be linked to the drug cartels. Besides those fired, 27 were suspended, 881 were reported fined and 998 others were reprimanded. A remaining 605 or about a quarter of this group were eventually cleared of wrongdoing. (Miami Herald: 23 Oct 94)

Yet, almost from the onset of his administration, Samper was plagued with drug-related scandals which not only incriminated himself but also other members of his government. A bitter Andres Pastrana, who had lost the presidential election to Samper by only about 1 percent of the vote (El Espectador: 28 Aug 95 and Miami Herald: 7 Feb 96), decided to provide the Country Team in Bogota with tape recordings of police wiretap intercepts of the Cali cartel's Miguel Rodriguez Orejuela arranging the movement of $3.5 million to help finance Ernesto Samper's presidential campaign. Pastrana hoped that the US would release the tapes, thereby causing a condemnation of Samper which might possibly create a voter backlash enabling the former to eventually win power. Samper and his campaign manager, Luis Alberto Moreno, banked on how important it was for the Bogota government to retain its credibility. US Ambassador Morris Busby approached his superiors in Washington on the issue, but was refused permission to release the tapes as the US government did not want to interfere with the Colombian election process. Here the matter appeared to rest. (Farrah 1996: 1-2 and Chernick 1996: 76)

Unknown to Ambassador Busby, the senior DEA official on the Country Team, Joe Toft, turned copies of the tapes over to the Colombian television media. Toft was frustrated that neither the US government nor the outgoing Gaviria administration, which also knew about the tapes' contents, had done anything in response. By 20 June the tapes were known across Colombia as the "narco-cassettes." The ensuing scandal cast a shadow over the new president-elect but did not deter Samper from taking office that 7 August 1994. Some months later a frustrated and visibly angry Toft resigned from the DEA and spoke out on Colombian television, declaring that the country had become a "narco-democracy" in which he could not "think of a single political or judicial institution that has not been penetrated by the narcotraffickers." He further charged that the Samper campaign had accepted millions of dollars from the traffickers and that the Cali cartel was exercising inordinate control over Colombia's political and economic institutions. (Lee 1996: 209; Farrah 1996: 3; and El Nuevo Herald: 28 Jan 96)

A year-long investigation took place led by Colombia's prosecutor-general. Accused and placed under arrest was Santiago Medina, Samper's former campaign treasurer. He in turn accused the Samper administration's Minister of Defense, Fernando Botero Zea, as having (as director general of the Samper campaign) coordinated the Cali cartel's contributions. Botero resigned, as did Interior Minister Horacio Serpa and Communications Minister Armando Benedetti - all of whom were accused of having arranged for the acceptance of up to $3 million from the Cali cartel. (El Nuevo Herald: 3 Aug 95) Over time Santiago Medina provided the Attorney General's office with some 400 incriminating documents which suggested that the Cali contribution was actually in the neighborhood of about $6 million. (Miami Herald: 13 Aug 95)

While Samper claimed that he was an innocent victim of a "narco-conspiracy" and for this reason would not resign (El Espectador: 28 Aug 95), the scandal shook the nation's confidence and the Bogota stock market dropped 25 points. (Miami Herald: 9 Oct 95) By this time the Committee of Accusations of the Colombian House or Chamber of Representatives, the only body constitutionally empowered to judge the president, also became involved in the investigation process which was now called "Case 8,000" (*Proceso 8000*). (Miami Herald: 6 Oct 95) While the Colombian Congress would initially condemn Samper, the president was eventually exonerated in June of 1996. The

Chamber of Representatives voted, 111 to 43 to absolve the president of any narco-related wrong doing during his election campaign. At this time nine members of the Chamber were in jail for having received money from the traffickers and another two dozen were under investigation for involvement with narco-trafficking. (Chernick 1995: 77 and Farrah 1996: 17) Since the Accusations Committee was made up of members of Samper's own Liberal Party with several of these also under investigation, the Chamber of Representatives' credibility was in question. (Miami Herald: 23 Jun 96 and Chernick 1996: 77)

Nonetheless, the scandal did not dissipate and in early 1996 Samper received another blow when the Liberal Party's Senator from the Boyaca Department, Maria Izquierdo, revealed that she had been personally instructed by Samper to go to the home of Santiago Medina to pick up some 30 million cash in Colombian pesos ($3 million) which presumably was from the Cali cartel. (El Nuevo Herald: 30 Jan 96) A week later the Attorney General, Alfonso Valdivieso, formally accused the president of illegalities involving the financing of his election campaign. A thousand pages of charges and supporting evidence were offered, indicating that the Samper election campaign had received some $6 million from the Cali cartel's leaders. The President was now formally charged with illegal enrichment, electoral fraud and cover-up. (Miami Herald: 7 and 15 Feb 96)

President Samper, acknowledging that his government was in crisis, fought back gamely, pointing to the 29,000 counter-narcotics operations to date that his government had carried out, the capture of six of seven of the key leaders of the Cali cartel, and the one-half (29,000 ha) of the estimated total coca crop which had been destroyed at a cost of $1 billion to the Colombian government. (Miami Herald: 20 Feb 96) But this was not enough, as the Clinton administration revoked Samper's US visa and refused to certify Colombia as a reliable partner in the fight against drug trafficking. (INCSR 1996: xxv-xxvi) Business and commercial elites who previously had supported Samper now began to distance themselves from him. (El Tiempo: 7 Mar 96) That influence peddling abounds in Colombian politics is well known. The legitimate economic sector is no exception. For example, Colombia's most powerful commercial conglomerate, The Santo Domingo Group, which owns Avianca Airlines and other oil, banking, brewery and media interests, donated about half of the $4 million limit that the 1994-95 Samper election campaign was authorized by law. (Miami Herald: 12 Apr 96) Still, time appeared to be working against Samper.

The Colombian President was now apparently being gradually

consumed by his own government's efficiency in carrying out the Case 8,000 process. By mid-1996 Samper's former military aide-de-camp, Colonel German Osorio, was placed under arrest for links to the Cali cartel. Holding Osorio in the greatest confidence, the President had suddenly transferred him to Italy as a "police-attache." This did not deter the Attorney General's office which recalled Osorio and placed him under arrest for ties to the traffickers. (El Nuevo Herald: 13 Aug 96) Threats of a possible military coup d'etat against the administration emerged at this time but came to nothing. (El Nuevo Herald: 14 Aug and 15 Sep 96) Additional complications involving the military surfaced when an investigation found that the President's official Boeing 707 of the Air Force's Air Transport Command was found with four kilos of cocaine stashed on board. (El Nuevo Herald: 2 Oct 96) This was not the first time the Air Force had been implicated in narcotrafficking as in June 1996 a kilo of heroin had been discovered on one of its C-130 Hercules aircraft. (El Nuevo Herald: 27 Sep 96)

A further blow to Samper personally was the resignation of his Vice-President, Humberto de la Calle, in protest over the President's alleged linkage to the Cali cartel and the tarnishing of the election results, stemming from the $6 million received from the traffickers. De la Calle also called for Samper's resignation in response to the perceived institutional crisis that was now shaking the government. (El Nuevo Herald: 6 Sep 96 and Miami Herald: 11 Sep 96) In turn, Fernando Botero, former Minister of Defense, now found himself receiving five years in prison for illegal enrichment and falsifying election campaign documents. Santiago Medina also received the same sentence. Serpa, meanwhile, was eventually absolved of any wrongdoing and resumed his post as Interior Minister. (Chernick 1996; 77 and Miami Herald: 7 Oct 96) In short, while Samper had avoided impeachment, his credibility was in question and his ability to govern was now significantly compromised.

The scandals involving the Cali cartel's financial contributions to the Samper election campaign generated tremendous pressures for the President and his administration to take some action against the traffickers. For the next couple of years significant successes were achieved. To initiate his counter-narcotics efforts in January 1995, Samper signed into law a new initiative to focus on the Cali drug kingpins. In addition, an anti-corruption law (Case 8000), seeking to combat trafficking, money laundering, illegal enrichment, and the embezzlement of public funding was promulgated. Now, for the first time, money laundering was illegal. (El Nuevo Herald: 7 Jun 95)

Highlighting the administration's law enforcement successes were the arrest or surrender of seven of the most notorious of the Cali cartel's leaders: Ivan Urdinola, brothers Gilberto and Miguel Rodriguez Orejuela, Jose Santa Cruz Londono, Helmer Herrera Buitrago, Victor Patino and Phanor Arizabateta. The entire principal cartel leadership was now in jail! (Chernick 1996: 77; INCSR 1996: 81; and El Nuevo Herald: 2 Sep 96)

By saturating the Cali city's urban area with some 3,000 police and soldiers under the DAN's Joint Special Command (Comando Especial Conjunto - CEC), the government's manhunt was able to work around the cartel's security cordon of a vast network of informants and employees which ranged from corrupt police officials to taxi drivers. Trafficker access to secret police communication codes had previously enabled the cartel members to monitor police radios and determine if an anti-drug operation was under way. To confound and throw police dogs off their scent, the cartel also used coffee and Vicks Vapo-Rub to conceal any tell-tale smell from the packages of cocaine. (El Tiempo: 18 Jun 95; El Espectador: 15 Oct 95; and Miami Herald: 10 Jun 95) This was now to no avail.

Additional drug interdiction operations were enhanced by two radars operated by US and Colombian personnel. These were established in the Amazonas region to augment the others already in place to points west and, over a four-month period, resulted in the shooting down or forced landing of 21 trafficker aircraft. Official Colombian policy had been modified and now authorized interceptions, provided no flight plan had been filed and the pilot ignored radio calls or refused to respond to visual signals to land. (El Nuevo Herald: 6 Dec 95 and Miami Herald: 7 Aug 95) There was an impact produced by the government's successes. Construction in Cali itself fell off some 40 percent and the price of coca paste per kilo dropped from an average of $1,647 to $750 due to the disruption of the Cali cartel's purchasing networks and the ensuing glut on the market. (El Nuevo Herald: 3 Jun 95)

Despite the initiatives by the Samper government, the ONDCP recorded that during 1994 US hospital emergency room admissions had involved some 142,000 cocaine users or the highest recorded number in years. (Miami Herald: 8 Nov 95) While Washington could criticize Bogota for a lack of will, some statistics showed that the anti-drug war for Colombia had been costly. Bogota recorded some 3,400 dead and another 5,000 wounded fighting the traffickers over a ten year period. During an anti-drug fumigation effort called Operation Resplandor, three government helicopters had been shot down and twelve others damaged by guerrillas in the pay of the traffickers. Included in the nation's total dead were now a minister of justice, four presidential candidates, 15 judges and thousands of police officials. Like the Medellin cartel before, the Cali groups also struck back with bombings and assassinations which frequently targeted the DAS. (El Tiempo: 18 Jun 95 and El Nuevo Herald: 10 Jun and 25 Nov 95) Bogota was now spending around $1.3 billion each year in its efforts to quash the narcotrafficking. (El Nuevo Herald: 13 Aug 96)

The anti-drug police (DAS and CEC), under the command of General Rosso Jose Serrano, relentlessly attempted to hunt down the traffickers. When Jose Santa Cruz Londono escaped from La Picota prison, passing through four distinct control points, he was eventually apprehended and then shot to death by the DAS. The implication was that trafficker escapes would be dealt with ruthlessly. (El Tiempo: 14 and 16 Jan 96) In another situation the anti-drug police captured and indicted Raul and Luis Grajales. The cousins ran a chain of supermarkets and fruit pulp export companies which served as a cover for trafficking activities to eastern Europe. Things were seemingly going well for the Grajales until the DAS intercepted four tons of cocaine mixed into a shipment of pulp. (El Nuevo Herald: 1 Mar 96)

To emphasize the US anti-drug policy in October 1995, President Bill Clinton declared that narcotrafficking presented "an unusual and extraordinary threat to the national security of the United States." Freezing narco-assets and outlawing any person or company from doing business with the traffickers was a major part of Clinton's initiative to deal with the situation. (Miami Herald: 16 May 96) US citizens were now prohibited from conducting transactions of any kind with the more than two-hundred cartel-linked businesses, including real estate, beef producers, construction companies, drugstore chains and radio stations. Fines of up to $250,000 and ten years in prison for individuals and up to $ 1/2 million for companies were established. US Ambassador Myles Frechette warned Colombian banks that they would be cut off from the US banking system if they were found to be doing business with any individual linked to the traffickers. The problem here was that the 80 or so large US manufacturing companies, such as Colgate, Palmolive and Proctor and Gamble, could not always be sure which Colombian distributor or middle men had links to the traffickers. Nonetheless, the affect of the policy was felt by the traffickers and the Rebaja drugstore chain controlled by the Cali cartel now found itself threatened with the specter of having to shut down. (El Nuevo Herald and Miami Herald: 26 Jul 96) Over time the Clinton administration froze the assets and bank accounts of 76 foreign businesses serving as front groups for the Cali cartel. The neutralizing of various pharmaceutical companies effectively cut Colombia off from its supply of Alka Seltzer and up to 300,000 Colombian employees found their jobs in jeopardy. (El Nuevo Herald: 6 Nov 95 and Miami Herald: 23 Oct 95)

Citing governmental corruption, insufficiently severe prison terms for the traffickers, an inability to obtain the forfeiture of all criminally-acquired assets, allowing the traffickers to continue to manage their operations while in prison, a general inability to dismantle completely cartel operations and a lack of commitment to cooperate on counter-narcotics matters, the White House formally decertified Colombia in March of 1996. For Washington, "Colombia remained the world's leading producer and distributor of cocaine and a major supplier of heroin and marijuana." (INCSR 1996: xxv-xxvi)

Decertification and the publicity it generated were not only embarrassing but also placed in potential jeopardy some of Colombia's cherished commercial enterprises. The $400 million flower export industry for example stood to lose all tariff exemptions, forcing it to pay US customs' duties which would cost it its competitive position in the US market. The coffee industry was likewise threatened. Also at stake was some $13.7 million in direct bilateral aid and the risk that the US might work to cut Colombia off from international financial aid. (Miami Herald: 7 Mar 96) Adding insult to injury, Washington further castigated the Samper government by revoking the US visas for a series of key officials, including the President himself. The Colombian Congress reacted by requesting that the Samper administration solicit the recall of Ambassador Frechette. (El Nuevo Herald: 28 Mar 96)

The Colombian government now struggled with its new status and negative international image. While the DAS could apprehend 278 traffickers during a one month period and Bogota hoped to confiscate the one billion dollars in the form of 109 properties and businesses owned by the Rodriguez Orejuela brothers, Gilberto himself reached a plea bargaining accord with judicial authorities. By admitting to several counts of trafficking in Louisiana and Pennsylvania, he would now serve twelve years in prison with the possibility of a reduced sentence to eight years or less for good behavior. (El Nuevo Herald: 4, 8 and 11 Jun 96) The issue of his properties was not addressed.

The DEA was able to sustain its assistance to Colombia by concluding with the Ministry of Defense and the DAS another anti-drug accord. The government agreed to intensify its operations with a goal of destroying some 39,000 ha of coca (of an estimated 50,900 then estimated to be growing) and up to 20,000 ha of poppy crops. (El Nuevo Herald and Miami Herald: 4 Aug 96) Later that Fall the Colombian Senate Commission for Constitutional Affairs entertained the idea of a possible amendment to overturn Article 35 of the 1991 Constitution, prohibiting the extradition of Colombian nationals. (El Nuevo Herald: 23 Oct 96) The Commission's recommendation for the elimination of the no extradition clause had a number of qualifications which also had to be met. Excluded from the extradition process would be those traffickers already in prison and those who had turned themselves in to the government voluntarily. (El Nuevo Herald: 24 Oct 96) Using the threat of revealing photos, tapes and bank checks that could embarrass publicly officials within the Samper administration and Congress, the Cali cartel leaders had attempted to blackmail the government into allowing the most favorable conditions possible on their behalf. (Miami Herald: 22 Jun 95) When blackmail did not seem to work, the traffickers targeted with death the key members of Congress, such as Senator Claudia Blum, who had sponsored the initiative to renew the extradition process. (El Nuevo Herald: 6 Nov 96) At about the same time the Congress only agreed to approve Samper's request for enhanced penalties (30 years in prison and stiff fines) for narcotrafficking, provided that ten of its own members then serving time in prison for narco-linked illegal enrichment convictions would have their respective five year sentences reduced to three years. (El Nuevo Herald: 3 Oct 96)

Plea bargaining had worked out well for several brothers and members of the Medellin cartel. Brothers Jorge Luis, Juan David and Fabio Ochoa Vasquez were released from prison in mid-1996, having received reduced sentences of only five years, instead of 20 years, because of confessions made, corrective courses taken and good behavior. Without prejudice they could now enjoy the 150,000 acres of land and other properties owned by the Ochoa Vasquez family - all acquired during the heyday of the Medellin cartel. (El Nuevo Herald: 16 Jun 96) Responding to US criticism of the light sentences, the Colombian government now promulgated new and stronger drug trafficking penalties which increased jail sentences up to 30 years and fines of up to $7.3 million, along with the confiscation of all properties and fortunes. (El Nuevo Herald: 21 Jul 96) In addition, Bogota agreed to a new anti-drug cooperation pact with the US and the Congress entertained the possibility of a new extradition treaty with the US. (El Nuevo Herald: 12 Jul 96) Not withstanding the new pact, Samper, still smarting over the decision to revoke his US visa and the embarrassment it entailed, lashed out at the US calling on all Colombians to "close ranks" and unite against the US pressure. (El Nuevo Herald and Miami Herald: 13 Jul 96) Tensions between Bogota and Washington were now exacerbated significantly. Colombian labor unions and the press urged that Ambassador Frechette be thrown out of the country for interfering with Colombia's sovereignty. (Miami Herald: 21 Jul 96) That the Colombian House of Representatives voted to absolve Samper of any wrongdoing during the election process and censored Frechette hardly ameliorated the situation in the eyes of the Country Team. (Farrah 1996: 17; and El Nuevo Herald: 31 Oct 96)

Despite the rising tensions between the two countries, Bogota began a major anti-drug and eradication operation (Operation Conquest) in the Guaviare region. Declared a "war zone," police forces, supported by 38 helicopters, 12 fixed wing aircraft, and 9 T-65 Turbo Thrush fumigation/spray planes as well as Army troops, attacked laboratories and coca plantations in earnest. People living in the relatively remote Guaviare Department, long considered a cocaine production haven, now found their personal movements and vehicular traffick restricted. Controls were also placed on the sale of cement and all chemicals that could be used in the production of coca. Some 5,000 coca farmers, not knowing what might be the consequences of the government's operations fled the area. (El Nuevo Herald: 17 Jul 96) Still under US pressure, by September 1996 Bogota was even willing to experiment with a new herbicide (Imazapyr) against coca bushes. (Miami Herald: 12 Sep 96) With considerable pride the DAS could already point to some 24,000 ha of coca having been sprayed during 1995. (INCSR 1996: 83) As a further incentive, the US House International Relations Committee granted the Colombian government $107 million for the purchase of UH-60 Black Hawk helicopters and reconnaissance aircraft to assist in anti-narcotics operations in the future. (Miami Herald: 31 Aug 96; and El Nuevo Herald: 12 Oct 96) Toward the end of 1996, Colombian anti-drug police were able to carry out their first raids on a series of heroin laboratory production centers in the vicinity of the Choco Department. (Miami Herald: 11 Oct 96)

In Caqueta during September 1994 government forces, accompanied by US Ambassador Myles Frechette, raided a laboratory complex defended by the FARC guerrillas. The complex, capable of processing 10 tons of cocaine HCl per month, was considered to be on a par with the Tranquilandia complex captured in 1984. (El Nuevo Herald: 24 Sep 94) Frechette's personal interest in Colombia's anti-drug operations helped foment a reappraisal of the coca eradication effort. Rather than attempting to coerce coca farmers to stop producing their relatively high value crops, the government was now willing to take a "carrot and stick" approach. Over a period of about a year, beginning in October 1994, $150 million had been designated for alternate development crops as a substitution for coca. (ANALDEX 1995: 2) The idea was to maintain a similar standard of living and income (the carrot) to that provided by coca. Failure to switch to the alternate crop(s) meant the farmer would most likely be liable to criminal charges (the stick) and lose not only his coca crop but also his land and all that had been involved in the production effort. As a backdrop to this strategy, the Colombian and US governments were facing the stark reality that there had taken place an overall 13 percent increase in coca, marijuana and poppy crop production throughout Colombia. With coca being farmed at the rate of three crops a year or about one complete crop every one-hundred days, the government calculated that each hectare's production of 2.2 kilos of coca paste was enabling the traffickers to obtain about 250 tons per year. (ANALDEX 1995: 1 and 14) It was not without reason that the ONDCP had concluded that Colombia was for the first time in decades now leading Bolivia (but second to Peru) as a top producer of coca. (INCSR 1996: 81) The crop substitution plan appeared to have considerable merit, but the key question was how this would resonate with the coca farmers themselves.

In terms of its eradication program, the Samper administration in 1994 and 1995 found itself confronted by some 20,000 irate, protesting campesino coca farmers, supported by armed FARC guerrillas in the area of San Jose de Guaviare. The issue revolved around the government's eradication effort based on aerial fumigation using glyphosate chemicals. The situation became tense and saw the chief of the anti-narcotics police in nearby Miraflores surrounded for a few days by supporting FARC guerrillas whose own small arms fire forced two police helicopters to the ground. The FARC was merely delivering on its security contracts with the various farmers to protect them against government intrusion. In return for its involvement in narcotrafficking in Guaviare Department, the FARC was now thought by Colombian authorities to be receiving as much as $4.8 million in profits. Easily prompted by both the guerrillas and the traffickers to protect their mutual interests, the peasant-farmer coca protest did have some impact as the national government in Bogota dispatched a commissioner and negotiating team to Guaviare to discuss the fumigation problem. In this way the Samper administration hoped to head off a more militant confrontation and possible civil war. Under pressure, the government commission agreed to allow up to three hectares (about 6.5 acres) to be planted by an individual farmer without fear of fumigation. This agreement did bring forth considerable criticism from Attorney General Valdivieso, the cousin of the slain presidential candidate Luis Carlos Galan. He pointed out that the coca growers could now divide their large plots and holdings into smaller ones and carry on much as before. In short, the government's efforts had ended up neutralizing the intent of the anti-coca fumigation campaign. (El Nuevo Herald: 18 Dec 94)

The coca farmers, still incensed that the government was trying to work around the situation and continue to use glyphosate on the larger coca crops, and at the urging of the traffickers, extended their demonstrations into the Putumayo Department along the Ecuadoran frontier. Here, with some support from the FARC guerrillas, they temporarily blocked roads leading into the villages of Orito, Hormiga and San Miguel. In addition, the Trans-Andean oil pipeline pumping systems were attacked and damaged enough so that the government reported a loss of $2.5 million in revenues due to lost production. The government, through its National Council for Economic and Social Policy (CONPES), now attempted to negotiate a fully funded crop substitution deal with the farmers, swapping their coca crops for other more traditional crops (citrus etc.). (El Nuevo Herald: 3 Jan 95 and Miami Herald: 7 Jan 95) Nonetheless, the farmers remained adamantly in favor of coca in the face of the government's inducements to switch. (Tokatlian: 1995; and INCSR 1996: 82) The apparent haplessness of the government in the face of the traffickers and the farmers caused US Senator John Kerry to call Colombia a "narcodemocracy." (El Nuevo Herald: 19 Dec 94)

In partial response to the US criticisms, the Samper administration announced in Bogota that an effort would be made to eliminate the entire poppy and coca crop over a two year period. The announced plan, called Operation Splendor, was to demonstrate the government's commitment to fighting the traffickers. Despite coca farmer protests to the contrary, the Ministry of the Interior under Horacio Serpa refused to back down. The US responded with support in the form of twelve additional fumigation airplanes, helicopters and glyphosate herbicide. Coca leaf production was now estimated to be about 50,000 ha (over 100,000 acres), or about on a par with Bolivia. Beginning in mid-1994, the anti-drug police, using three airplanes to spray glyphosate, had destroyed about 5,000 ha of coca. (Miami Herald: 7 Jan 95; El Nuevo Herald: 10 Jun 95) This operation and the implications it held for the future had actually touched off the coca farmers' backlash in southern

Colombia. Continuing to execute Operation Splendor throughout 1995 and into 1996 meant that the government was now backing off its agreement with the farmers to allow up to 3 ha of coca to be grown in small plots.

Feeling pressured by the government's coca eradication and crop substitution program in the Putumayo Department in 1996, coca farmers once again began to demonstrate. Undaunted, the Colombian anti-drug forces began to carry out project "Plante," a $45 million campaign effort to eliminate the coca bush plantations growing along the Ecuadoran frontier. (El Nuevo Herald: 5 Jan 96) Having eradicated some 24,000 ha of coca throughout Colombia during 1995, there was considerable confidence that all would go well again. (INCSR 1996: 83) The initial indications of anti-drug success could be seen in some of the smaller towns in the region.

La Hormiga, a small tropical town near the Putumayo River saw the bottom fall out of its coca market and the 120 prostitutes that served the town's some 6,000 inhabitants were with little or no work. The eradication impact was only temporary as trafficker networks were reconstituted under new directors. The coca production business there resumed much as usual. In this part of Colombia a coca leaf picker could earn $15 per day and one kilo of coca paste was selling for $1,000, earning a $200 profit for the farmer or crude paste laboratory producer. Economic realities meant that, while coca farmers might prefer to grow corn, yuca or potatoes, the prohibitively high costs of farm-to-market transportation for their more traditional crops negated any possibility of making a profit. Coca and its paste derivatives dominated an otherwise unworkable market. With traffickers purchasing the coca paste with a door-to-door pickup service, a coca farmer with several hectares or more of coca plants could make a small fortune compared to the small-plot farmers growing traditional crops in other parts of Colombia. (El Nuevo Herald: 25 Mar 96)

As the government's eradication effort spread to other departments in southern Colombia, the farmers, in conjunction with the FARC guerrillas, began to organize to try and stop the glifosate fumigation and spraying of their coca crops. To support the coca eradication goal of 30,000 ha for 1996, the Colombian government deployed large numbers of Army troops to the region under the command of General Herold Bedoya Pizarro. Bedoya's troops now found themselves confronting some 20,000 irate coca farmers in the Guaviare Department. Despite the demonstrations, Interior Minister Serpa stood firm, stating that the eradication policy was not negotiable, although land titling and financing for alternate crops could be. (El Nuevo Herald: 23-24 Jul 96)

By late Summer 1996 the situation began to resemble a civil war as the Putumayo Department became convulsed and the demonstrations became ever more violent. The Army's 4th Brigade of several thousand men was hard pressed to restore order and casualties in the form of dead and wounded in the vicinity of Puerto Asis mounted. Now feeling the pressure, Serpa announced the government's intention to enter into a dialogue with the farmers in an effort to reach an accord. Health, rural electrification, human rights and agrarian reform were all issues that the government was willing to discuss. Stopping eradication and the legalization of coca were out of the question as far as Serpa was concerned. (El Nuevo Herald: 4 Aug 96)

As the negotiations took place, Serpa offered to pay $30 a day to any campesino who would be willing to pull up coca bushes. About $17 million had been allocated by Bogota for this purpose alone as part of the $300 million authorized Operation Splendor's eradication and crop substitution effort. (El Nuevo Herald: 6-7 Aug 96) In time the government was forced to admit that there was no viable marketing infrastructure which could support an alternate crop program on any large scale in this part of Colombia. Indeed, the remote areas of southern and eastern Colombia had received little or no government support in terms of roads and markets. Health, education and road communications were sorely lacking. This complicated the situation and played into the hands of the FARC guerrillas who could point to Bogota's deficiencies and corruption as evidence and a razon d'etre or just cause for the coca farmers to support the formers' revolutionary war effort against the government. (Semana: 5 Mar 96 and El Nuevo Herald: 7 Aug 96)

As the government remained intransigent in its position that coca farmers would have to first eradicate their entire coca crop before being allowed to begin the crop substitution process (also the US Country Team position), prolonged and violent demonstrations ensued. In part this was due to the government's failure to provide the previously promised crop substitution payments and land titles rapidly enough. Demonstrations escalated to the point where some 75,000 farmers attempted to march on Florencia, the capital of Caqueta Department. (El Nuevo Herald: 18 Aug 96 and El Tiempo: 15 Jan 96) The impact of the demonstrations reverberated throughout Colombia and, while crop eradication and substitution appeared to be at a standstill, the farmers were now able to get the government to promise credits, land, and a price payment system which was supposed to be equal to that of coca.

(El Nuevo Herald: 14 Aug 96) Later, after further promising to allocate $14 million for education, health and various public works projects, the government's negotiators were able to achieve a partial settlement towards the eradication of coca and the introduction of a crop substitution program. In addition, the government offered to pay $2,300 for each eradicated hectare of coca and a further subsidy of about $1,800 to enable the coca farmer to survive throughout the next growing season or until the substitute crop(s) would be available for marketing. (El Nuevo Herald: 13 Sep 96) On this basis the issue appeared to rest. Whether the government could really deliver on its promises remained very much in question.

The government's anti-drug efforts throughout rural Colombia were further complicated by the guerrilla war which was well into its fourth decade. The alliance between the FARC, ELN and EPL meant that the guerrillas could field a combined force of some 17,000 fighters against Bogota's army of about 120,000 men. (Miami Herald: 19 May 95) Being a revolutionary was a lucrative business and guerrilla earnings were reported at an estimated $2 million per day, obtained through narcotrafficking, kidnapping and extortion, or a total of around $720 million per year. (El Nuevo Herald: 6 Nov 96) This was not a new phenomenon as in 1994 reported earnings were: FARC $336 million, ELN $240 million, and the ELP $36 million. In general the guerrillas were earning more than the National Coffee Foundation's $460 million for the same year. (El Nuevo Herald: 19 Jul 95) Captured documents also showed that the FARC, as part of its protection fee extortion racket, charged coca farmers $11 per month to "protect" each hectare of coca bushes and $5 as a tax for each kilo of coca paste produced. Traffickers were charged $11,000 weekly for each laboratory being protected and $15,000 for each flight from a clandestine airfield. To this end, narco-guerrilla linkages had been established in about half of Colombia's departments. (El Nuevo Herald: 8 and 25 Nov 95 and 7 Feb 96) In addition to this, counter-drug operations conducted by the Army in the Caqueta Department discovered that the FARC was producing acetone for use in its own coca-cocaine refining laboratories which brought in further profits. (El Nuevo Herald: 26 Nov 96)

This infusion of funds now enabled the FARC to obtain weapons on the international market and to operate in over 500 municipalities throughout Colombia in which some 130 mayors were known to be paying war taxes to the guerrillas' cause in order to survive. (El Espectador: 25 Nov 95 and El Nuevo Herald: 6 Nov 96) The expansion of the FARC's influence was actually several times that of the 1980's.

(El Nuevo Siglo: 25 Nov 95) In 1995 alone seven mayors were assassinated and 500 others were threatened with death if they did not cooperate and pay the guerrillas' taxes. This meant that at least half of Colombia's key municipal officials were under continuous threat. (El Nuevo Herald: 12 Jun 96) The guerrillas were now strong enough to attempt to directly contest the government for control of its territory in such regions as the Uruba banana region of the Antioquia Department. (El Tiempo: 21 and 23 Sep 95) The ensuing violence involving over 600 deaths and some 20,000 displaced persons over a peroid of a few months caused fruit companies such as DOLE (which handled 65 percent of Colombia's fruit export crops) to suspend operations. (El Tiempo: 25 Sep 95 and El Nuevo Herald: 25 Sep 95)

Pacing the guerrilla operations in Colombia were a series of 27 attacks against urban areas during the Summer and early Fall of 1995. (El Espectador: 15 Oct 95) With guerrilla violence escalating and the country facing still another year of some 30,000 homicides and 700 kidnappings, President Samper declared a state of emergency. (El Nuevo Siglo: 16 Dec 95 and El Nuevo Herald: 17 Aug 95) A distraught Colombian press argued that there was no effective government counter-insurgency strategy in play to deal with the situation. (El Tiempo: 26 Nov 95)

The guerrillas appreciated full well that a successful government crop eradication and substitution campaign would seriously undermine their financial earnings from the coca growing regions, as well as trafficking in general. It would also enable the government to assert its control over more and more of the population and Colombian territory, thus reducing a source of potential recruits and the always protective maneuver space needed to provide security for the guerrilla forces. During a two-month period (Operation Conquest) anti-drug police and supporting Army forces still destroyed 64 cocaine laboratories and 1,600 ha of coca plants in the face of guerrilla counter-measures. (El Nuevo Herald : 11 Jul 96)

To exploit the coca farmer's determined and high-spirited demonstrations and marches against the government's anti-drug effort in the southern part of Colombia, the FARC and ELN opened a series of violent offensives aimed at inhibiting or blocking the coca eradication operations. Their purpose, in part, was to distract the armed forces away from the coca growing regions. Beginning in the Summer and continuing on into the Fall of 1996 the guerrillas attacked 26 distinct urban locations in 13 of the nation's 32 departments. (El Nuevo Herald: 2 Sep 96) Reported as the most intensive series of guerrilla operations in 32 years, the guerrillas challenged the government's presence in the coca growing departments of Meta, Tolima, Cauca, Valle, Santander, Sucre, Magdalena, Cundinamarca, Cesar, Huila, Arauca, Putmayo and Caldes. (El Nuevo Herald: 1 Sep 96 and Miami Herald: 2 Sep 96) Sometimes operating with units of up to two-hundred men, the FARC blew up bridges, trains, trucks, petroleum pumping stations, oil pipelines, Army and police outposts and ambushed an Army troop convoy. (El Nuevo Herald: 1, 5-6 Sep 96 and Miami Herald: 25 Jul and 2, 9-10 Sep 96) The guerrillas effectively blocked for a period of weeks about half of the country's main roads and highways, displacing some 750,000 people. The ELN followed the FARC's lead and conducted operations in eight departments (Cesar, Tolima, Bolivar, Antioquia, Santander, Norte de Santander and Valle), intercepting and burning trucks, bombing oil pipe-lines, banks and electrical pylons and shooting up Army and police outposts. (El Nuevo Herald: 21 and 23 Sep 96) Attacks on the Cano Limon-Covenas pipe-line alone were now costing the government over $1 billion a year. (El Nuevo Herald: 25 May 95) The Ministry of Defense in Bogota acknowledged that the guerrillas had inflicted serious blows against the government. (El Nuevo Herald: 3 Sep 96) This was despite the Army having, with US aid, created 44 new infantry battalions (25,000 men) to deal with the civil war. (El Nuevo Herald: 4 Oct 96) Under considerable pressure to respond to the intensified threat, President Samper announced that he would have to impose his own form of war tax on the wealthy (about 370,000 people or about 1 percent of the population) in order to collect $500 million needed to equip and support the Army's counter-insurgency operations in the field. (El Nuevo Herald: 6 Nov 96) The Army was all too frequently finding itself outgunned and outmaneuvered by the agile guerrillas. With the vast expanse of Colombia's mountains and savanna lowlands being too much for the 32-helicopter airmobile squadron to cover, the Colombian government began to purchase additional helicopters from as far away as Russia in an effort to alleviate the problem. (El Espectador: 14 Mar 96) In short, the guerrillas had demonstrated their power throughout the length and breadth of Colombia. Not helping the government was the critical report by Gustavo Gallon, President of the Commission of Andean Jurists, who, after visiting the coca growing regions to the south, denounced the government for committing human rights violations, burning down campesino homes and arbitrarily detaining local citizens without cause. (El Nuevo Herald: 7 Aug 96)

The surprise, nation-wide guerrilla attacks did catch the attention of Washington. To assist Colombia against both the guerrillas and the traffickers, the US government sold the Colombian military twelve additional armed UH-60 Blackhawk helicopters. (El Nuevo Herald: 11 Oct 96) The now open willingness of Washington to allow the Colombian military to use US equipment to fight guerrillas, as well as narcotraffickers, was a tacit acknowledgement by Washington that the insurgency was now recognized as a major complicating factor in the success of the drug war. That adverse socio-economic conditions throughout much of Colombia were exacerbating the problem of trying to deal with both the traffickers and the guerrillas were now more than ever appreciated by the Samper government.

President Samper, smarting from the negative US comments about his administration, had sent in late 1994 both his foreign minister and minister of defense to Washington to persuade the Clinton administration that his policies were in fact in lockstep with the interests of the US. At stake was $29 million in badly needed anti-drug monies which could be withdrawn if suitable certification was not forthcoming from the White House. (El Nuevo Herald: 4 Feb 95) At the same time, in order to deal with some of the socioeconomic problems facing the country, Samper announced plans to invest up to $82 million in social development and badly needed infrastructure. The financing for this was to come from the Colombian oil fields which had produced over $900 million in revenues in 1994 alone. The Cusiana oil fields, located about 135 miles northeast of Bogota, were expected to triple Colombia's oil experts to about $3 billion or far better than the up to $2 billion produced by coffee. According to the government's plan, over a four year period about $1.8 billion was to be invested in the development of potable water systems for 8.5 million persons who still lacked this basic service. Nonetheless, the Comptroller General in Bogota was reporting that over $20 million in government funding had been embezelled by a reported 1,244 government officials, including ambassadors, tax collectors and municipal treasurers. (El Nuevo Herald: 8 Feb 95 and Miami Herald: 10 Apr 95) This noted lack of civic consciousness and fiscal responsibility on the part of the government officials was nothing new, but did not bode well for the reforms that Samper had in mind.

Narco-linked corruption was very prevalent throughout the government's highest levels. Indicative of this were the accusations delivered by the Attorney General's office against the former Chief of the National Police, General Jose Guillermo Medina, for illegal enrichment. In just two years (1986-1987) Medina was able to amass a small fortune of $250,000 on a salary of about $1,000 per month. (El Nuevo Herald: 13 Apr 94) In 1996 the Supreme Court (Corte Suprema de Justicia) found the general guilty of linkages to the Medellin Cartel and an unexplained fortune of some $400,000. Fined $200,000, Medina was sentenced to 52 months in prison. (El Nuevo Herald: 19 Jul 96) Documents captured as part of the Samper directed crackdown on the Cali cartel indicated that some 2,800 persons were being paid off or otherwise bribed by this cartel alone, costing the traffickers a still very affordable $3.7 million per year. (El Nuevo Herald: 24 Jul 95) Other sources indicated bribery spending as high as $100 million annually. (Lee 1996b: 207) Corruption had indeed also reached the 160-person House of Representatives which found over time that its own 15-member Committee of Accusations had twelve of its own under investigation for criminal activities involving narcotrafficking of one sort or another. (Miami Herald: 12 Apr 96) At this same time twenty other congressmen were facing charges of having accepted drug monies. When 56 of 102 Senators attempted to pass a bill to quash the up to two-dozen drug related investigations against their fellow legislators, it was only in the face of public outcries and media denunciations that the full Congress eventually quashed the bill. (Miami Herald: 6 Feb 96)

Apart from these events, the Colombian media, a year into the Samper administration, was reporting that the Senate was providing millions of dollars to individuals and friends who otherwise were not performing a function on behalf of the government. (El Espectador: 28 Aug 95) Corruption also affected the Attorney General's offices. Acting Attorney General Luis Eduardo Montoya was arrested for illegal enrichment and links to the traffickers. Montoya had previously replaced former Attorney General Orlando Vasquez, himself accused of linkages to the traffickers. Both Montoya and Vasquez falsely charged the government's General Prosecutor, Alfonso Valdivieso, with links to the traffickers in a vindictive effort to oust him from the government. (El Nuevo Herald and Miami Herald: 8 Jun 96) Even such icons as former Attorney General Gustavo de Greiff were not immune from investigation and, while serving as Colombia's ambassador to Mexico, de Greiff was linked to the Cali cartel's Gilberto Rodriguez Orejuela through being a co-owner of the El Dorado Airline in 1980. (El Espectador: 28 Aug 95)

Other examples illustrate the ubiquitous nature of the narco-linked corruption in Colombian politics. Samper's election opponent, Andres Pastrana, eventually found that his own campaign organizer, Beda Malca, was linked to a money laundering scheme involving the mysterious Bogota branch of the Miami based Bank Atlantic. (El Nuevo Herald: 16 May 96) Previous to this, eleven members of the national telephone company were arrested, convicted and sent to prison for intercepting and passing on government and armed forces' communications to the Cali cartel. Further evidence of trafficker payoffs implicated most of the Cali airport police, employees of the El Valle telephone system, 6 of 22 Cali city councilors and the mayors of four of Colombia's major cities, including Medellin. (Nuevo Herald: 26 Oct 95 and Lee 1995: 208-209)

The trafficker's influence was pernicious, extending even into the religious community. Similar to the Italian Mafia or gangsters in the US, the Colombian groups maintained their Church connections. Dozens of churches owed their beautiful architecture, opulent interiors and well-kept gardens to the large and ever frequent donations made by the cartels. Contaminated by narco-dollars, Church critics of the Samper administration found their now tarnished images as an obstacle, muting any form of moral condemnation of the traffickers or those accepting financial gifts and bribes. (Miami Herald: 6 May 96) Narco-influence was also infamous in terms of the national prison system. Traffickers were almost without exception able to corrupt prison officials to unprecedented degrees. In one instance prisoners, serving sentences at La Picota prison for murdering Justice Minister Rodrigo Lara Bonilla, were found to be spending weekends partying at local discos. (Miami Herald: 11 Oct 94) In another, Jose Santa Cruz Londono walked through three key control points and out of the La Picota prison posing as a government anti-drug prosecutor. (Miami Herald: 12 Jan 96) At the maximum security Modelo prison the Cali cartel leaders hosted parties with fashion models, whiskey and music, while otherwise continuing to conduct their nefarious business activities. (Miami Herald: 31 Oct 96)

Colombia's traditional contraband operations continued apace throughout this time and the Minister of Defense announced in the mid-1990s that he would need help to deal with the estimated $3.5 billion in untaxed merchandise which was passing back and forth over the Colombian frontiers. The World Bank estimated Colombian contraband as accounting for about $5.5 billion. Whether one agreed or not with the specific amounts, the respected economist and co-director of the Banco de la Republica, Salomon Kalmanovitz, estimated that the levels contraband were about double of those recorded for 1994. (El Espectador: 26 Nov 95 and El Nuevo Herald: 23 May 95)

The Colombian government's attack on the Cali cartel leadership did inhibit this group's operations, but also revealed the resiliency of the traffickers in general. The intensified counter-drug operations against the Cali group discovered that the traffickers were using state of the art equipment to defy the government's efforts to suppress them. Satellite-linked communications systems with voice scrambler devices to confound police intercept monitors, voice distortion microphones and even signal intercept/monitoring systems to eavesdrop on government and competing trafficker communications were captured. Vast complexes of holding companies and proxy ownerships, such as those belonging to the children of Cali cartel members were also discovered. Trafficker infiltration was so ubiquitous that even most of the private security guard companies in Cali were found to be owned by the cartel and provided a form of citywide trafficker intelligence network in which local police movements could be reported by radio. Nine companies were eventually found to be compromised in this fashion and, accordingly, lost their licenses. (Miami Herald: 12 Apr 95)

The Cali cartel for years had founded phantom firms which were then used to funnel funds in the form of payoffs to politicians. Using bribes, not bullets, as their modus operandi, the cartel had attempted to penetrate the Congress, police, airlines companies and even the office of the president. Government investigations indicated that about $7 million were paid out from March through June 1994 alone through a series of dummy coffee ventures and companies. That major banks allowed the phantom companies to overdraw their accounts by large amounts brought further suspicion on the banking industries involved. (El Nuevo Herald: 14 May 95 and Lee 1996: 208) The Colombian public more or less accepted the Cali group despite Samper's declarations that the government was attacking the narco-kingpins and the traffickers' financial infrastructure, communications, transportation and logistical support systems. (El Nuevo Herald and Miami Herald: 18 May 1995) Albeit the US government was impressed by the Samper administration's efforts to confront the Cali traffickers, a more somber note was registered by other US and Colombian officials.

Despite the principal Cali cartel leadership being dead or in jail, some 40 smaller trafficking groups affiliated with the cartel continued to operate the business. In short, the remnants of the cartel reorganized, formed new linkages and consolidated their respective networks, continuing to manufacture and distribute cocaine, heroin and even marijuana to markets in Europe, Africa, the Middle East, Asia and the Americas. (El Nuevo Herald: 25 Nov 95 and 11 Jan 96) Over a short period of time Colombia's DAS was reporting the formation of 15 other mini-cartels or organizations of varying sizes throughout Colombia which were now competing for and taking up the market slack from the somewhat fragmented Cali organization. Even elements of the former

Medellin cartel were reported by the Ministry of Defense as having reconstituted themselves to engage once again in trafficking operations. (El Nuevo Herald: 21 Jun 95, 3 Sep and 3 Dec 96)

The disruption of the Cali cartel did have some fallout in the form of small, but vicious drug wars between the surviving and new, would-be heads of the Cali group and others in the surrounding departments (such as the North Valley cartel). The North Valley group sent their sicarios to attack the Cali traffickers. Despite years of apparent cooperation, basic commercial rivalries and the greed for profits (an estimated $4 billion to $7 billion annually) and market share were driving forces in Colombia's always dangerous and highly contentious drug-trafficking world. (El Nuevo Herald: 21 Jun and 31 Jul 95 and 23 and 27 May 96 and Lee 1996: 207) To this end there were indications that the Cali group, with the aid of modern communications and the computer revolution, had decentralized its operations and was tending to operate more and more from Miami. This included the supply and distribution of cocaine and heroin via New York, Chicago and Texas, using a cellular system of contacts. While one cell coordinated regional smuggling operations, another rented the cellular telephone systems in use and still another was responsible for the secret storage and stashing of cocaine etc. DEA officials estimated that the Cali cartel's operations were actually earning upwards of $8 billion a year. Exploiting the technology boom, commercial demand markets and the technical training of its personnel in the US and Europe, the cartel was operating in true transnational form. (El Nuevo Herald: 4 Jan 96 and Miami Herald: 2 Mar 96)

Testifying before a US Senate committee, former US General Barry McCaffrey, now Director of the ONDCP, admitted that despite the elimination of Cali's narco-kingpins, some 840 tons of cocaine were still being produced and transshipped world-wide to meet the international demand. (El Nuevo Herald: 15 May 96) Of this amount around 334 tons of cocaine were estimated as flowing through the Caribbean alone. (El Nuevo Herald: 24 Sep 96) This possibly reflected in part the ability of the Rodriguez Orejuela brothers who, despite fines of $105 million, still were able to coordinate their trafficking activities from their respective Colombian prison cells. (El Nuevo Herald: 21 Sep 96) When all else appeared to fail, other cartel family members could always be relied upon to continue the cartel's operations. (Schrieberg 1996: 24 and El Nuevo Herald: 30 Oct 96)

The Colombian traffickers proved themselves to be determined adversaries of the Washington-Bogota anti-drug alliance, leaving no stone unturned in their often ingenious and incessant efforts to produce and transship their illegal products to the international market. Venezuela, for example, continued to be a major route in this effort and some 15 tons or more of cocaine moved by boat and air through the Orinoco River's 150 tributaries and 3,000 channels to the Atlantic Ocean. On the backhaul arms and other contraband were brought back into Colombia. The primitive Warao Indians living in the Orinoco region served as the traffickers' guides for this effort. (El Nuevo Herald: 14 May and 30 Sep 96 and Miami Herald: 15 Jul 96) Documents captured by Colombia's DAS indicated that the Cali cartel alone was annually able to funnel some 210 mt of cocaine through Venezuela and on to forwarding points in Honduras, Guatemala and Mexico before making the transit into the US. (El Nuevo Herald: 11 Jun 95 and INCSR 1996: 110) Facilitating the Venezuelan drug trade were the efforts of the likes of General Guillen Davila, Chief of the Venezuelan National Guard, who was formally charged by the US Federal Court in Miami with expediting the smuggling of up to 22 mts of cocaine into the US. As a top counter-narcotics chief, Davila exploited his Caracas based CIA contacts to foster the drug trade. (El Nuevo Herald: 23 Nov 96) In the Sierra de Perija region of western Venezuela, gum opium poppies were also reported to now be growing with some 1,660 targeted for destruction by government authorities (INCSR 1996: 113)

The arrest of the leading Cali narco-kingpins, in conjunction with successful radar guided intercept operations of trafficker aircraft coming out of Peru, did cause the prices of coca leaf to plummet about two-thirds in Peru and Bolivia. (Miami Herald: 2 Mar 96) Nonetheless, when the Peruvian trafficker, Demetrio Chavez Penaherrera was jailed by government authorities for having collaborated with the Sendero Luminoso guerrillas, he was merely replaced by Abelardo Cachique Rivera who transhipped some 4,000 kilos of cocaine and paste per month into Colombia. Cachique's eventual capture, in turn, caused others, lured by the immense profits to be had, to replace him. (El Nuevo Herald: 12 Jan and 21 Jul 96) Other lesser but otherwise competent traffickers such as Diego Leon Montoya Sanchez (coordinating the Mexico-US smuggling routes) and Arcangel de Jesus Henao (running Bolivian and Peruvian coca paste shipments) kept the system functioning and the cocaine flowing. (Miami Herald: 2 Mar 96) Transportation expenses and bribes generally cost the traffickers about $2,000 per kilo transshipped, but this was offset by the wholesale profits such as those in Miami where a kilogram (2.2 pounds) of cocaine brought in $17,000 (in Europe the price oscillated between $40,000 and $90,000 per kilogram), and the same amount of heroin $100,000. With drug couriers able to carry up to several pounds of heroin on their bodies (about $150,000 in market value) the system appeared to be worth the risks of capture, as many were. McCaffrey noted that in the early 1990s Colombia had produced virtually no heroin but was now producing in the range of 65 tons a year! (ANALIDE 1995; 15 El Nuevo Herald: 4 Sep 96 and Miami Herald: 8 Sep 96)

Inhibiting the interdiction effort was the report by customs officials in Miami that they were able to inspect "only a small fraction" of the 400,000 or so of twenty-foot containers moving through that port on an annual basis. (Miami Herald: 8 Sep 96) Among the many techniques used, drug smugglers also hid cocaine in concrete corner stones and construction material. (Miami Herald: 11 Aug 96) Sometimes successful and sometimes not, the traffickers often faced major losses such as the 11 mt cocaine shipment captured in a boat along the Pacific Ocean coast by a joint Colombia, Ecuador and US anti-drug police effort. (El Nuevo Herald: 24 Oct 96) This, however, did not daunt the traffickers who continued their operations apace.

Trafficker money laundering remained a major problem for the US anti-drug policy. In June 1996 it was revealed that the Bank Atlantic of Miami was maintaining 1,100 secret, unregistered accounts through which $5 million flowed each month. Bank personnel then redirected the money back to their Bogota branch where it was further dispersed to other outlets. (El Nuevo Herald and Miami Herald: 6 Jun 96) Other favored laundering sites included Sao Paulo and Rio de Janeiro, Brazil. It was in this manner that the Cali cartel was able to amass a fortune over a ten-year period, which captured documents indicated was upwards of $10 billion. The money was generally then invested in dozens of business ventures involving furniture, construction, transportation, pharmaceutical laboratories, farming and cattle ranching, money exchange houses and other enterprises. (El Nuevo Herald: 21 Jun and 21 Oct 96) In the Cali area alone narco-dollars constructed a reported 7,841 homes and other buildings as part of a $1.6 billion investment effort. (El Tiempo: 30 Oct 95) Cartel family members ran the supermarket chains, discount drug stores and retail outlets. (Schrieberg 1996: 24) Nonetheless, the Colombian media reported a 25 percent decrease in marketing sales in Cali as one by one the cartel kingpins were captured. (El Tiempo: 19 Nov 95)

Because of the pervasive economic influence of the traffickers, Colombian Army commander Harold Bedoya thought that "a third of

Colombia" was most probably in their hands. (El Nuevo Herald: 2 Sep 96) The Colombian Agricultural Society (Sociedad de Agricultores de Colombia - SAC) reported that some 42 percent or about 4 million ha of the most productive farmland in 13 of 32 departments was now owned by the traffickers as part of their money laundering schemes. (El Nuevo Herald: 1 Dec 1996) It was estimated that trafficking was generating two times the export earnings of the coffee crop or all other contraband and smuggling operations combined. (El Tiempo: 30 Oct 95 and El Nuevo Herald: 11 Jun 95) The US government found itself frustrated by the fact that, despite the principal narco-kingpins being in jail or even dead, their possessions such as the several hundred ranches and properties of Jose Santa Cruz Londono, estimated at a value of over a billion dollars, would revert to their respective wives and children. Of some 994 ranches and farm properties seized by the Colombian government from the traffickers, 566 reverted back to their families for lack of evidence that the properties had been obtained illegally. (El Nuevo Herald: 11 Aug 95 and Miami Herald: 7 Mar 96)

Echoing the Colombian government's own position since the Cartagena conferences of the early 1990s, the then US Southern Command's Commander-in-Chief, General Barry R. McCaffrey, testified to a US Congressional committee on the issue of the validity of the US source-country focus in the drug war. Speaking to the Senate Armed Forces Committee, General McCaffrey commented that the vast arsenal of the drug war was still accomplishing little in the face of a strong appetite for drugs on the streets of the US. "As long as there is a national demand, someone will find a way to satisfy it." (El Nuevo Herald: 17 Feb 1995) President Samper stated the situation in other terms during a commentary made to CNN during a September 1996 trip to the US: "In Colombia there isn't a Colombian who is either indirectly or directly involved with narcotrafficking." (El Nuevo Herald: 3 Oct 96)

# Chapter 8

## Observations And Conclusions

From its onset, the US anti-drug policy in Colombia has faced a series of challenges in the form of countervailing socioeconomic and political factors. Some of them it was able to overcome to some degree, but others have remained to plague it even today. The socioeconomic setting in which narcotrafficking flourished in Colombia could not have been better from the point of view of the traffickers. The relatively skewed economy and levels of income in the face of an elite sector attempting to protect a status quo in its favor and the general impoverishment of the rural sector meant that a ready supply of poor, peasant, *campesino* labor would always be available to the traffickers. This socioeconomic factor, when combined with the entrepreneurial prowess of the traffickers themselves, their propensity to use violence as it suited their needs, Colombia's highly creative contraband-smuggling tradition and huge black market, a weak state which has lost control over much of its territory and a general social condition of corruption and debased values whereby people tend to flaunt the law of the land whenever convenient, has produced conditions which have sustained the traffickers' efforts throughout the years. Professor Francisco Thoumi perceived the situation in Colombia as offering the traffickers the "best package of incentives for the development of the industry." (El Nuevo Herald: 11 Jun 95)

As pointed out in this case study, the risks to the traffickers in Colombia were initially rather minimal at the beginning of the 1980s.

This condition tended to ameliorate the impact of the fledgling US anti-drug policy, which for all intents and purposes had little or no serious impact on Colombian drug trafficking. As time went on, however, the risks became ever more greater for the traffickers, forcing them to modify their operations accordingly. The Colombian traffickers displayed considerable versatility and sensitivity to market demand signals by shifting to heroin as an adjunct product to be exploited on the international drug scene. Since trafficking in cocaine was merely a profit seeking business for most, it was also perfectly logical to traffick in heroin where the profits were potentially several times higher still. With experienced black market smuggling systems already in place, the traffickers mixed loads of heroin and cocaine together as they made use of all possible transshipment modes and techniques, including sea planes and submarines, to bring their products to market via the Caribbean and Central American/Mexican access routes into the US. Over time, domestic coca production became a significant factor in Colombia as it competed with and then surpassed Bolivia in this role, while the traffickers continued to receive coca paste/cocaine shipments from Peru and Bolivia to the south.

Complicating the situation for the government in its attempts to deal with coca and gum opium poppy farming was the ubiquitous presence of the various guerrilla groups which intimidated both coca and poppy growers, traffickers and government law enforcement personnel alike. Thus, the initially limited coca cultivation that did take place did so on a protected basis, continuing to gradually expand over the years through the thousands of mom-pop coca-paste production enterprises which in their way served to replace any coca paste lost at larger laboratory sites and enabled independent cocaine producers to compete and gain experience without antagonizing the major cartel groups. This contrasted to marijuana production which from the beginning confronted significant government counter-measures which suppressed much of its activity through the use of herbicides and thus became a modest success for the US anti-drug policy, although it too began to make a steady come back in the mid-1990s.

Offsetting the anti-drug policy's apparent counter-marijuana success was the Colombian military's negative experience during the early 1980s with the corrupting influence of the traffickers' bribes which badly tarnished the former's image. Out of this experience the Colombian Army tended to maintain an ambivalent attitude towards the traffickers and preferred to focus on the guerrilla-insurgency threats to national security as its leading priority. Only under the pressure of extremely high levels of trafficker violence did this reluctant attitude change and the willing participation of the military in the drug-wars became intermittantly more forthcoming. The guerrillas have had a vested interest in the maintenance of the trafficking activities within Colombia. With the intellectual appearance of a just cause now lacking due to the impact of the political and human rights reforms of the 1991 Constitution, the guerrillas have been thrown back onto their own devices in order to survive. To this end they have exploited the bandolero, bandit-style tradition of Colombia in the form of continuing to levy extorsive taxes on the coca and poppy planters, traffickers, ranchers, and petroleum and commercial business interests alike in exchange for providing "protection." In addition to the extortion-protection racket, the kidnapping of members of Colombia's wealthy elite also provides them considerable income. In the rural Colombian outback, the still limited opportunities for education and economic enhancement make this type of life for a number of people appear lucrative and relatively painless. As such, the guerrillas as an effective force in the field have stalemated the government, controlling at least a third of the countryside, and remain an obstacle to any anti-drug policy which seeks to bring into play an eradication process.

Endemic corruption as a countervailing anti-drug policy factor has been a key element in the success of the Colombian traffickers. Over time no single government agency could be said not to have been tainted by the corrupting influence of narcotraffickers' bribes. The police, military Congress and officials and actors at all levels both within and outside the government have been highly vulnerable and more often than not have succumbed to the temptation to accept bribes in return for protective favors. Nobel Prize winner Gabriel Garcia Marquez commented on this situation calling it the "moral catastrophy" afflicting politics in Colombia. (El Tiempo: 28 Feb 96) For those who had direct influence on the formation or application of the government's anti-drug policy there was always the choice of *plata o plomo*. This highly coercive narco-terrorist threat to one's own life as well as to close family members, combined with the limited ability of the government to provide protection, sorely tempted most people to acquiesce in the traffickers' interests rather than risk lethal retribution for non-compliance. This form of narco-terrorism effectively paralyzed Colombia's criminal justice system throughout most of the 1980s and into the 1990s. In this manner most of the traffickers were able to avoid prosecution or extradition to the US, all the while protecting their illegal trade interests.

The cartels themselves, while often thought of as highly structured organizations due the prominence given some of the drug kingpins, were well organized, but also highly flexible in all their operations. As smaller independents and subcontracted traffickers numbering in the scores of thousands from all parts of Colombia gained experience over the years, they too expanded their smaller scale operations to meet the ever constant international drug market demands. Increasing market demand necessitated the expansion of the cartels' cocaine production, refining and transshipping capabilities. Since international market demand was so strong and the profits so immense, particularly during the 1980s, even with the arrest and extradition of a number of important traffickers, there were always others ready, able and willing to take their place. This ability to recapitalize and regenerate lost production capacity totally undermined the popular conceptions held by the US government about the rigidity of a cartel organization's structure, transshipping components, and leadership which were perceived as being vulnerable in the form of *key centers of gravity* to attack by US and Colombian counter-drug efforts. This situation remains true even today.

While appearing deceptively simple, the traffickers' loose system of highly flexible yet well-coordinated operations were quite amorphous and could not be precisely attacked in the same manner that one might approach an opposing military force's fighting components, headquarters, leadership or supporting logistical systems as centers of gravity which, when destroyed or neutralized, would enable one to achieve decisive results. Narcotrafficking is a business enterprise and not a structured military operation which makes the myriad of traffickers as a whole a less than ideal target. The self-generating nature of the business based on strong market demand does not provide a finite end-game for the US supply side strategy solution. Conventional interdiction might put small traffickers out of business by wiping out their entire capital investment in a single seizure, but this is not likely to happen within larger groups with multiple enterprises or with any trafficker who has some profits held in reserve as a hedge against this very possibility or has the ability to recapitalize the production process by receiving financial loans from the marketing end of the business.

Even when most if not all of the trafficking kingpins were either dead, in prison, or on the run, cocaine refinement and transshipping operations have continued unabated, indicating that others have stepped in to fill the marketing gaps. All-out offensives on the part of the government in reaction to the murder of noted Colombian officials and prominent citizens have provided no more than a temporary setback to the traffickers who reorganized and adjusted their operations to the changing conditions. Successes against both the Medellin and Cali cartels merely caused a redistribution of power within the cocaine-heroin industry with other groups and personalities coming to the forefront of the trafficking business in an effort to garner some of the potentially huge profits available to any newcomer. As an indicator of overall trafficker successes in the face of US and Colombian anti-drug efforts during the period of 1981 to 1992, Colombian economist Dr Salomon Kalmanovitz estimated that total narcotrafficking earnings were divided about equally between the US and European markets, realizing between $7 and $8 billion in profits annually. (Kalmanovitz 1992: 6) This came in large part from the 500 mt that the Cali cartel and its related enterprises alone were moving through Colombia. (El Nuevo Herald: 5 Dec 93)

Some fluctuations in coca leaf prices in the Central-Andes did result from the Colombian government's anti-drug backlashes, as happened in 1987, 1989, and again in the 1990s. There were major disruptions lasting some months in the flow of cocaine products out of both Peru and Bolivia into Colombia as the local governments seized or destroyed quantities of airplanes and laboratories among other trafficker assets. The traffickers were only then forced to take the time to make new arrangements, establish new contacts, renew their basic coca product sources of supply, recapitalize and otherwise replace destroyed or captured production equipment and supporting chemicals and supplies. Due to the persistently strong market demand and high profits as powerful incentives, this invariably took place and trafficking resumed again where it had left off.

Throughout the period of the US anti-drug policy effort in Colombia, the issue of Colombian national sovereignty has always been at the forefront of the relationship between the two countries. This was reflected in the general intransigence of the Colombian government to adhere to the extradition agreements with the US except under extreme circumstances so as to project an image that it was in control of its own domestic policies and was not being unduly influenced by the US hegemon to the north. To this end Colombia refused to allow the US to have operational control of specific anti-drug operations. As a result, the US anti-drug policy was forced to achieve its ends by working through the Colombian government's judicial, police and military bureaucracy. In the end the US was quite successful at this and the ever increasing monies spent on behalf of the Colombian government's efforts did engage the police and from time to time the military against the traffickers.

While the US (especially after 1985) did consider trafficking to be a threat to national security, the Colombian government generally did not. The US anti-drug policy naturally wanted to see the traffickers perceived as a threat to national security within Colombia with a total effort in the form of a great anti-drug crusade taking place. Nonetheless, both the Colombian military and the government tended to perceive the guerrillas as the primary threat to society. This perspective dominated some officials attitudes to the degree that from time to time the military joined hands with the traffickers, as in the Magdalena Valley, to defeat the insurgents as the opportunity presented itself. That the Colombian government preferred to principally engage its police in the anti-drug effort reinforced the point and was initially a partial rejection of the US anti-drug policy's efforts at a larger militarization of the drug war. This also reflected the effort of the Colombian state to maintain sovereignty over its own domestic affairs, a perfectly normal reaction.

The exception to the state's perspective on the issue of sovereignty took place when certain traffickers used violence in an attempt to intimidate the Bogota government through the assassinations of known and highly respected personalities. This produced a short duration but highly inflammatory uproar on the part of the entrenched elites who now felt themselves directly and seriously threatened. Nonetheless, this mercurial reaction and reflection of public opinion was generally offset by the otherwise ambivalent elite attitudes toward trafficking in general and their tendency to be tolerant of narcotrafficking activities as long as they were not threatening to them personally.

Colombians have tended to treat narcotrafficking as one would any other criminal activity involving the production and transshipment of an illegal product. Ironically it was only the Medellin cartel's high profile murders of Lara Bonilla (1984), Guillermo Cano (1986), Carlos Mauro Hoyos (1988) and Luis Carlos Galan (1989) that roused in each case a violent government backlash influenced by elite perceptions of insecurity and outrage. These murders and the escape from prison of Jorge Ochoa (1986) and Pablo Escobar (1992) produced serious government crackdowns specifically targeting the Medellin cartel. This was fundamentally because the elites sensed that the Medellin group was now a direct threat to themselves, whereas the relatively pacific Cali cartel and other groups were not generally seen in this light. Ironically, the Medellin cartel's use of violence provided the US anti-drug policy with an invigorating series of positive shocks which, while not continuous over the years, did shake the Colombian government out of its lethargy and propelled it headlong into a confrontation with the traffickers. Had the Medellin cartel group and Pablo Escobar in particular been less confrontational in their modus operandi and more subtle in their use of violence as the Cali group tended to be, it is difficult to say where the US anti-drug policy would be today, if at all. In sum, the violence produced a fruitful effect which generally aligned the Colombian anti-drug policy with that of the US.

Ironically, the government's counter-drug backlash produced by the violence tended to focus on the Medellin cartel, leaving the Cali groups and a myriad of smaller but very aggressive independents to pick up the slack of trafficking opportunities left by the fragmentation of the Medellin group. Only with the advent of the Gaviria and Samper administrations was the Cali cartel, in turn, singled out and almost by default became the government's next principal target. Here too, as the Cali traffickers now found themselves in disarray, dozens of independent traffickers expanded their operations to service the continuing international market demand and increased opportunities to acquire some of the immense profits from the drug trade.

The lack of a comprehensive US and Colombian anti-drug policy strategy and related, integrated campaign plans to deal with all aspects of the trafficking operations simultaneously further inhibited the achievement of decisive results. The US anti-drug policy sponsored numerous operations over the years, but in all cases, while monies were allocated and dispensed and successes were recorded, there was always a loophole, some externality or even a shortcoming which undermined the effort. As an example, the US anti-drug policy was eminently successful in reducing the flow of chemical precursors, including acetone, ethyl ether, methyl-ethyl-ketone, toluene and others from being exported from the US into Colombia. Nonetheless, this success in the decrease in precursor chemicals flowing into Colombia from the US was offset by an equally proportional increase of chemicals flowing into Colombia from Europe. (ONDCP 1992c: xi). The inflows of chemicals into Colombia for narcotrafficking refining operations virtually never slackened. This, in itself, is indicative that there was a constant trafficker demand for the required precursor chemicals used in cocaine and heroin manufacturing. As cocaine production increased from about 500 mt in the mid-1980s to around 1,000 mt in the early to mid-1990s (Figure 5), when sufficient precursor chemicals were not available from US and European sources or there was a shortfall in the supply, the traffickers then obtained what they needed in Brazil. Here a balloon effect was now in play in terms of precursor chemicals being available to the traffickers from a multitude of sources.

The balloon effect was not only reflected in the smuggling of precursor chemicals but also in the production and refining of ever increasing quantities of cocaine. During the early-1980s, the traffickers generally had the choice of establishing a few large laboratory complexes to provide upwards of 100 mt on an annual basis or a series of dispersed, smaller efforts to accomplish the same end. Beginning in 1984 when the surprise, post-Lara Bonilla murder crackdown took place under the Betancur administration, the operational risks began to increase and the traffickers took precautions, decentralizing a number of their operations by looking to Panama, Peru, Brazil, Ecuador and Venezuela on Colombia's periphery as potential areas for replicating the norcotics production then taking place inside Colombia.

Given the dynamics of the Colombian scene and the relative agility of the trafficking operations, it was difficult at best for the US government, the Bogota based US Embassy Country Team and Colombian anti-drug planers to determine exactly what ends needed to be achieved, how or by what ways this could be done and what type and how many resources should be brought into play to support the contemplated strategy. All too often monies were proposed and allocated in support of the anti-drug policy in Colombia and only then was a strategy formulated, inevitably spending the monies but not accomplishing decisive or permanent results. Despite generally full Colombian cooperation, the Andean Initiative with its quantum rise in funding did little more than temporarily disrupt narcotrafficking operations. This indicates that the supply side strategy of the US anti-drug policy in Colombia is focused on a false center of gravity (supply and organizational structure) and not focused where it ought to be (demand) as the first priority. For this reason anti-drug planners and operators alike have met considerable frustration in bringing the anti-drug effort to a successful close in Colombia.

Over the years, with US funding, logistics, and operations and training support made available to it, the Colombian government did make some progress in terms of its interdiction and repression campaigns as is evidenced by the ever increasing amounts of coca and poppy bushes eradicated and cocaine base and cocaine HCl and heroin seized. Nonetheless, the narcotrafficker production capacity more than kept pace with the government's success, producing an estimated 1,000 mt of cocaine by the 1990s (up from 500 mt in 1986). In addition, US market prices generally remained fairly stable throughout the years and only for short periods such as in 1989-90 was there an increase in the wholesale price on the US market.

The US anti-drug policy did record some operational successes against the traffickers. The extradition effort caused dozens of traffickers to be sent to the US for trial and eventual confinement in prison. The Colombian military was focused from time to time on the traffickers as part of the process of government sponsored backlashes and herbicides were used with considerable effect against coca, marijuana and poppy cultivation efforts. Operation Green Ice may have been the most successful anti-drug operation of all in terms of hampering trafficker operations and at least limiting the enjoyment of the latter's illegal profits. Certainly the decimation of the Medellin and Cali cartel's leadership and the fragmentation of their structures could be considered as a tactical success of some importance. Nonetheless, the ability of the Cali cartel remnants and other similar trafficking enterprises to immediately step in and pick up the temporary slack to meet the ongoing high demand of the international drug markets served to neutralize the strategic impact of the derailment of the major cartels.

SOUTHCOM's support of the US anti-drug policy also enjoyed some successes. Its contribution in the form of providing timely intelligence on trafficking air flows was potentially very valuable. Nonetheless, the scores of likely trafficker targets discovered each day were impossible to service as a whole, given the humanitarian Chicago Agreement being in effect until March 1994 and the traffickers' ability to fly at night, outclassing the Colombian Air Force. As it was, the difficulty of tracking all the potential narcotrafficking aircraft as they dispersed into the thousands of airfields available to them throughout Colombia and adjacent countries made this type of interdiction a monumental if not futile task. The riverine operations appeared to have a better margin of success and were an unpleasant surprise to the traffickers. Despite the SOUTHCOM successes, the traffickers still were able to adapt themselves to the new conditions and continued to operate. The GAO reported that most of the $397 million in military and law enforcement aid and other loans was used to equip and train forces to better engage in counternarcotics activities. The airlift capability of the police, the riverine capability of the Colombian Marine Corps, the support and surveillance capabilities of the Air Force and the ground capability of the Army were all substantially increased. Yet when measured against the ONDCP goals of the early 1990s in reducing cocaine shipped into the US by 15 percent in 2 years and 60 percent over 10 years, the Colombian anti-drug policy in its implementation is obviously failing. The US and Colombian efforts can pressure the traffickers to change their aerial routes and methods of producing and distributing cocaine and heroin, but not prevent the trafficking from occuring. (GAO 1993a: 17 and 20)

Interestingly enough, when things did not go well for the US anti-drug policy in terms of the Colombian government's own activity, the US responded by threatening the Colombian economy, delaying Colombia's exports into the US, and harassing Colombian citizens and officials attempting to enter the US. In this manner Washington acted in a way which was prejudicial to its own anti-drug interests and may have even jeopardized to a degree its own anti-drug policy by increasing unemployment inside Colombia and reducing the export income tax base on which the government relied in part to finance its own anti-drug efforts. While this did not occur with any great frequency, combined with the veiled threat of possible intervention on the part of US naval forces, these activities did cause some friction in the US-Colombian relationship. In addition, Washington's decertification process of 1996, while intended to spur Bogota on to greater action, appeared to do nothing more than place the two nations in an adversarial relationship, thoroughly demeaning to Colombia and prejudicing what ought to be an anti-drug *alliance*.

The Gaviria and Samper governments use of plea bargaining, in conjunction with a repressive backlash as a policy, was not well received by US leaders, but it did influence a number of the traffickers to turn themselves over to government authorities. This policy only backfired somewhat when narco-kingpin Pablo Escobar and others flaunted their influence and continued to run their respective cartel operations from their prison cells. Escobar's and later Londono's escape called into question the government's effectiveness and produced yet another anti-drug backlash which further decimated the remaining elements of the Medellin cartel, elements of the Cali group, and some independent traffickers. The US government sent some of its foremost anti-drug policy specialists such as Ambassadors Thomas McNamara and Myles Frechette to Colombia to keep the anti-drug policy on track. This effort was reinforced by the Andean Initiative which enabled Colombia to receive over a half-billion dollars ($607 million) in US aid for the prosecution of the anti-drug war effort. The US support for reform of the Colombian judicial system and its approach to law enforcement was successful in terms of restructuring the system and increasing the number of successful prosecutions of various traffickers. This has been a favorable legacy of the Andean Initiative in terms of reestablishing some form of less corrupt rule of law in Colombia. The establishment of a separate Prosecutor General and a system of courts under the 1991 Constitution was a signal event in terms of enhancing the independence and efficiency of the courts and the prosecuting system. The US, in conjunction with the Colombian government, did accomplish portions of its anti-drug policy objectives for Colombia. It did curb to some degree drug production and processing structures. It did immobilize and prosecute dozens of major traffickers, as well as hundreds of lesser ones. It did temporarily interdict, destroy and disrupt the flow of narcotics and processing chemicals as well as disrupt and seize large amounts of trafficker profits. Likewise the democratic process continued apace within Colombia and the government's institutional capability to confront the cocaine trade was strengthened as significant damage was inflicted on some trafficking organizations. To this end both the visibly enhanced anti-drug police and military were by the mid-1990s conducting continuous operations on land, in the air, and on the rivers and seas against the traffickers. Despite all this, the US anti-drug policy in Colombia only appears to have reduced the flow of cocaine and heroin being produced and transshipped by Colombian traffickers by about ten to twenty percent. Despite ever increasing spending on the part of the US Government, the traffickers have merely increased their levels of production to offset their losses to a point where the international drug market today still remains fully supplied, if not saturated, in meeting the demands of its customers (Figure 5).

A first and primary lesson learned which one might deduce from the US anti-drug policy experience in Colombia is the need for a government to *study all sides of an issue* to ferret out all the potential factors which can negatively effect a policy before it is seriously considered for implementation. That this lesson has not been learned very well over the years can be seen in the previous quagmire-like cases of Vietnam and Somalia where policy failure was largely assured from the beginning due to an inadequate analysis of the countervailing socioeconomic and political factors in play. In the case of Colombia the US attempted to apply a supply oriented anti-drug policy to a situation which was preeminently demand driven. As a result, despite the capture or destruction of numerous trafficker assets, personnel and products, which are impressive statistically, there was no viable attrition end-game in favor of the US anti-drug policy as long as the self-generating condition of narcotrafficking remained in play as a result of an intense demand driven factor. All indicators are that demand remains a pervasive and urgent problem inside the USA. (Miami Herald: 21 Aug

96)

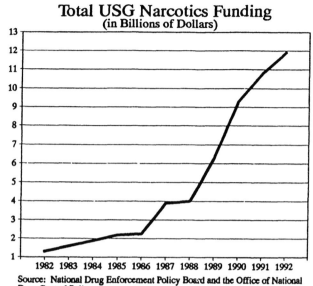

## Total USG Narcotics Funding
### (in Billions of Dollars)

Source: National Drug Enforcement Policy Board and the Office of National Drug Control Policy

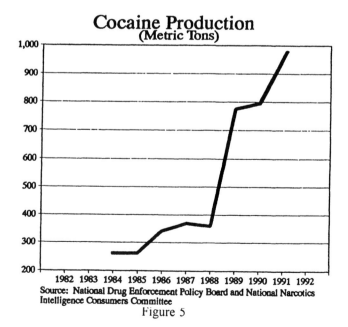

## Cocaine Production
### (Metric Tons)

Source: National Drug Enforcement Policy Board and National Narcotics Intelligence Consumers Committee

Figure 5

Another lesson learned from the Colombian experience is the transnational nature of the narcotrafficking phenomenon and the related *balloon effect* which often takes place in Colombia. Despite all efforts to the contrary, the US and Colombian anti-drug policies tended to merely push the traffickers around, often causing them to move their operations into countries adjacent to Colombia, rather than completely destroying them. Any supply oriented anti-drug policy must be prepared to address this aspect of the drug-trafficking phenomenon if it expects to achieve a decisive success at all. If this is not possible and a multinational effort is not forthcoming, it is unlikely that a supply side anti-drug strategy can ever decisively defeat the traffickers who can operate with relative impunity across most international frontiers.

A third lesson learned is the inevitable policy conflicts that will arise when one nation such as the US attempts to impose a virtual *single issue foreign policy* on a country such as Colombia. Colombia perceived its problems as being several in nature, involving state threatening insurgencies, economics and violence. Narcotrafficking, except when it threatened the lives of key segments of the population, was not viewed as a threat so much as it was a criminal nuisance. The US viewed narcotrafficking as a critical national security threat imperative and as a result became frustrated when the Colombian government did not give this issue the same high priority as did Washington. To this end the US attempted to resolve the conflict of interests by imposing economic penalties on Colombia which merely inhibited the latter in the pursuit of its own anti-drug policy. In this case, by reacting the way it did, the US inadvertently was potentially placing in jeopardy its own anti-drug policy in Colombia.

A last lesson learned deals with *anti-drug policy strategy formulation*. A strategy should not be resource constrained in its initial conceptual formulation. This will enable the planners to see reasonably well what the total resources will be required to support the operations or ways needed to accomplish the sought after ends or objectives. Doing this will enable one to better visualize whether the strategy can even succeed and hopefully prevent the often incremental or piecemeal approaches taken wherein monies are all too often allocated first, and only then are plans and operations considered and brought into play. The fallacy of the resource or money constrained modus operandi is that the implementers often do not really know where they are going and merely operate for the sake of operating without achieving decisive results. In the anti-drug effort in Colombia, the monies did get spent and the policy was carried out, but the results have proven indecisive. The US has only begun to realize this after operating for more than a decade in Colombia. If a viable end-game is not apparent or not obtainable at a reasonable cost, then an alternate solution needs to be sought out. The Colombian anti-drug problem may have appeared deceptively simple to some anti-drug policy planners and, if so, this was a blunder of no small proportions. As this study has shown there are numerous potentially conflicting factors which need to be addressed by the policy planner. In the case of Colombia this was not done adequately enough and years of effort and national treasure have been spent in an indeterminate effort.

In Colombia it is essential that the local government be able to enforce the law and administer justice in a fair and evenhanded manner as part of its institutional capacity to govern and promote the social-economic welfare of its people. There is no doubt that the government will attempt to continue in this direction and the state will generally preserve itself in the face of the current criminal and insurgent activities. The greatest societal threats remain intimidation through violent means and corruption of human values (*plata o plomo*) which provide a dynamic and basis for the delegitimization of the governing authority in the national conscience and the eyes of the people. Nonetheless, societal values being what they are and the general tolerance of the contraband tradition on the part of Colombian society indicate that the ambience conducive to narcotrafficking will remain, prejudicing the successful conclusion of any US anti-drug policy in Colombia.

Professor David Bushnell in his survey of Colombia concludes pessimistically that the severe inequality of income between the rural and urban populations due to the inefficiency of the country's productive structure and the government's failure to provide essential services to all areas equally have caused people to continue to question the legitimacy of the state in many of the rural sectors. (Bushnell 1993: 283) Until such time as the government can effectively resolve the rural population's social-economic inequality as conditions conducive to supporting insurgency activity, it is likely that the guerrilla threat will continue indefinitely and even strengthen as it appears to be doing in the late-1990s.

The guerrillas and the traffickers, while often antagonistic toward each other, do depend to some degree on each other in their often symbiotic and mutually supporting roles. Narcotrafficking provides an extensive extorsive rent resource for the guerrillas on the one hand and on the other the guerrillas do provide some protection for certain trafficker and coca and poppy farming activities. Indeed, the guerrillas have even found it lucrative to enter into the cocaine production business themselves. The traffickers support the guerrillas because they do serve as a distraction to the Colombian military, keeping it busy while otherwise controlling large tracts of rural Colombia where drug crops can be cultivated in relative obscurity. This situation is likely to remain to plague the Colombian government in its efforts to curb both the guerrillas and the traffickers well into the next century. In short, the US anti-drug policy currently finds itself only able to raise the risks somewhat of the traffickers inside Colombia, pushing the demand-driven narcotrafficking phenomenon around, but not stamping it out. This is the legacy of the balloon effect. In sum the traffickers will continue to produce, refine and transship their products both inside Colombia and over its neighbors' respective frontiers and border regions indefinitely. Despite the capture of thousands of traffickers, the destruction of hundreds of laboratories of all types and the seizure of hundreds of metric tons of cocaine and other drugs, due to the self-generating nature of the demand inspired narcotrafficking business and its immense profits, the US anti-drug policy in Colombia finds itself producing inconclusive results. This is due to the fact that narcotrafficking is a business and nothing more. As long as the profits are sufficiently high enough to outweigh the visible risks involved, this type of business will continue to flourish indefinitely.

For Colombia, the strong countervailing effect stemming from *a strong international market demand has maintained the narcotrafficking business as a viable enterprise* in the face of the US anti-drug policy. This means that the basic driving force behind trafficking in Colombia lies outside that country. As such, the solution to the Colombian problem also begins at this point. Until the *demand side* of the drug phenomenon is addressed and the associated high profits reduced significantly, narcotrafficking in Colombia will undoubtedly continue into the foreseeable future.

In sum, the US anti-drug policy for Colombia will remain less than fully successful and eventually fail in the long run because there has been insufficient reduction of the demand side and its related high profits which provide the basic incentive for Colombians to engage in this form of illicit activity. In the end the US anti-drug foreign policy in the North-Andes has failed to achieve decisive results because it could neither effectively address the high demand, capitalist oriented market processes which have exploited the abject poverty which is the norm in rural Colombia today, the corrupted societal value systems in play, nor the extraordinary entrepreneurial flexibility and agility of the trafficking organizations which have continued to operate despite any and all efforts to obstruct their respective operations. To this end Colombia remains a unique ambience conducive to narcotrafficking in general - a veritable *cocaine quagmire*, hamstringing the US anti-drug policy implementation at every turn.

# Bibliography

## Primary Sources

### Government/Official Reports:

Agency For International Development (AID). 1992. *Andean Counter- Drug Initiative Objective IV: Alternate Development Quarterly Report (January - March 1992)*. Washington, D.C.: AID.

Craig, Frank. 1982. NAU Deputy Director *Memorandum* "Coca Leaf Analysis by the DEA Special Testing and Research Laboratory." Bogota: US Embassy, 10 June.

Department of State (DOS). 1991. *International Narcotics Control Foreign Assistance Appropriation Act Fiscal Year 1992 Budget Congressional Submission*. Washington, D.C.: US Government Printing Office.

_____. 1992. *Colombia Fact Sheet*. Washington, D.C.: Department of State.

_____. 1992a. *Declaration of San Antonio*. Washington, D.C.: Department of State. 30 July.

_____. 1993. *The Budget in Brief Fiscal Year 1994*. Washington, D.C.: Department of State.

_____. 1994. *Cable 087397*. "Presidential Certification For Major Narcotics Producing And Transit Countries." 2 April

Department of State (DOS). Bureau of International Narcotic Matters (INM). 1992. *International Narcotics Control Strategy Report (INCSR) 1991*. Washington, D.C.: US Government Printing Office.

_____. _____. 1993. *International Narcotics Control Strategy Report (INCSR) 1992*. Washington, D.C.: US Government Printing Office.

_____. _____. 1994. *International Narcotics Control Strategy Report (INCSR) 1993*. Washington, D.C.: Department of State.

_____. _____. 1995. *International Narcotics Control Strategy Report (INCSR) 1994*. Washington D.C.: Department of State

_____. Bureau for International Narcotics and Law Enforcement Affairs. 1996. *International Narcotics Control Strategy Report (INCSR) 1995*. Washington, D.C.: Department of State.

Drug Enforcement Administration (DEA). 1987. *National Narcotics Intelligence Consumers' Committee (NNICC) Report 1985-1986*. Washington, D.C.: US Department of Justice.

_____. 1991. *Operation Green Ice (Briefing)*. San Diego: San Diego Field Division.

_____. 1992. *The NNICC Report*. Washington, D.C.: Department of Justice.

_____. 1993. *Source to the Street. Mid-1992 Prices for: Cannabis Cocaine Heroin*. Washington, D.C.: Department of Justice.

Economics Section. 1992. *Economics Trends Report Colombia 1992*. Bogota: US Embassy.

Ejercito Nacional. 1992. *Resultados Generales Plan Aguila*. Bogota: Fuerzas Militares de Colombia, 3 December.

General Accounting Office (GAO). 1993. *The Drug War: Colombia Is Undertaking Programs, But Impact Is Uncertain*. GAO/NSIAD-93-158. Washington, D.C.: General Accounting Office.

_____.1993a. *Drug Control: Heavy Investment In Military Surveillance Is Not Paying Off*. GAO/NSIAD-93-220. Washington, D.C.: General accounting Office.

_____. 1992. *Promising Approach to Judicial Reform in Colombia*. GAO/NSIAD-92-269.

_____. 1991a. *The Drug War*. GAO/T-NSIAD-92-2. Washington, D.C.: US General Accounting Office.

_____. 1991b. *Drug War Observations on Counternarcotics Aid to Colombia*. GAO/NSIAD-91-296. Washington, D.C.: US General Accounting Office.

_____. 1988. *Drug Control U.S.-Supported Efforts in Colombia and Bolivia*. GAO/NSIAD 89-24. Washington, D.C.: US General Accounting Office.

Narcotics Affairs Section (NAS). 1991. "Talking Points: Coca Eradication." Bogota: US Embassy, 9 July.

_____. 1993. *Counternarcotics Support Program For Fiscal Year 1992*. Bogota: US Embassy, 13 January.

Narcotics Affairs Unit (NAU). 1987. *Briefing*. "The Narcotics Situation In Colombia." Bogota: US Embassy, June.

National Institute on Drug Abuse (NIDA). 1990-1991. *NIDA Notes*. Washington, D.C.,: Department of Health and Human Services.

Office of National Drug Control Policy (ONDCP). 1989. *National Drug Control Strategy*. Washington, D.C.: US Government Printing Office.

_____. 1990. *National Drug Control Strategy*. Washington, D.C.: US Government Printing Office.

_____. 1991. *National Drug Control Strategy*. Washington, D.C.: US Government Printing Office.

_____. 1992. *National Drug Control Strategy: A Nation Responds to Drug Use*. Washington, D.C.: US Government Printing Office.

_____. 1992a *Selected Seizure Statistics (fact sheet)*. Washington, D.C.: ONDCP, April.

_____. 1992b. *1992 National Drug Control Strategy Executive Summary*. Washington, D.C.: US Government Printing Office.

_____. 1992c. *Two Years After Cartagena in House Committee on The Judiciary*. Washington, D.C.: US Goverment Printing Office.

_____. 1993. National Drug Control Strategy. Washington, D.C.: U.S Goverment Printing Office.

_____. 1994. *Clinton National Drug Control Strategy*. Washington, D.C.: US Government Printing Office.

Policia Nacional de Colombia (PNC). 1992a. *Balance Actividades Antinarcoticos 1992*. Bogota: Policia Nacional.

_____. 1992b. *Operativo Realizado En Cartagena - BTA*. Bogota: Direccion Antinarcoticos.

_____. 1992c. *Operativo Realizado En Bogota*. Bogota: Direccion Antinarcoticos.

_____. 1992d. *Operativo Meta*. Bogota: Direccion Antinarcoticos.

_____. 1992e. *Operativo Puerto Asis*. Bogota: Direccion Antinarcoticos.

_____. 1992f. *Operativo Cauca*. Bogota: Direccion Antinarcoticos.

_____. 1992g. *Operativo Cesar*. Bogota: Direccion Antinarcoticos.

President's Commission on Organized Crime. 1986. *America's Habit: Drug Abuse, Drug Trafficking and Organized Crime. Report to The President and Attorney General.* Washington, D.C.: US Government Printing Office, March.

United Nations (UN). 1990. *Handbook of International Trade and Development Statistics*. New York: United Nations.

_____. 1990a. *Basic Indicators*. New York: United Nations.

_____. Children's Fund (UNICEF). 1989. *State of The World's Children*. New York: United Nations.

US Agency For International Development (USAID). 1986. *A Review of AID's Narcotics Control Development Assistance Program (AID Evaluation Special Study No. 29)*. Washington, D.C.: Agency For International Development.

US Department of Health and Human Services (DHHS). 1987. *Trends in Drug Abuse Related Hospital Emergency Room Episodes and Medical Examination Cases for Selected Drugs DAWN 1967-1985*. Rockville, Maryland: CSR Incorporated.

_____. 1987a. *Cocaine Client Admissions 1979-1984*. Rockville, MD: CSR Incorporated.

_____. 1991. *Drug Abuse And Drug Abuse Research*. Maryland: CRS Incorporated.

_____. 1991a. *Annual Emergency Room Data 1990*. Maryland: CRS Incorporated.

_____. 1991b. *National Household Survey on Drug Abuse: Highlights 1990*. Rockville, MD: Research Triangle Institute.

US Embassy (USE) Colombia (CO). 1990. *Fact Sheet*. Bogota.

_____. 1991. *Coca Cultivation In Colombia: Quality Up Only A Little*. Cable 1484. Bogota: 29 January.

_____. 1991. *The Counternarcotics Andean Strategy: The Fifth Objective*. Cable 6299. Bogota: 25 April.

_____. 1991. *Monthly Report Of The U.S. Funded Narcotics Program -- Colombia -- June 1991. Cable 11260.* Bogota: July.

_____. 1992. *Colombia: Key Economic Indicators*. Bogota: Economics Section.

_____. 1992a. *Monthly Report Of The U.S. Funded Narcotics Program -- Colombia -- November 1992. Cable 19022.* Bogota: 23 December.

_____. 1992b. *Monthly Report Of The U.S. Funded Narcotics Program -- Colombia -- October 1992.* Cable 17638. Bogota: 27 November.

_____. 1992c. *Monthly Report Of The U.S. Funded Narcotics Program -- Colombia -- September 1992.* Cable 16357. Bogota: 30 October.

_____. 1992d. *Monthly Report Of The U.S. Funded Narcotics Program -- Colombia -- February 1992.* Cable 4009. Bogota: 17 March.

_____. 1993. *Monthly Report Of The U.S. Funded Narcotics Program -- Colombia -- December 1992.* Cable 1749. Bogota: 3 February.

_____. 1993b. *Narcotics Activities Report: May 1993.* Cable 9015. Bogota: 11 June.

White House. 1987. *National Security Strategy of The United States.* Washington, D.C.: US Government Printing Office.

_____. 1991. *National Security Strategy of The United States.* Washington, D.C.: US Government Printing Office.

**Congressional Hearings and Reports:**

US Congress. 1988. Senate Caucus On International Narcotics Control. *Hearing.* 100th Congress. 2d Session. S. Hrg. 100-1021. 16 March. Washington, D.C.: US Government Printing Office, 1989.

_____. 1988a. Senate Committee On Foreign Affairs. *Drugs, Law Enforcement And Foreign Policy.* Senate Print 100-165. Washington, D.C.: US Government Printing Office.

_____. 1989. Senate Committee On The Judiciary. *Hearing.* 101st Congress. 1st Session. S.Hrg 101-591. 17 August. Washington, D.C.: US Government Printing Office, 1990.

_____. 1989-90. House Committee on The Judiciary and Senate Caucus On International Narcotics Control. *Joint Hearings.* S. Hrg. 101-1228. 101st Congress. 1st and 2d Sessions. 6 November 1989, 18 January and 27 March 1990. Washington, D.C.: US Government Printing Office, 1991.

_____. 1990a. House Committee On Government Operations. 101st Congress. 2d Session. *Report 101-991.* 30 November. Washington, D.C.: US Government Printing Office.

_____. 1990b. House Committee On Government Operations. *Stopping the Flood of Cocaine With Operation Snowcap: Is It Working? Report 101-673.* 14 August. 101st Congress, 2nd Session. Washington, D.C.: US Government Printing Office.

_____. 1991a. House Committee On Armed Services. *Hearing.* H.A.S.C. Rpt. No. 102-19. 30 April. 102d Congress. 1st Session. Washington, D.C.: US Government Printing Office, 1992.

_____. 1991b. House Committee On Foreign Affairs. *Hearing.* 10 July. 102d Congress. 1st Session. Washington, D.C.: US Government Printing Office.

_____. 1992a. Senate Committee On Foreign Relations. *Hearing.* S.Hrg. 102-652. 20 February. 102d Congress. 2d Session. Washington, D.C.: US Government Printing Office.

_____. 1992b. House Committee On Foreign Affairs. *Joint Hearing.* 7 May. 102d Congress. 2d session. Washington, D.C.: US Government Printing Office.

_____. 1992c. House Committee On Foreign Affairs. *Hearings.* 3-4 and 11-12 March. 102d Congress. 2d Session. Washington, D.C.: US Government Printing Office.

_____. 1992d. Senate Judiciary Committee and the International Narcotics Control Caucus. *Fighting Drug Abuse.* Washington, D.C.: US Government Printing Office.

**Official Statements, Interviews, And Briefings:**

Callahan, Robert. 1993. USIA official interviewed by author in Washington, D.C., 27 April.

Camacho, Dr Alvaro. 1993. Professor of Political Science at the Institute of Political Studies of the National University of Bogota. Interviewed by author 4 February.

Carlucci, Frank. 1988. *Testimony* before US Senate and House of Representatives Committee on Armed Forces. 100th Congress, 2nd Session. Washington, D.C.: Mimeo of 15 June.

Cassman, Joel. 1993. Economic Counselor of US Embassy, Bogota. Interview with author in Bogota 3 February.

Chernick, Dr Mark. 1993. Professor of Political Science at Colombia University doing field research on violence and the state in Colombia. Interview with author in Bogota 2 February.

Clinton, Bill. 1993a. *Press Release*: "Remarks by The President In Announcement of Lee Brown as Director, Office of Drug Control Policy." White House: Office of the Press Secretary, 28 April.

_____. 1993b. *Executive Order 12880*: 16 Nov 1993 in Federal Register, Vol. 58 No. 221 (18 Nov 93), p. 60989.

Country Team Official (CT:CO) 1993. US Embassy in Bogota. Interview with author in Bogota 3 February.

Craig, Frank. 1982. Narcotics Assistance Unit (NAU) Deputy Director *Memorandum* "Coca Leaf Analysis by the DEA Special Testing and Research Laboratory." Bogota: US Embassy, 10 June.

Department of Defense (DOD) official. 1993. Interview by author in Washington, D.C. 28 April.

Deering, John S. 1993. Office of Inspector General. US Department of State. Interviewed by author in Washington, D.C. 27 April.

Department of State (DOS) official. 1993. Interview by author in Washington, D.C. 30 April.

Drug Enforcement Administration. 1991. *Operation Green Ice (Briefing)*. San Diego, CA: San Diego Field Division

Drug Enforcement Agency. Official (DEA:CO). 1993. US Embassy in Bogota. Interview with author in Bogota 3 February.

Eli Lilly and Company. 1993. *Letter* to author signed by Edward A. West. 30 April.

Falino, Lou. 1993. Director, United States Information Service (USIS) of US Embassy in Bogota. Interview with author in Bogota 1 February.

Gallegos, Karen E. 1993. Human rights specialist with the US Embassy in Bogota. Interview with author in Bogota 7 February.

International Narcotics Matters (INM), Bureau of, official. 1993. Interviewed by author in Washington, D.C. 28 April.

Joulwan, General George A. 1993. *Statement* before Senate Armed Services Committee. Washington, D.C.: Senate Armed Services Committee, 21 April.

Kalmanovitz Krauter, Dr Salomon. 1993. Professor of Economics at the National University (Universidad Nacional) in Bogota. Interview with author in Bogota 1 February.

Levitsky, Melvyn. 1991. *Statement* before Legislation and National Security Subcommittee of the Committee On Government Operations, House of Representatives. Washington, D.C.: US Department of State, 23 October.

Lupsha, Dr Peter. 1993. *Letter* to author from Department of Political Science, The University of New Mexico. 26 May.

Martinez, Robert. 1992. Speech. 28 October before the Contraband and Cargo Inspection Technology International Symposium. Washington, D.C.: *Mimeo* of 29 October.

Narcotics Affairs Section official (NAS:CO). 1993. Field agent with extensive experience at US Embassy in Bogota. Interview with author in Bogota 7 February.

Narcotics Assistance Unit (NAU). 1987. *Briefing.* "The Narcotics Situation In Colombia." Bogota: US Embassy. June.

National Security Council (NSC) official. 1993. Interview by author in Washington, D.C. 30 April.

ONDCP 1. 1993. Key official in Office of National Drug Control Policy (ONDCP) during the 1980s. Interviewed by author in Washington, D.C. 29 April.

ONDCP 2. 1993. Key official in Office of National Drug Control Policy (ONDCP) during the 1980s and 1990s. Interviewed by author in Washington, D.C. 26 April.

Reuter, Peter. 1990. "Statement" in Senate Caucus on International Narcotics Control ed. *US International Drug Policy.* Washington, D.C.: US Government Printing Office.

Ross, Timothy. 1993. A ten-year veteran newspaper reporter covering Colombia for both the *Independent* and *The Guardian.* Interviewed by author in Bogota 3 February.

Rutledge, Alvin. 1993. Colombian insurgency specialist at the US Embassy in Bogota. Interviewed by author 2 February.

Silva Lujan, Gabriel. 1993. Presidential advisor on international affairs. Interviewed by author in Bogota 5 February.

SOUTHCOM. 1990. *Briefing*: "SOUTHCOM 2000".

SOUTHCOM (US Southern Command) J3. 1993. Briefing for author at Quarry Heights and Howard Air Force Base, Panama. 8 February.

Stickney, Brian. 1993. Director of the Narcotics Affairs Section (NAS) at the US Embassy in Bogota. Interview with author in Bogota 4 February.

Toft, Joseph. 1993. Director DEA at US Embassy in Bogota. Interviewed by author in Bogota 5 February.

Tokatlian, Dr Juan Gabriel. 1993. Director of the Center for International Studies at the University of The Andes (Universidad de los Andes) in Bogota and acknowledged expert on narcotrafficking in Colombia. Interview with author in Bogota 3 February.

_____. 1995. June 9.

US Air Force Mission official (USAF:CO). 1993. US Embassy in Bogota. Interview with author in Bogota 6 February.

US General Accounting Office (GAO) official. 1993. Interviewed by author in Washington, D.C. 26 April.

US Navy Mission official (USN:CO). 1993. US Embassy in Bogota. Interview with author in Bogota 5 February.

## Secondary Sources

**Books:**

Arango Jaramillo, Mario. 1988. *Impacto del Narcotrafico en Antioquia*. Medellin: J.M. Arango.

Arango Jaramillo, Mario and Jorge Child Velez. 1985. *Los Condonados de la Coca: El Manejo Politico de la Droga*. Medellin (Colombia): J. M. Arango.

Arrieta, Carlos Gustavo et. al. 1990. *Narcotrafico En Colombia*. Bogota: Ediciones Uniandes and Tercer Mundo Editores.

Bagley, Bruce M. 1991. *The Myths of Militarization*. Miami, FL: North-South Center.

Bushnell, David. 1993. *The Making of Modern Colombia*. Berkeley: University of California Press.

Castillo, Fabio. 1987. *Los Jinetes de la Cocaina*. Bogota: Editorial Documento Periodisticos.

Clawson, Patrick and Lee III, Rensselaer. 1992. *The Negative Economic, Political and Social Effects of Cocaine on Latin America*. Washington, D.C.: US Information Agency.

Clutterbuck, Richard. 1990. *Terrorism and Guerrilla Warfare*. New York: Routledge Press.

Eddy, Paul et al. 1988. *The Cocaine Wars*. New York: W.W. Norton.

Gugliotta, Guy and Jeff Leen. 1989. *Kings of Cocaine*. New York: Simon And Schuster.

Lee, Rensselaer W. III. 1989. *The White Labyrinth*. New Brunswick, NJ: Transaction Publishers.

MacDonald, Scott B. 1989. *Mountain High, White Avalanche.* New York: Praeger.

Sheahan, John. 1987. *Patterns of Development in Latin America.* Princeton, NJ: Princeton University Press.

Smith, Peter H. ed. 1992. *Drug Policy in The Americas.* Boulder, CO: Westview Press.

Walker III, William O. 1989. *Drug Control in the Americas.* Albuguerque: University of New Mexico Press.

WOLA (Washington Office On Latin America). 1990. *Going To The Source.* Washington, D.C.: WOLA.

_____. 1991. *The War In The Andes: The Military Role in US International Drug Policy.* Washington, D.C.: Washington Office on Latin America.

World Bank. 1992. *World Table 1992.* Baltimore: John Hopkins University Press.

**Journal Articles/Presentations/Chapters In Books:**

Asociacion Nacional de Exportacion (ANALDEX). 1995. "Politica Antidrogas y Efectos de la Aplicacion de Dicha Politica en La Economia Colombiana" in *FEDESAROLLO,* October.

Bagley, Bruce Michael. 1987. "Colombian Politics: Crisis or Continuity?" in *Current History,* January.

_____. 1988. "Colombia And The War On Drugs." in *Foreign Affairs,* Fall.

_____. 1989-90. "Dateline Drug Wars: Colombia: The Wrong Strategy." in *Foreign Policy,* Winter.

_____. 1990. "Narcotrafico: Colombia Asediada" in Francisco Leal Buitrago y Leon Zamosc eds. *Al Filo Del Caos.* Bogota: Tecer Mundo Editores.

_____. 1992. "After San Antonio," in *Journal of Interamerican Studies.* Vol. 34, Fall.

Bejarano, Ana Maria. 1990. "Estrategias de Paz y Apertura Democratica: Un Balance de Las Administraciones Betancur y Barco." in Francisco Leal Buitrago y Leon Zamosc eds. *Al Filo del Caos.* Bogota: Tercer Mundo Editores.

Camacho Guizado, Alvaro. 1991. "El Ayer y El Hoy De La Violencia En Colombia: Continuidades y Discontinuidades." in *Analisis Politico No 12.* January-April.

Chernick, Marc W. 1996. "Colombia's Fault Lines" in *Current History, February.*

Claudio, Arnaldo. 1991. "Failure Of A Security Strategy." in *Military Review,* December.

Collett, Merrill. 1988. "The Myth of The Narcoguerrillas." in *The Nation.* 13 August.

Dziedzic, Michael J. 1989. "The Transnational Drug Trade And Regional Security" in *Survival,* November-December.

Farah, Douglas. 1996. "The Crackup" in *The Washington Post.* 21 July. Washington, D.C.: LAC NEWS/LATAMCOM INC. July.

Gomez, Hernando. 1988. "La Economia Ilegal en Colombia: Tamano, Evolucion, Caracteristicas, e Impacto Economico." in *Coyuntura Economica.* September.

Greiff, Gustavo de. 1994. "Produccion, narcotrafico y consumo" in *El Nuevo Herald.* 23-24 May.

Gros, Christian. 1992. "Los Campesinos de Las Cordilleras Frente A Los Movimientos Guerrilleros y A La Droga: Actores o Victimas?" in *Analisis Politico* No. 16, May-August.

Gugliotta, Guy. 1992. "The Colombian Cartels and How to Stop Them." in Peter H. Smith, ed. *Drug Policy in The Americas.* Boulder: Westview Press.

Gunter, Frank R. 1991. "Colombian Capital Flight." in *Journal of Interamerican Studies.* Spring.

Harmon, Lt. Col. Robert E. et al. 1993. "Counterdrug Assistance: The Number One Priority." in *Military Review.* March.

Kalmanovitz Krauter, Salomon. 1992. "Analisis Macroeconomico Del Narcotrafico En La Economia Colombiana Desde 1975 Hasta 1992." Presentation (manuscript) in Bogota, Colombia at the Centro de Investigacion Para El Desarollo - CID - Universidad Nacional de Colombia. 1 December.

Kolton, Major Randy J. 1990. "Combating The Colombian Drug Cartels." in *Military Review.* March.

Lee, Rensselaer W. III. 1992. "Colombia's Cocaine Syndicates." in Alfred W. McCoy and Alan A. Block, eds. *War On Drugs.* Boulder, CO: Westview Press.

———. 1995. "Global Reach: The Threat of International Drug Trafficking" in *Current History.* May.

Maingot, Anthony. 1988. "Laundering Drug Profits: Miami And Caribbean Tax Havens." in *Journal of Interamerican Studies.* Summer/Fall.

Martz, John D. 1994. "Colombia: Democracy, Development, and Drugs" in *Current History*. March.

Ortiz Crespo, Dr. Gonzalo. 1990. "Ecuador" in Diego Garcia-Sayan, ed. *Narcotrafico: Realidades y Alternativas*. Lima: Comision Andina de Juristas.

Perl, Raphael Francis. 1988. "Congress, International Narcotics Policy, And The Anti-Drug Abuse Act of 1988." in *Journal of Interamerican Studies*. Summer/Fall.

_____. 1994. "Clinton's Foreign Drug Policy" in *Journal of Interamerican Studies*. Vol 35, Spring.

Reyes Posada, Alejandro. 1990. "La Violencia Y La Expansion Territorial Del Narcotrafico" in Juan G. Tokatlian and Bruce M. Bagley eds. *Economia y Politica del Narcotrafico*. Bogota: C.E.I. Uniandes.

_____. 1991. "Paramilitares En Colombia: Contexto, Aliados y Consecuencias." in *Analisis Politico* No. 12, January-April.

Sohrieberg, David. 1996. "Sins of the Fathers" in *Newsweek*. 12 Aug.

Sharp, Kenneth E. 1988."The Drug War: Going After Supply." in *Journal of Interamerican Studies*. Summer/Fall.

Thoumi, Francisco E. 1990. "Las Politicas Economicas Ante Los Desafios del Desarrollo" in Francisco Leal Buitrago y Leon Zamosc eds. *Al Filo Del Caos*. Bogota: Tercer Mundo Editores.

_____. 1992a. "The Economic Impact of Narcotics in Colombia." in Peter H. Smith, ed. *Drug Policy in The Americas*. Boulder: Westview Press.

_____. 1992b. "Why The Illegal Psychoactive Drug Industry Grew In Colombia." in *Journal of Interamerican Studies*, Fall.

White, Peter T. 1989. "Coca" in *National Geographic*. January.

Zamosc, Leon. 1990. "El Campesinado y Las Perspectivas Para La Democracia Rural" in Francisco Leal Buitrago y Leon Zamosc eds. *Al Filo Del Caos*. Bogota: Tecer Mundo Editores.

**Newspapers:**

*Christian Science Monitor*: 3 Jun and 8 Dec 92

*Economist* (UK): 14 Nov 92; and 30 Jan 93.

*El Espectador* (CO): 13 Dec 84; 1 Aug 85; 29 Mar 86; 26 Jan 88; 8 and 11 Jan 90; 18 Oct 91; 3, 9, 15 and 19 Nov; 9-13 and 29 Dec 92; and 14 Feb 93; 28 Aug; 15 Oct; 25-26 Nov 95; and 14 Mar 96.

*El Mundo* (CO): 18 Oct 92.

*El Nuevo Herald* (US): 29 May 91; 7 Jan; 14-15 Aug; 4 Sep; 4, 7, 8, 10, 21 and 23 Oct; 4, 8, 10, 12-14, and 26-27 Nov 92; 4, 19-21, 23 and 25 Jan; 2, 14 and 23 Feb; 5 and 22 Mar; 2, 7-8 May; 16 Jun; 14 and 19 Jul; 2, 7-8, 19, 22 and 28 Aug; 15, 23 and 26 Sep; 1 and 7 Oct; 29 Nov and 5 Dec 93; 3, 6 and 25 Jan; 5, 13, 21, 23-25 Feb; 3, 14, 16 and 30 Mar; 11, 13, 15, 19 and 24 Apr; 3-5, 14, 23-24 and 27 May; 24 Sep 11 and 29 Oct 94; 23 Nov; and 18-19 Dec 94; 3 Jan; 4, 8 and 17-18 Feb; 12 Apr; 5, 14, 18 and 25 May; 3, 7, 10-11 and 21 Jun; 19 and 31 Jul; 3, 11 and 17 Aug; 25 Sep; 26 Oct; 6,8 and 25 Nov 95; 4-5, 11, 28 and 30 Jan; 1, 25 and 28 Mar; 14, 16, 23 and 27 May; 4, 6, 8, 11-12, 16 and 21 Jun; 11-13, 17, 19, 21 and 23-24 Jul; 4, 6-7, 11, 13- 14 and 18 Aug; 1-6, 12-13, 15, 21, 23-24, 27 and 30 Sep; 2-4, 11-12, 21, 23-24 and 30-31 Oct; 6, 23 and 26 Nov; 1 and 3 Dec 96.

*El Nuevo Siglo* (CO): 25 Nov and 16 Dec 95.

*El Tiempo* (CO): 7 Jul 84; and 9 Feb 88; 11 Dec 91; 7 Aug; 2 Sep; 30 Oct; and 16 and 29 Nov; 23-24 Dec 92; 8 and 31 Jan ; and 3 Feb 93; 18 Jun; 21, 23 and 25 Sep; 30 Oct; 19 and 26 Nov 95; 14-16 Jan; 28 Feb; 7 Mar and 26 Jul 96.

*Excelsior* (MX): 29 Jan 93.

*Independent* (UK): 21 Jun; 17 Aug; 18 Nov 91; and 27 Feb 92.

*Insight*: 2 Apr 90.

*La Prensa* (CO): 11 and 18 Dec 91; 6 Aug; and 8 Nov 92.

*Latin American Report* (Andean Region): 5 Oct 89.

*Los Angeles Times*: 2 Jul 90.

*Miami Herald*: 26 Jul; 2 Sep; 21 Nov; and 15 Dec 91; 6 Jan; 2 Feb; 24 May; 13-14 Aug; 7, 12, 31 Oct; 8, 13-15 and 19 Nov 92; 4, 10, 14, 19, 21, and 23 Jan; 2-3, 10, 16-17 and 27 Feb; 22 Mar; 10 Apr; 8-9 and 24 May; 1-2, 7, and 13 Aug; 23 and 26 Sep; and 1 and 29 Oct; 3 and 15 Dec 93; 22, 24-25 Jan; 2, 10 and 20 Feb; 13-14 and 16 Mar; 4, 9, 10-11, 15-16 and 21 Apr; 2, 7, 18, 23-24 and 27-28 May; 10 Aug; 6 Sep; 23 Oct; and 18 Dec 94; 7 and 25 Jan; 10 and 12 Apr; 3, 8 and 18-19 May; 10 and 22 Jun; 7 and 13 Aug; 6-7 and 23 Oct; 8 Nov; and 6 Dec 95; 12 Jan; 7, 15 and 20 Feb; 2 and 7 Mar; 12 and 24 Apr; 6 and 15-16 May; 6, 8 and 23 Jun; 13, 15, 21, and 25-26 Jul; 4, 7, 21 and 31 Aug; 2 and 8-11 Sep; 7, 11 and 31 Oct 96.

*Nacional* (VE): 25 Jul 92.

*New York Review*: 22 Dec 88.

*New York Times*: 13 Jan and 21 Dec 88; 7 Jan; and 12 Aug 90; 1 and 27 Sep; and 27 Oct 91; and 14 Feb 93

*Pais* (CO): 10 Nov 92.

*Prensa* (PN): 16 Feb 93.

*Semana* (CO): 29 Aug; and 5 Dec 88; 23 Jan 90; 8 Jan 91; 7 Jul; 11 Aug 92; 24 Nov 92; 12 and 19 Jan; 2 Feb; and 2 Mar 93; 5 Mar 96.

*United Press International* (UPI): 28 Sep 92.

*Washington Post*: 30 Mar; 17 Apr; 13 Aug and 4 Sep 90; 18 Jan, 20-21 Jun 91; 26-27 Jul; and 31 Dec 92; 15 and 24 Feb; and 16 Apr 93.

*Washington Times*: 24 Feb 91; and 12 May 92.

# Index

# Author Biographical Sketch

Sewall H. Menzel earned his Ph.D. at the Graduate School of International Studies, University of Miami (Coral Gables). A graduate of The Citadel (B.A., history), he also holds a M.P.A. in public administration from the University of Oklahoma.

Dr. Menzel is a faculty member of Florida International University, where he has taught courses in Latin American politics, U.S. foreign policy, national security affairs and goverment. He spent the better part of the 1980s as a serving U.S. Army lieutenant-colonel foreign area specialist on Latin America, working in Colombia, Bolivia, Peru and Panama. Other books by the author include:

*Fire in the Andes:*
*U.S. Foreign Policy and Cocaine Politics in Bolivia and Peru*

*Bullets Versus Ballots:*
*Political Violence and Revolutionary War in El Salvador, 1979-1991*

*The Potosi Mint Scandal And Great Transition of 1652*